W9-CPE-525

Unlimited Challenge

Unlimited Challenge

The autobiography of
GARRY KASPAROV

with Donald Trelford

Grove Weidenfeld
New York

Copyright © 1987, 1990 by Garry Kasparov

All rights reserved.

No part of this book may be reproduced, stored in a retrieval
system, or transmitted in any form, by any means, including
mechanical, electronic, photocopying, recording, or otherwise
without prior written permission of the publisher.

Published by Grove Weidenfeld
A division of Grove Press, Inc.
841 Broadway
New York, NY 10003-4793

First published in Great Britain in 1987 by Hutchinson Ltd,
an imprint of Century Hutchinson, under the title *Child of Change*

This revised edition first published in Great Britain in 1990
by Fontana Paperbacks

Library of Congress Cataloging-in-Publication Data

Kasparov, G. K. (Garri Kimovich)
    Unlimited challenge / the autobiography of Garry Kasparov, with
Donald Trelford. — 1st American ed.
       p.   cm.
    Rev. ed. of: Child of change.
    Includes index.
    ISBN 0-8021-1103-3 (alk. paper) : $19.95
    1. Kasparov, G. K. (Garri Kimovich)   2. Chess players—Soviet
Union—Biography.   I. Trelford, Donald.   II. Kasparov, G. K. (Garri
Kimovich) Child of change.   III. Title.
GV1439.K38A3   1990
794.1'092—dc20
[B]   90-45098
                                                                 CIP

Manufactured in the United States of America

Printed on acid-free paper

First American Edition 1990

10 9 8 7 6 5 4 3 2 1

PUBLISHER'S NOTE

This book was originally published in Great Britain in 1987 under the title *Child of Change*. Subsequently Garry Kasparov rewrote and updated the text, making extensive revisions and retitling it *Unlimited Challenge*. As a student at the Institute of Foreign Languages in Baku, he was taught to speak and write "the Queen's English," and for that reason British spellings and locutions have been retained in the American edition.

In memory of
my father
Kim Moiseyevich Weinstein
1931–1971

CONTENTS

ILLUSTRATIONS

Defending my world title – press conference in London
    (*John Wildgoose, Observer*)
My parents
Deepest concentration
A game at the Pioneers' Palace, Baku
My first game against Karpov
Simultaneous against Korchnoi
Three World Champions
Tigran Petrosian (*Camera Press*)
Mikhail Tal (*Popperfoto*)
Victor Korchnoi (*Tony Prime, Observer*)
Boris Spassky (*Michael Kupferschmidt*)
Lev Polugayevsky (*Camera Press*)
Alexander Belyavsky (*Novosti Press Agency*)
The World Championship match begins (*Associated Press*)
The day of shame (*Associated Press*)
World Champion at last (*Novosti Picture Agency*)

ACKNOWLEDGEMENTS

This book is a joint venture between a Soviet citizen and an English writer, a rare form of cooperation that would have been unlikely before Mr Gorbachev's policy of *glasnost*. It would not have been possible without the assistance of Phyzchltura y Sport and Victor Chepizhny, whose cooperation is gratefully acknowledged. The authors met to discuss the material at various times and places over the past year, including Moscow, Baku, Dubai, London, Zurich and Brussels. They wish to thank the many friends in many countries of the chess world who gave more help than they sometimes knew, by facilitating access to tournaments, providing personal anecdotes or the books they have written. Acknowledgements are also due to the newspapers and periodicals quoted in the text. The authors give special thanks to Clara Kasparova and Leonid Weinstein for confiding their memories; to Raymond Keene, David Goodman, Andrew Nurnberg and Andrew Page for their general advice and encouragement; to Natalia Pavluchenko for her translations; to Ratko Knezevic, for his pictures, his advice and his hospitality; to our patient and resourceful editor, Tony Whittome of Century Hutchinson; and to Barbara Rieck for typing, retyping and then uncomplainingly typing yet again the various drafts against an ever-looming deadline.

AUTHORS' NOTE TO THE 1990 EDITION

Since completing this book, Garry Kasparov has become directly involved in the political changes sweeping the Soviet Union. He has resigned from the Communist Party and taken an active part in the new democratic opposition forces.

INTRODUCTION

'Child of Change'

On 10 November 1985, the day after I became world champion, Rhona Petrosyan said something very strange to me. 'Garry,' she said, 'I am sorry for you.' In my heart I rejected her words immediately, particularly as they were said at the time I was celebrating my victory in Moscow with my friends. Why should she feel sorry for me? I had just won the world title and was, at twenty-two, the youngest chess champion in history.

But I knew that Rhona was close to events and a person of long experience. I had good reason to trust her instinct in these matters, for it was not the first time in my life that she had delivered an important warning. 'And what is there to feel sorry about?!' I asked point-blank. 'I'm sorry for you, Garry,' she said, 'because the happiest day of your life is already over.'

It is too soon in my life to say whether Rhona, the widow of the ninth world champion, was right. After all, I am still only twenty-six now. But at the time I sensed another, deeper meaning in her words. They expressed some sort of vague concern, almost an omen of my troubles to come. Deep down inside me, it rang an alarm bell.

My mother thinks the most important day in my life was another one – 13 April 1963, the day she gave birth to me. In fact, my birthday was almost the day afterwards, for I came into the world at a quarter to midnight. In some ways she would have preferred me to be born a day later. But the 13th it was, and, despite all the superstitions, thirteen has turned out to be my lucky number – even to the extent that I became thirteenth world champion.

For myself, I would choose yet another date as the most memorable one in my life – 15 February 1985 – that day of shame in the history of chess when Florencio Campomanes, the President of the world chess organisation FIDE, with the blessing of the Soviet sporting authorities, cut short my first match for the world title against Anatoly Karpov. The years may have passed, but the dramatic events which unfolded that day at the press conference in the Hotel Sport in Moscow reverberate to this day in the world of chess.

I now realise that in the few seconds it took me to make my way up to the podium to protest against that improper decision, I was making the most important choice in my life. It was the day I threw down the challenge to my opponents. My private struggles became public.

We shall probably never know all the details of the private deal cooked up in advance between Campomanes, Karpov and the USSR Sports Committee. But of one thing we may be sure: it was not designed to 'save' Kasparov. And yet, through a curious twist in circumstances – of a kind that has recurred at several dramatic moments in my life – I was able to turn it to my advantage. Every time I watch the video recording of that press conference I freeze the shot of Campomanes with his floundering expression and darting eyes, and I am reinforced in the faith that the fight I began that day is a just fight: one that goes far beyond the realms of chess and touches on that most fundamental question of the way people should, and should not, behave towards one another in this world.

The ending of the return match in October 1986 was not only the crowning point of all the ordeals I had faced during my struggle for the world title; it also gave me at last something of a breathing space. It was then that I conceived the idea of gathering up all the facts and trying to piece together a complete picture of everything I had been through, so that the world would understand the true significance of the battle I continue to fight and the nature of the forces ranged against me. I realised that when you come to write about events that are still fresh, much of it will inevitably bear the stamp of uncompleted action. But in this case I was able to describe a complete stage in my life: I had become world champion.

The poet Yevgeny Yevtushenko, after writing his autobiography (which was published in the West) in the early 1960s, called it 'precocious', and a quarter of a century later, addressing a gathering in the Central Writers' Institute, he openly admitted: 'People don't write that sort of book at the age of thirty.'

What, then, if you are only twenty-four? But let us not jump to hasty conclusions. As we grow older, of course, we do become more objective, more restrained in our judgements. But do we become more truthful? I think that the passing years dull that sharpness of reaction, that freshness with which we view much of what has taken place, and subconsciously we begin to tailor the facts to suit later events.

There was something else, too, that spurred me to write my autobiography at such an early age: the realisation that such a book is a part of your struggle, that you should as soon as possible formulate and openly proclaim the principles by which you live . . .

I should add at this point that the publication of *Child of Change* in the Soviet Union was not originally part of my plans. Not, of course, because I did not want it to be published, but simply because I had very little hope that it would be. However, life in our country is evolving at a rapid rate, including the sphere of chess.

All the circumstances were favourable for writing the book. *Perestroika* in our country was gaining ground, *glasnost* had begun to penetrate every nook and cranny of political life, and people in the West were taking a heightened interest in the events taking place in the Soviet Union. My co-author was Donald Trelford, the distinguished British political observer and editor of the *Observer* Sunday newspaper. My experience of giving interviews, including interviews to the Western press, gave me grounds for believing that what was a difficult job could be successfully accomplished. In fact, *Child of Change* was not actually written: I simply dictated it on to a recorder in English, which I can speak, though of course nowhere near as well as my native Russian. What was more, time was short: as I was completing work on the book, I was getting ready for the match in Seville.

Unfortunately not all the difficulties could be overcome. Despite Trelford's marvellous adaptation, my ideas and opinions did not find their full expression in the book. Nevertheless, what I did succeed in was gaining the necessary experience and discovering my own form of presentation.

The publication of *Child of Change* simultaneously in six European languages ruffled the feathers of certain people who had hoped, by means of an obedient Soviet press, to portray their own actions in a flattering light. It came as no surprise that immediately the match in Seville was over, the Soviet press launched an almighty campaign against the book.

But the question was, since the book had not been published in Russian and no one there had read it, how could anyone begin to discuss it seriously, let alone arrange for it to be condemned? Was this not in the spirit of a time past, of which one writer said, tongue-in-cheek: 'We knew every single error that Feuerbach made without reading a single line he wrote'?

Interestingly, my other book *Two Matches*, which came out on the eve of the duel in Seville, was simply not noticed by the 'people concerned' and no discussion of it ever appeared in the press, although it was no less incisive, and by and large blatantly controversial. The reason for that would seem to be that it was published in the Soviet Union. If anyone had taken it into their head to pull a quote out of its context and then put their own interpretation on it, as some of my opponents do when they speak about *Child of Change*, any reader would quickly decide that the critic was being unscrupulous. When that possibility does not exist, critics have free rein to say what they like.

Unfortunately Soviet chess followers remained for a long time in ignorance about the conflicts and intrigues surrounding the world championship play-off. The stereotyped picture of 'an honest sporting combat between two top Soviet chess players', which became ingrained thanks to the endeavours of our journalists, was supposed to symbolise the indissoluble unity and cohesion of the Soviet school of chess. That is why chess fans had to content themselves in the main with rumours and titbits of information from abroad, where the intense 'political' struggle being fought at the top of the chess pyramid was discussed in all its detail. Ultimately, the problems that first reared their heads in our country were to boomerang back . . .

The result of the work I did on the Russian edition of *Child of Change* was somewhat unexpected. It turned out in fact to be a new book, mostly because two years had passed since the first publication, and in that time new events happened and interesting facts came to light. As far as the general direction of the book and my fundamental judgements on various events are concerned, these have not only remained unchanged, but are now backed up by documentary and other evidence.

What is more, the genre itself has undergone a radical change. At that time I was speaking – now I am writing. When a person speaks, he tends to be more verbose, more categorical and less precise in the way he expresses himself. A clean sheet of paper quenches over-emotion and compels you to look for words of precise meaning. What is the use in simply calling someone a coward, spy, mafioso or bribe-taker? Far more important for the reader are the documents, the facts, logic, and a clear-cut argument. Then he can work out for himself who is what.

My book was written for people who want to know about my life, my battles, my thoughts and beliefs. It is for them that I have tried to be truthful, even if somewhere I might have been mistaken.

ONE

A Boy from Baku

How do biographies of famous chess players begin? Usually with some memorable episode that happened in very early childhood. To take a classic example: the five-year-old Capablanca, while watching his father play, points out that he has made a wrong move, although no one has ever explained the rules of chess to him before.

I shall not break with tradition, either, and shall begin with my early childhood. My parents used to like solving the chess problems which were published in our local Baku newspaper, *Vyshka*. At the time, I did not play chess, although I was always close by, studiously following each move of the pieces on the board. Once, to my parents' utter amazement, I suggested how to solve a problem. My father said, 'Well, since he knows how the game ends, he ought to be shown how it begins', and with that he began explaining the rules to me. In a short time, it became difficult to drag me away from the game, and a year later I was already beating my father.

Who knows what might have happened if I had not shown an aptitude for chess at that time. I would probably, like my father, have gone to music school. That was what my father's parents had great hopes of my doing (my father, to their great dismay, had broken the family tradition by giving up music and going into engineering). His father, Moisey Rubinovich Weinstein, was a composer and operatic director of the Baku Philharmonic Society. His mother, Olga Yulievna, was a music teacher. They believed that everyone should have a musical education. It didn't matter that I had no ear for music. 'The most important thing is a sense of rhythm,' Olga Yulievna would say. 'It was the same thing with Leonid: his musical talents only began to develop when he was eleven.' And how they developed! Today Uncle Leonid, my father's younger brother, is a composer of some renown and an Honoured Artiste of Azerbaijan. He has written three operas, six symphonies, numerous chamber and vocal works, and film music.

But my father was categorically against my studying music. 'The boy has a fine analytical brain,' he said. 'He shall study chess, not music!'

It was an unexpected decision. My father had never been a serious chess player. My mother, however, did have a talent for the game. When she was six, she used to beat older boys and even some adults. But her preference was for more active games. When she was thirteen, a trainer came to see her parents and tried to persuade them to let her play for the republican basketball team. But my grandmother would not allow it. She did not like the idea of the inevitable travelling that it would involve for her daughter to take part in competitions.

So my mother, Clara Shagenovna Kasparova, took up neither chess nor basketball. By profession she is an engineer, a specialist in automation and remote control systems. She was a senior scientific associate, and later Secretary, of the Azerbaijani Electrical Engineering Research Institute until she left in 1981 to devote herself entirely to her son's chess career.

By then I was already a grandmaster, world junior champion and national champion, and was starting to dream of greater things. This is what I wrote about my mother in a school essay: 'My mother plays a big part in my life. She taught me to think independently, she taught me how to work and to analyse my own behaviour. She knows me better than anyone else because I discuss all my problems with her – school problems, chess problems, literature problems. My mother taught me to appreciate fine things, to be principled, honest and frank.'

My father, Kim Moiseyevich Weinstein, died when I was just seven. My time with him was so short, yet how great was his influence on the rest of my life! My mother recalls how I would virtually keep sentry duty by the door waiting for him to arrive home from work. After lunch he and I usually went out for a walk. It was during those walks that my father little by little instilled in me his own perceptions of things and laid down the foundations of my own future outlook on life. Our relationship was always an adult-like one.

I began to read when I was four. They say that I learnt to put the letters together to make syllables from newspaper headlines. The way it happened was this. I knew that before my father took me out for a walk he would look through the newspapers, and I would wait patiently for him to finish. As soon as he had finished one newspaper and put it aside, I would unfold it and, with a completely serious expression, also at an unhurried pace, 'look through' it. My wish to imitate everything my father did was of great amusement to my parents. Thus was I introduced to 'reading' the newspapers.

Like all children, I went to kindergarten, but I was often away ill, and on those long days that I had to spend in bed I had nothing to do. Toys I didn't like, but reading – that was another matter entirely. At the age of six I amazed a friend of my mother's who came to visit and saw me reading aloud from a newspaper: 'Si-tu-at-ion in Ca-i-ro', followed by the whole report to the end. When she asked whether I remembered what I had read, I told her everthing I knew about the conflict in the Middle East.

My father loved geography and would often tell me stories about the travels of Magellan, Columbus, Marco Polo . . . One morning when I woke up, on my sixth birthday, I found an enormous globe by my bedside. I quickly shut my eyes and opened them again, but no, it wasn't a dream, the globe hadn't disappeared. The happiness it gave me! The favourite game of me and my father was to trace the journeys of famous navigators across that globe. Soon I knew by heart the capitals of all the countries, their populations, land areas, and masses of other useful information. What a valuable gift a globe is, given to a child at the right age.

At the same early age, this time thanks to my mother, I

developed an interest in history. Unable to do anything by halves, I immersed myself in the history of Ancient Rome, France, Spain and Britain. Those were the countries that fired my imagination. When I was eight I read a book on Napoleon by Tarle which made an enormous impression on me. I always loved to read the life stories of strong individuals who forged their own destinies.

In 1970 my father fell seriously ill. He spent many months in Moscow, at the Oncology Centre in Kashirka, then died of lymphatic sarcoma at the age of thirty-nine. The last time I saw him was 1 January 1971, when he gave me a chess clock as a present – the day after I qualified for category three . . . After that, they would not let me see him. It was my father's wish: he wanted me to remember him healthy and cheerful, just as I had always known him. They didn't take me to his funeral, either, fearing that it might upset me too much. I remember saying to my mother: 'Let's pretend that Daddy has gone away on business.' And in school I continued for a long time afterwards to speak about my father as if he were still alive.

My mother and I went to live with her parents. My grandfather, Shagen Mosesovich Kasparov, used to be an oil engineer. After the war they began extracting oil from the sea bed, and it was there that the first offshore drilling rigs in the world were erected. Later an entire town called Neftyanye Kamni ('Oil Rocks') grew up on the sea. When I was nine I went there to give a simultaneous chess display. That trip of mine gave Shagen Mosesovich particular pleasure – for a good twenty years he had been chief engineer of a large offshore oil field.

After my father died, my grandfather retired and the two of us became very close. He being an old communist, we spent hours together talking about politics, and he introducd me to books on philosophy. Occasionally we argued, and it was not always Kasparov Senior who won the argument. Ever since I was small I have tried to think through, analyse and question everything I hear or read, and to have an opinion of my own on everything. My grandfather, though, I have to admit, did not greatly approve of my spirit of contrariness.

My grandmother, Susanna Bagdasarovna, although a graduate of the Moscow Institute of Finance, devoted the greater part of her life to bringing up first her daughters, then me. She taught me to be truthful, to trust people, and to appreciate everthing created by Man. A strict woman of strong character and good sense, my grandmother enjoyed universal love and respect. Although she had lived through hard times, she never lost her natural optimism and kindness. As I recall today her favourite saying – 'It's wonderful that all my grandchildren are of different nationalities' – I think what a wise woman she was. Among my cousins there are Armenians, Azerbaijanis and Jews. But my grandmother singled none of us out for special attention; she cherished the right of each of us to her warmth and love.

The family never spoiled me, nor was there ever a hint of nannying. They brought me up by persuading me of what was right. I remember my mother's 'inoculations' against conceit, when they started praising me in the newspapers: 'Everyone has a talent for something,' she would admonish, 'but that talent doesn't always surface. You are lucky that your abilities have shown themselves so early on. Just lucky!' Then she would give me jobs to do, like sending me down to the shop for bread and milk, or leaving me to look after my two younger cousins . . . When I did take chess up seriously, I had virtually no free time left.

In my third year at school I began taking part in tournaments. Life immediately became divided into dull days and happy days. The happy days were the tournaments; all the others were dull days. But soon I began to get pleasure from the daily chess lessons too. The dull days disappeared!

Here is one of my first schoolboy interviews for the magazine *Yunost*: 'Be deprived of chess? What do you mean deprived? If I found myself alone on a desert island? No problem! I'd start by making myself a chess set. How would I manage without someone to play with? I think I could manage for a few years without them. And if there was nothing to make a chess set out of? Then there wouldn't be a solitary thing to do on the island: chess is the absolute bare minimum! But if I made a chess set and some evil being destroyed it? In that case . . . well, in that case he and I would have to get a few things sorted out!'

In everyday life, too, I preferred to 'get things sorted out' with people. Like all little boys, I used to quarrel and fight. My closest friend at school was Vadim Minasian, who remains my friend to this day. We got into many a schoolboy scrape together. But our most exciting escapades had something to do with fire. On one occasion we lit a bonfire in the school itself and started jumping through it to show off to the girls . . . Though until I was sixteen I was not particularly interested in girls and was rather disdainful of them (although they used to scare me a little, too). I once asked my mother: 'Why do girls spend so long preparing for class lessons? Why have they got such limited minds? I hate them!' Now, when she tells this story, she adds, with a gale of laughter; 'Just six months later he was in love.'

I remember while I was in the third year at school a girl sent me the following note: 'I love you. I want you to marry me.' I'm afraid my reply was not terribly gallant. Fortunately (or unfortunately), my message was intercepted by the teacher before it could break my admirer's heart.

When I finally did fall in love, the whole situation was reversed. She was younger than me and was in a different class, so I somehow had to attract her attention. But how? I arranged for my friends to set her up. They met her on the street and pretended to pester her. A moment of anxiety, and then I appeared on the scene like a knight in shining armour, to save the damsel from distress. Afterwards I arranged a firework display in her honour, with real rockets.

My mother had a lot of trouble with my health, or rather my sickness. When I was nine I had my appendix out. A day after the operation my uncle came to hospital only to find my bed empty. He was alarmed, but the nurse calmed him down and led him to the doctors' room. Looking in he saw me, lying on a trolley blindfolded and playing a chess 'simul' with the doctors.

When I was ten the doctors began to be concerned about my heart. They diagnosed rheumatic carditis and said that I should avoid catching colds because it might strain my heart. After that, my mother learned how to give me injections herself, and wherever we travelled she carried a syringe with her because until I was fifteen I had to have injections of antibiotics. Afterwards, thanks to my sporting activities, I resumed a normal life, swimming, playing football, badminton and cycle racing.

I began travelling abroad to chess tournaments when I was thirteen. Before every trip I would prepare myself thoroughly for the country I was going to, hungrily absorbing all the information I could find and discussing it with my school teachers.

I would come back so full of impressions that at first I couldn't sleep. Only after I had released all my emotions and told my classmates everything I had seen could I calm down. I remember being hugely impressed in Paris by the fact that in the parks you were actually allowed to sit on the grass.

With my childish curiosity and the same thoughtfulness that I applied to chess, I would compare what I had seen with the way we lived. Occasionally this got me into trouble. Certain adults would tick me off for criticising my own country. But even at that age I felt that every problem should be tackled objectively and that you should not be afraid to say exactly what is on your mind. My father was a man of firm principles, uncompromising, and I am glad that I have inherited those traits of his character.

I always carry a photograph of my father with me. I notice that outwardly, too, I am becoming more and more like him. People tell me that when I speak on the telephone, I gesticulate in exactly the same way that he used to. Like him, too, I get easily excited, but cool down again just as quickly.

In school, one subject that came quite easily to me was mathematics, especially algebra. Solving difficult problems was for me pure enjoyment. The teacher even insisted that I should take extra classes to develop my mathematical abilities, but my mother was against it. She was of the opinion that a combination of mathematics and chess was unlikely to lead to the development of a rounded person, and she wanted me to study literature. Life has proved her to be right.

Deep down inside I am a romantic, a person of feeling, or at least that is how I like to view myself. This may surprise certain people, but only those who think that chess is basically a scientific pursuit played by impassive human computers. I firmly believe that chess belongs to the world of art, because a chess player, in addition to his other qualities, must have a well-developed imagination and rich fantasy.

Unlike chess, the literary genius does not usually emerge in childhood. Writing books requires knowledge of the world and experience of life (though children do sometimes show a gift for poetry). Music, mathematics and chess, because of their abstract nature, do not require this kind of experience. So you find Reshevsky at the age of five playing simultaneous chess games against adults, Mozart at four composing music, and a boy called Kim Ung-Yong in South Korea also at four performing integral calculus.

The American linguistic philosopher George Steiner advanced the theory that talents for chess, music and mathematics are all related to a powerful but narrowly specialised area of the human brain. This can somehow be triggered into life in a very young child and can develop in isolation from the rest of the psyche, he suggests. Well, it's quite possible. In any case, his theory would explain the appearance of the musical or chess *wunderkind*.

After school I went on to the Baku Institute of Foreign Languages. My school teachers had each in turn advised my mother that I should pursue their own particular subject, the

mathematics and literature teachers being especially persistent. But we decided that the most useful thing for my chess
career would be a knowledge of foreign languages.

Many people wonder why I changed my name from Weinstein to Kasparov. After my father died I went to live with my
mother's parents. It seemed natural to use the name Kasparov,
particularly as they had three daughters and no son (my
mother has two sisters: Nelli, a doctor, and Janna, a teacher).

The origin of my first name is odd. It was one of those
single-minded decisions by my father which, in the seven
short years that fate gave us to live together, by and large
determined my character. 'My own name, Kim, is short and
really rather soft-sounding,' my father said. 'The boy should
have a name you can clearly hear. It should have a hard sound
to it, with the letter R. Our son shall be named Garry.'

The little Garik Weinstein who once wrote essays at school
in Baku and the Garry Kasparov who today upholds the cause
of justice in chess are one and the same person. The values I
represent are the same. They have not changed over the years,
nor will they change in the future, regardless of the successes
or failures that await me.

TWO

School

I made my first acquaintance with chess at the age of five, began playing seriously when I was seven, and at ten I was already studying in the Botvinnik School. By the age of fourteen I realised that chess was destined to become the most important thing in my life.

Chess lessons and travelling to take part in tournaments took up a lot of my time, and I came to spend less and less of it in the company of children my own age. I was destined from an early age to mix with older people. Maybe it was not such a bad thing. Adult men served as some replacement for the early loss of my father and ensured that there were masculine elements in my upbringing to balance the strong influence of my mother's love. But still I was living a life that was somewhat unnatural for a boy of my age, and even then felt to a certain extent deprived of my childhood. Sometimes I yearned to be a normal boy, just like the rest.

Unfortunately there were few children of my own age with whom I could mix easily. Full of stories from an unknown world and unchildlike problems, I must have seemed to them something like a creature from another planet. My stories may have made some of them resentful or even envious, although everything I said and did was out of a natural desire to share my fears and joys.

When I saw the Gagarin Young Pioneers Palace in Baku, a white, two-storey building looking out over the Caspian Sea, it seemed like some sort of fairy-tale castle of chess. I was taken there by Rostik Korsunsky, an older boy from a neighbouring flat. When I was a child, my favourite piece was the bishop. Once I played a unique type of match with Rostik in which all my pieces could move like a bishop and all his like a knight . . . Later on, Korsunsky became a chess master. Incidentally, in the thirty years of its existence, the chess circle of the Young Pioneers Palace has produced over 300 first-category players, twenty-five candidate masters, a good dozen masters, Baku's first grandmaster Vladimir Bagirov, and a world title challenger, Tatiana Zatulovskaya.

My first trainer was Oleg Privorotsky. He remarked immediately on my memory for the moves and my ability to cut myself off from my surroundings during a game. 'I don't know whether other cities have similar beginners, but there is certainly no one like him in Baku,' he said with amazement after my first few lessons.

When I was nine I reached the final of the Baku lightning championship and thereby earned my first mention in the press: 'Third-year schoolboy Garik Weinstein, playing whilst standing up (when sitting down he cannot reach all the pieces!), achieved the topmost result in stage one – nine points out of nine . . . The fourteen winners in stage two comprised thirteen candidate masters and . . . one category 2 player.' After a successful performance coming third in the Baku youth championship, I was made a member of the Azerbaijani republican youth team.

The national youth team championship, which was held in Vilnius in the summer of 1973, was my first baptism of fire. And although all my opponents were four or five years older than me, I did not lose a single game in the final. At the closing ceremony I was presented with the first prize I had ever won, the prize for the youngest player in the tournament.

The most important result of my performance in Vilnius, however, was my meeting with Alexander Sergeyevich Nikitin, the national team trainer. At the time he was looking for promising young pupils for the Botvinnik School. Nikitin watched my play throughout the whole tournament, but approached me only after it had finished. Thus began our long friendship, which continues to this day. I value him greatly, not just because he is a fine trainer and chess expert, but also for the important fact that he has stood by me during the most difficult times in my life.

Nikitin is a native Muscovite and by profession a radio engineer, but he quit his job to devote himself entirely to training chess players. Passionately fond of chess, he became a master at a very early age and in his youth played for the national students team alongside Boris Spassky.

For many years we had studied under the system of opening preparation that Nikitin had developed. And then, in August 1973, he arranged for me to be invited to a session of the Botvinnik School. Together with other children, I was called to Moscow for an interview with Mikhail Moiseyevich. Each of us spent two hours alone with the famous champion, showing him games we had played, answering his questions and analysing positions that he set. I passed the rigorous examination and was enrolled in the school. To come under Botvinnik's wing was beyond doubt a stroke of good fortune.

The Botvinnik School had begun back in 1963 as part of the sports society 'Trud' and in its first phase lasted for only eighteen months. Karpov was among the first pupils. The school started up again in 1969, and from around the mid-1970s onwards its pupils began to achieve remarkable successes.

Three times a year – in February, May and August–September – twenty boys and girls from various cities in the Soviet Union came together for the sessions. The winter and spring sessions would be held near Moscow, and the autumn session in the 'Orlyonok' young pioneers' camp by the Black Sea.

'I conduct the studies in accordance with a system tried before the war in the Leningrad Pioneer Palace,' Botvinnik wrote in his book *Achieving the Aim* (Moscow, 1978). 'We work together, but we examine the play of one of the students . . . This is the way to get to know a player's spirit, to study his good points and his failings.'

Botvinnik went into greater detail about how the studies

were conducted in his book *From Chess Player to Machine* (Moscow, 1979): 'The standard report delivered by a student about what he had done since the previous session would be a statement to the class about his successes in his school work, his sporting activities, his participation in competitions and how far he had accomplished his personal target. Then the student would demonstrate four of the matches he had played since the last session. After that, we would collectively make a preliminary diagnosis of the young player's chess health . . . But the course of treatment was not yet prescribed: that would come after the end of the practice games held during the study session, and these were of great importance: there was no selecting of simply the ones you wanted to discuss . . . and no hiding the fact if you exceeded your time limits! Those games would be analysed by the whole class together. Then the final diagnosis would be made and the treatment prescribed, in other words the target was set.

'Students would come with their own local trainers, who liaised with the head of the school, or if they were little, they would come with their mothers or fathers . . .'

At least as valuable as the formal lessons were the various subtleties of preparing for tournaments that Botvinnik passed on to us. In this area he had achieved the highest level of professionalism, and the importance of what he taught us is hard to overestimate.

Botvinnik's wisdom lay in the fact that he never tried to overwhelm us with his authority. He never tried to impose his own style on his pupils. On the contrary, he tried in every possible way to help us develop our own talents. He didn't push, but with his intrinsic tact as a teacher prompted you in the right direction. From the outset he sensed my ambition to have a dynamic, attacking style, and I don't think it was by chance that he included an analysis of Alekhine's matches as part of my first homework.

Botvinnik tried to take the mystery out of chess, always relating it to situations in ordinary life. He used to call chess a typical inexact problem similar to those which people are always having to solve in everyday life, and would say: 'In order to solve inexact problems it is essential to limit the scope of the problem so as not to get entangled in it, and only then is there the chance of finding a more exact solution. Hence it is a mistake to think that chess does not reflect objective reality. It reflects man's thinking.'

That is typical of Botvinnik's approach to chess, and indeed to life itself: reduce the problem to a manageable size.

There was a period when I became fascinated by the boundless variations that could be achieved in the game. Someone once calculated that if you were able to solve every possible variation in just one minute, it would still take forty thousand years, day and night, to exhaust the 208,089,907,200 ways of placing the pieces on the board. After just three opening moves by each player, more than nine million different positions are possible!

I am still constantly amazed at the inexhaustibility of chess and am becoming more and more convinced of its unpredictability. Millions of games have been played and thousands of books about the game have been written, but no chess formula or method which can guarantee victory has yet been found. To this day there are no mathematically valid, precise criteria for evaluating even a single move, let alone a position. As with Cleopatra, so with Caissa; 'Age cannot wither her nor custom stale her infinite variety.'

Botvinnik used to warn me against this love of complications for their own sake, and once said: 'You will never be like Alekhine if you allow the variations to govern you rather than the other way around.' That upset me very much but of course he was right. He wrote about this episode later: 'It was clear from the beginning that Kasparov stood out among the other boys because of his ability to calculate the variations very skilfully and for many moves ahead. But Garry was a very excitable boy. I had to insist he think before making a move. Quite often I would tell him that there was a danger of his becoming a new Larsen or Taimanov. Even at a mature age those outstanding players would sometimes make a move first and then think . . .'

I must have heeded Botvinnik's advice, because just four months after that first school session at a tournament in Baku I succeeded in scoring my master norm. Incidentally, another player in that tournament was Alexander Shakarov, a great expert in openings theory who was to become my future assistant.

The following year, 1974, began for me with a fresh victory. To many people's amazement, the Baku team of Young Pioneers won the qualifying stage of a tournament for the *Komsomolskaya Pravda* prize. I had four wins and one draw.

The final of the national Young Pioneers tournament took place in Moscow. We were to play simultaneous games against the grandmaster captains of the rival teams. In the very first round I was dumbfounded to see before me a living legend – Mikhail Tal. I could even shake his hand! In later life I considered it my direct duty to take part in these 'tournaments of chess promise' (as the Young Pioneers competitions rightly came to be known), realising how important it was for the young ones to meet a renowned grandmaster over the board.

That meeting with Tal was one of the most memorable events of my childhood. I had heard about the intimidating, hypnotic glare with which he would fix his opponents. To 'overcome' me, though, Tal had no need to stare. I also lost to Taimanov and Polugayevsky, but on the other hand I beat Averbakh and drew with Kuzmin, who told a correspondent: 'I never dreamt that a ten-year-old boy could play such a competent end-game.'

At the USSR Junior championship in Vilnius in January 1975 I came seventh out of more than thirty contestants. Given my age, it was not bad, but it could have been better. During the last round, playing against Alyosha Yermolinsky from Leningrad, I missed an easy winning trick and lost. I remember being so upset by it that I almost burst into tears there and then, not because I lost, but simply because I was angry with myself for making a stupid mistake. Even now blunders like that make me furious.

By an irony of fate the championship was won by the then seventeen-year-old Zhenya Vladimirov, who subsequently became one of my trainers. He had stunning positional sense, and people forecast a great future for him.

Soon after the Vilnius tournament, Leonard Barden, the chess columnist for the London *Guardian*, made the following forecast: 'Whatever happens to the world title in 1975, most experts predict that Karpov will be Fischer's successor – this year, in 1978, or in 1981. But who will be world champion after Karpov? In my opinion there is a clear favourite for world champion in 1990. He is eleven-year-old Garry Weinstein from Baku, youngest player in the USSR junior championship and youngest candidate master since Karpov.'

Barden's forecast was five years out, but the very fact that it was made is noteworthy, albeit because it was the first honourable mention that I received in the Western press. At the time, luckily, this very flattering assessment never reached my ears, otherwise it might have turned my head.

In November of the same year, 1975, I finally made the acquaintance of Anatoly Karpov. We met in Leningrad at a Young Pioneers tournament. Karpov was acting as captain of a team from Chelyabinsk. He was twenty-four years old and had only recently inherited the world championship title from Fischer.

Yet my encounter with Karpov did not give me the same quiver of excitement as the game with Tal had. The other boys, though, were nervous, and went into the game looking rather lost. In the hotel lobby where the tournament was taking place I said to them: 'What's there to be afraid of? Karpov may be world champion, but he can still make mistakes.' This remark was evidently overheard, because the next day one of Karpov's backers, A. Tupikin (then secretary of a Leningrad district Party committee), told my mother: 'Bear in mind that Karpov never forgets a slight.'

In its report on that round, *Sovietsky Sport* wrote: 'During A. Karpov's session with the schoolchildren from Baku, the point came where the world champion had just one opponent left, twelve-year-old candidate master Garik Kasparov. Karpov sat down opposite the young player, and naturally it was a moment that the photographers did not fail to catch. The thing is that Garik is one of the most talented young chess players, and who is to say whether one day there may not be another Karpov–Kasparov fight . . .'

Who would have thought then that a few years later we would have played some 150 games together and spent more than 600 hours at the board?

That game I lost, although just before I had had a clear edge over him. This was my interview with a correspondent for the Baku newspaper *Sport*:

- What would you say were the reasons for your defeat by the world champion?
- Maybe because I was left facing him alone. You can imagine what it's like to have the best chess player in the world sitting opposite you. I just didn't see his combination.
- And what lesson have you drawn from the encounter?
- That you have to go on fighting to the end, even if you are in a winning position.

My next challenge was the USSR junior championship in Tbilisi in January 1976. I didn't expect to win, since I was so much younger than my opponents. But deep down I felt I had a chance and, as it turned out, I wasn't wrong.

When it came to the last round I was standing first equal with Rafik Gabdrakhmanov. But then he lost to Zurab Sturua, who moved half a point ahead. I needed a win, but, as ill luck would have it, I played dreadfully and, in deep trouble, adjourned my game with Zigurds Lanka.

Everybody thought I was bound to lose, except Alexander Aslanov, one of the Baku coaches. He and Oleg Privorotsky helped me analyse the adjourned position. We worked hard on it until at last, together with the Yerevan coach Albert Arutyunyan, we found a stunning idea for a defence.

In the event of a draw, the first two places would have been shared, and the Buchholz tie-break system would have been applied. But in this case the situation was unclear because not all the games in the last round had been completed. Be that as it may, the Georgians were already celebrating in anticipation of a double gold: Maia Chiburdanidze had already become the Soviet girls' champion, and Sturua, they all believed, was about to join her.

We sat down to finish the game. After a few moves I happened to glance out into the hall and saw Aslanov gesticulating wildly, obviously excited about something. Ten moves later our game was recorded as a draw.

What happened afterwards became engraved forever in my memory. Aslanov covered the distance from the seventh row to the stage in an instant, and with a yell of 'Garik, Garik, you're the champion!' lifted me up in his arms.

Unable to believe what had happened, I kept repeating to myself over and over, probably for another hour: 'I am the champion, I am the champion . . .'

THREE

Adult Games

My first trip abroad came in July 1976, when I played in the world junior championship at Wattigny, near Lille, in France. I was the youngest chess player ever to represent the Soviet Union at an international match. That, however, was my only achievement. In all other respects the trip brought me nothing but disappointment.

I suppose I didn't play badly: I shared 3-6th place [that is, third place with six others] out of thirty-two contestants, and that indeed was the verdict of the weekly chess magazine *64-Chess Review* on my performance: 'not bad'. But my own private verdict was more critical. I felt that I could have played the front runners far better than I did, and that upset me.

I was also unhappy that the tournament left me practically no time to see anything of France itself. Before I went to France, I tried to find out everything I could about its history and customs and pored over my grandfather's map of the country. And what happened? We simply swept past all the historical monuments I had been so looking forward to seeing. But I couldn't help noticing that the way of life there was substantially different to ours, although I was too small to draw any conclusions from it. I simply accepted it as a fact of life, as the result of our troubled history.

The following January in Riga I was to defend my title of national junior champion. It's common knowledge that defending a title is always more difficult than fighting to win it: everyone plays twice as hard against a champion. What's more, there were some strong players in the field, including Chernin, Yusupov and my old foe Sturua.

What happened, however, came as a surprise to everyone: I

methodically won one game after the other. And it did not go unnoticed that I had especially prepared a number of new opening systems and variations which I had never played before and which served me well in the tournament. As a result I beat the runner-up, Sasha Chernin, by two clear points. The junior team coach Anatoly Bykhovsky described my performance as follows: 'To become national junior champion twice in a row is something that no one up to now has ever achieved. Kasparov's style was varied: he conducted an excellent attack in his game against Pigusov, beat Lanka and Sturua by purely positional manoeuvres, put up a resourceful and tenacious defence against Yusupov, and caught out Gitsin in the opening. This whole diverse arsenal of fighting manoeuvres was demonstrated by a boy of just thirteen years old!'

Yes, that was my most significant victory, and a particularly sweet one after my not terribly successful debut abroad. Soon afterwards in Leningrad there was a qualifying tournament for two world junior championships: one for the under-20s and the other for the under-17s. Among the eight contestants I was the only candidate master; the others were masters. The tournament was a bitterly-fought one, with only a third of the games ending in a draw. The tone was set by the youngest players: Artur Yusupov and I took it in turns to lead over the entire distance. It was amusing that initially they wanted to play off each championship separately, so that the little ones wouldn't get under the feet of the big ones. And that's just what we tried to do – not get under their feet. The victor was Yusupov, who went on to win the world championship in Innsbruck in the same confident way. I came half a point behind him and won my second trip to the junior championship, which was again taking place in France.

This time we played in the picturesque town of Cagnes-sur-Mer on the famous Riviera, whose boulevards reminded me of Baku in the summer. The tournament was held according to the Swiss system, with a very tough schedule. There would be a round in the evening, uncompleted games finished off the following morning, then play again in the evening. So it carried on through the whole tournament without a single day off.

I had a successful start: three victories. Then defeat. After an important win in the eighth round against the future champion Jon Arnason from Iceland, who was in the lead and one point ahead of me, I managed to correct the situation. But I didn't have the strength to push any harder. Three draws in the last three rounds fought against not the strongest of opponents and my final result was eight points and third place. Success went to the older and physically stronger boys, Arnason and Whitehead (USA). Incidentally, it was at this championship that the British boy Nigel Short made his first appearance: two years younger and two points behind me, he too noticeably lost his stamina at the last. When I returned home, Botvinnik pointed out a number of major faults in my playing, but still said he thought it was a good result. I myself had a lingering feeling of dissatisfaction.

It was a crucial time for me, perhaps one of the most decisive moments in my life. Soon I would be fifteen, and I knew that if I didn't soon qualify to be a master it would be time to start thinking about finding another career. I had been a promising player for long enough: now it was time to come up with results. No one, including me, guessed that I was on the verge of taking a qualitative leap in my chess development. It was then that I found my own style.

I am a follower of the investigative school of chess to which Botvinnik belongs. It is from him that I learnt really to study chess, to find new ideas and work constantly at perfecting them. It is a scientific approach, based on a profound analysis of our heritage from the past, the quest for new opening variations and methods of play in the middle-game, and the development of fundamentally new strategic plans. All chess players study old games in the same way that people learn the words of a foreign language. But once you have some sort of vocabulary, you have to learn how to use it to give expression to your creative thoughts. Especially if you aim to become world champion.

A turning point for me was the A. Sokolsky memorial trophy tournament in Minsk in January 1978. I had done some good preparation, particularly with regard to openings: I had some ideas up my sleeve for the seemingly most well-studied positions assessed by theory as being on a par. As a result I was able to create acute, off-beat situations, which I loved. It was only here that the game in fact really began for me. I managed to beat several well-known masters, but I had one draw with a candidate master which to this day I cannot forgive myself for. I had a completely won position when Albert Kapengut, the famous Belorussian coach, came up to me and said that the book *The Count of Monte Cristo* was waiting for me at the hotel. I was so overjoyed that I immediately made a clumsy mistake. Nevertheless I managed to maintain a very high pace: 4 points out of 5, 8 out of 10, 12 out of 15.

Throughout the whole tournament I was hotly pursued by the international master Viktor Kupreichik. In order to become the outright winner, I had to beat grandmaster Anatoly Lutikov in the last round. 'Beat' is easy to say, but what if it's your first game against a grandmaster (not counting 'simuls')? There is, however, such a thing as beginner's luck.

My triumph in Minsk (thirteen points out of seventeen!) was picked up by the experts. In his book *From Chess Player to Machine*, Botvinnik recalled: 'It was difficult to get Kasparov accepted as one of the players. He had not yet qualified as a master, and naturally there were objections – why should a candidate be allowed to play in a masters' tournament? The outcome proved that it was the right thing to do: Garik won first place, getting three and a half points more than he needed to qualify as master. It was the greatest success ever achieved by such a young chess player in the Soviet Union!'

Still there were people who said that the tournament was not significant. Coming up in the summer was the national qualifying tournament in Daugavpils: that really would be a serious test!

Straight after Minsk I hurried off to the session of the Botvinnik School, where my strict mentor had more than just words of congratulation. During that same session Mikhail Moiseyevich asked me if I would like to be his assistant. I was brimming with pride: it meant I had reached the stage where I could give some help to Botvinnik himself.

At one point Botvinnik asked me whether I hoped to gain one of the top places at Daugavpils. I gave a vague reply. Then he said that if that was how I felt, there was no point in going to the tournament, which was being held according to the Swiss system and from a training point of view would be ineffective.

The national qualifying tournament in Daugavpils started in July. Out of sixty-four competitors just one was at USSR top league level, while another six were facing a replay in the first league. A total of seven top places for the whole lot!

Initially the coaches set me the relatively modest task of getting 'plus 2'. Perhaps that is why I played calmly. I began to get anxious when I saw my name highlighted in red in the tournament table – four and a half points out of six. Nikitin modified the original plan: the sights were set on a place in the first league! And after another two wins the targets had to be set still higher.

Fortune was kind to me. Igor Ivanov and I gained nine points out of thirteen, but under the Buchholz tie-break system I was ahead. The road to the top league was open!

'Chess today is becoming more and more for young people,' the Latvian chess magazine *Shakhmaty* wrote. 'But even so, when a fifteen-year-old boy shows an encyclopaedic knowledge of openings, a rich imagination, the ability to make a rapid calculation in extremely complex middle-game situations, and possesses the highly skilled technique of utilising his advantage in the end-game – all this cannot but give rise to astonishment.'

So in two leaps I jumped straight into adulthood. I was full of energy and any doubts about my future had vanished. From now on my life would be devoted to chess.

While preparing for the national championship in Tbilisi in December 1978, I did not set myself any ambitious targets, believing that first and foremost I should demonstrate a good game and gain some experience. Nikitin always used to say that the main thing was to play well, because success would then come along of its own accord. I found out later, though, that back in 1975 he had shown my mother a timetable for my future sporting results. The entry against the year 1978 read 'USSR top championship league'.

Only a short while before, at the tournament in Minsk, I had been anxiously awaiting my first game with a grandmaster. Now there were sixteen holders of the top title ranged against me all at once. Botvinnik's strategic directive had been abundantly clear: 'Play seventeen good games and don't think about the result.' I couldn't, of course, help thinking about the result, but I wasn't aiming too high: as long as I didn't drop below the first league. But the start of the championship turned out successfully for me: I beat Polugayevsky and Kuzmin, got four points out of six and . . . decided to stay in the top league. My optimism, however, was a little dampened when I was beaten by Timoschenko and Razuvayev.

In the chess bulletin I read the following dialogue:

> 'Do you think we should congratulate you on your victory over a fifteen-year-old schoolboy?' was the question put to Yury Razuvayev.
> 'Yes, I think you should,' the Muscovite grinned. 'It looks as though that was my last chance to beat him.'

That hint of my guaranteed future, however, was a poor consolation to me at the time.

Yet fortune smiled on me once again. I scored a difficult win against Belyavsky, adjourned a game against Gulko with the winning chances on my side, and achieved a threatening position against Mikhalchishin. At that point I was picturing myself somewhere among the dizzy heights of the winning three! The moment of reckoning was not long in coming. So busy celebrating, I made a mess of my game with Mikhalchishin and lost. Then I was unable to beat Gulko. And when I played a talentless game and lost to Tseshkovsky, I came down out of the clouds not just to earth, but to the very bottom of a deep ravine.

Nevertheless I managed to get a fifty per cent result, which put me in clear ninth place and enabled me to stay in the top league. At the end of the tournament I had a chance to try my strength in a lightning match against Mikhail Tal, who had won his sixth gold medal as USSR champion in Tbilisi. Our hard-fought battle ended, to my joy, in a 7-7 draw. To this day I recall how two Alexanders – Bakh and Roshal, members of Karpov's close entourage – followed our game with unflagging interest. Probably they would have agreed with Tal, who during an interview gave this highly flattering assessment of my playing:

'Kasparov is without doubt a unique phenomenon in chess. There are only two other people I could name who gave such successful performances at the age of fifteen in major tournaments: Fischer and Spassky. Clearly, no matter what high position the boy achieves in the next championship, it won't be such a sensation.'

But the sensation came earlier than that. In the spring of 1979 I left to take part in my first 'adult' foreign tournament at Banja Luka in Yugoslavia. The tournament contestants were very strong players: in addition to former world champion Tigran Petrosyan there were another thirteen grandmasters!

Petrosyan, renowned for his dogged defensive play, had an astonishing sense of danger. It used to be said that he took measures to counter his opponent's attacks even before his opponent thought of them. Max Euwe once said: 'If Petrosyan had ever adopted an offensive style, all heads would have been beheaded, without exception.' It was also said that if

Petrosyan had been Tal's coach, and vice versa, neither of them would have become world champion.

Having drawn in the initial round with the 'iron Tigran', I then beat Sibarevic, Browne, Hernandaz, Marovic, Marjanovic and Knezevic, and drew only with Smejkal. In order to achieve my International Master norm, I had to beat two Yugoslav grandmasters, Bukic and Vukic.

Before the tournament started, Vukic had been complaining loudly that the organisers had invited a player that nobody knew. 'Kasparov doesn't even have an international rating,' he moaned. 'So why should a grandmaster play such a weak player? The Russians are sending us children. They're insulting us.'

The spectators, however, seemed to think differently: I felt they were on my side from the very first few rounds. But they gave me particularly hearty support during my match with Vukic. The Yugoslav grandmaster got angry with the public and even started arguing with them. My victory over Vukic gave rise to noisy delight in the hall. Never before had I had such enthusiastic support!

After drawing with Andersson and Matanovic, and with still three more rounds to go, I assured myself of victory in the tournament and achieved not only the International Master's norm, but my first grandmaster title! The final games therefore, with Garcia, Kurajica and Adorjan, were held, to use the diplomatic phrase 'in a spirit of peace and mutual understanding'. And still I was two points ahead of my closest pursuers. I was happy with my playing, and with good reason: in one single tournament I had stepped up two rungs of the chess ladder!

The British master Robert Wade was unstinting in the comparisons he drew: 'Kasparov's remarkable performance at this tournament should be forever enshrined among the epics of chess. Is there such a precedent in chess history? Robert Fischer at Zurich in 1959 or Boris Spassky at Bucharest in 1953? Both were also sixteen.'

After making the top league I asked if I could have my Elo-rating, which should have been 2545. Our chess officials were in no hurry to give me one. 'There's plenty of time for that,' they said. But my result in Banja Luka corresponded to an international rating of 2695! It was then, finally, that I was given my rightful 2545.

I said earlier that by this time I had found my own chess style. I should explain what I mean by this. Every chess player has a different style because we all have different natures. The style reflects the man. For me, brought up on Botvinnik's scientific method, the ability to concentrate is the key to everything else. Seemingly a simple thing. But what about when you are in an extreme, crisis situation? Few people acknowledge that the ability to focus one's thoughts during the decisive moments in a game is virtually the most important quality that a chess player can have.

Unfortunately modern life is not conducive to concentration. We are used to doing a mass of things at the same time: reading, watching television, taking part in conversation. Earlier on, when I was sixteen, seventeen, or even twenty, I was completely engrossed in chess. Over the years, my range of interests has grown, numerous problems have appeared, and my public activities demand ever more time and attention. All this is wildly distracting from chess. Yet without working at it constantly and purposefully, you will never penetrate the secrets of a position, nor will you find a truly new and original idea. But people expect it of you. It is to champions that they look for fresh ideas, in the belief that it is a gift from heaven, that they suddenly can see the light. But it is not like that. I am sure that each one of us is capable of making his own discovery, so long as he is dedicated and persistent.

Some people, seeing me during a game with my head in my hands and a fixed stare at the board, think that I am deliber-ately trying to influence my opponent, intimidate him or upset him, much as Tal's famous glare was said to do. That is not so at all. Essentially, all my efforts are being channelled into excluding outside interference and being able to concentrate to the maximum.

Karpov has said on several occasions that the investigative approach to chess is outmoded, that it belonged only to the 'stagecoach era'. In his opinion, the most important thing is practical playing, keeping in form by continuously taking part in tournaments. Not surprisingly, his style is characterised by rationalism. He never tried to play like Fischer, putting everything into it. He always expended exactly the amount of energy that was required for the given situation.

I have a different approach. I am not used to avoiding complications, be it on the chessboard or in life. Until recently this philosophy was unwelcome. But then, as they say, nothing is permanent under this sun . . .

To play creatively without being afraid of risky ventures and to possess a refined chess style in no way releases you from the need to work hard. On the contrary you must constantly perfect your playing, enrich and expand your opening repertoire, fine-hone your techniques, and analyse complicated end-games. Chess, after all, is not some body of knowledge learned once and for all. Chess is dynamic, and any final result may turn out in actual fact to be simply an intermediate one. The truth has to be proved every time. I do not even regard my own commentaries on matches as being written in stone. I like to keep updating them: in time, many ideas come to be re-assessed, including, of course, one's own ideas. I am eager to go back to my mistakes and analyse them. 'When a chess player comments on a match, he frequently tries to conceal his own slips and omissions,' Botvinnik wrote in 1980. 'Kasparov does not do that. He seeks out the truth and tries to be objective.'

The first work I had published was when I was fifteen. It was an analysis of my game with Lutikov, which was published in *Shakhmaty*. For two years my match commentaries appeared only periodically in the press, but after 1981, when *Shakhmaty* first came out in Baku, my journalistic activity became more regular. After each tournament I used to comment on practically all my matches. It was hard but exceptionally interesting work.

I began publishing my match analyses at the insistence of Botvinnik and Nikitin who said that the results of my work should be made available for other players to discuss. My mother got me into the habit of taking notes during my competition trips abroad. She believed that a major chess player should be widely educated and able not only to analyse matches, but to write for the public about chess events. Fresh horizons began to open up before me.

The most important thing for me in 1979 was to consolidate my positon in the top league and to try and improve my result. I didn't want to repeat the common mistake of giving myself a breathing space after my super-efforts of the year before.

Serious preparation began. Two months before the championship, Botvinnik wrote me the following: 'The thing that worries me most of all is when you play Black. After your success in Yugoslavia they're going to be pulling out all the stops against you, and the prime trouble will be the Whites. So as Black you'll need to play solid systems, without risk. However, a passive game isn't for you, so those systems must allow the possibility of counter-play.'

But at the 47th national championship in Minsk I began playing very circumspectly, so much so that Salo Flohr, Botvinnik's old friend and rival from the 1930s, was amazed at my uncharacteristic restraint. 'No sacrifices – it's more like the style of Karpov or Petrosyan,' he commented on my victory in the first round over Georgadze. My next win, this time against Sveshnikov, was also gained by good, solid positional play. But in the third round I broke out of the ambush and beat Yusupov in a style which one commentator even compared to Alekhine's. So that in his article summarising the championship, Flohr came to a different opinion about my playing: 'Garik was like fire at the chessboard.'

After three wins at the start, I had six draws in a row,

although they were far from quiet battles. After that, it worsened. First of all I lost to Lerner because of one impulsive move, then I didn't make the most out of the good positions I had in my games with Anikayev and Belyavsky, and also lost. Nevertheless I managed to alter the unfavourable course of the battle and at the finish I beat Kupreichik and Dolmatov. As a result I won a bronze and shared 3-4th place with Balashov (after Geller and Yusupov). Out of eleven games with the grandmasters I won four, drew six and lost just one.

In six months my international rating had increased by fifty points and by the start of 1980 stood at 2595. Not bad, but still a whole 130 points behind Karpov.

The next European team championship was to take place in January. The venue chosen was the little Swedish town of Skara, near Goeteborg. I was included in the USSR team, which was defending its championship title. To play in the same team as Karpov, Tal and Petrosyan was a great honour for a sixteen-year-old schoolboy. Even though I was only second reserve, I still felt on top of the world: it was, after all, the first time I had played for a full adult national team. I had to justify the trust placed in me, and I made a contribution to the overall victory, losing just half a point in six games.

I came back from Sweden with a gold medal, and was now eagerly looking forward to the spring, when an international tournament was due to be held in my home town of Baku. I needed a second grandmaster norm, and had no intention of letting the chance slip by.

The tournament exceeded all my expectations. I played freely and easily; it must be true what they say about fighting on your home ground. How the people of Baku supported me! Anyway, I managed not only to exceed the grandmaster norm, but to come top with eleven and a half points out of fifteen, half a point ahead of Belyavsky.

The opportunity of playing in the world youth championship naturally made me happy. The thing that had eluded me previously in the junior tournaments in Wattigny and Cagnes-sur-Mer was now within my grasp in Dortmund.

As the player with the highest rating, I was expected to win. However, such expectations can come to nothing, especially if, after getting used to adult games, you don't adjust yourself to playing with people your own age. But this time it all turned out well. Taking the lead fairly quickly, I came in first at the finishing line, beating the silver medallist Nigel Short by one and a half points. Nigel says he still remembers the impression that I made on him across the table: 'I have never faced such an intense player, never felt such energy and concentration, such will and desire to win burning across the board at me.'

Now I was a prince of chess! I was overjoyed. My trainers, Nikitin and Shakarov, were happy, as were my teachers and schoolmates, or rather my former schoolmates, because three months before the championship I had graduated from school with a gold medal.

That remarkable year of 1980, the year I won four gold medals, ended for me with the Olympiad in Malta. After a grim battle lasting two and a half weeks, our team managed to beat the Hungarians, but only in a tie-break. Playing on the last board, number six, after Karpov, Polugayevsky, Tal, Geller and Balashov, I gained the highest points of all – nine and a half out of twelve.

By January 1981 my international rating went up to 2625, while Karpov's stood at 2690. The gap between us was closing, a fact which had certainly not gone unnoticed by either Karpov or his entourage. Was I perhaps beginning to get a little too close for comfort?

FOUR

'We Don't Need Another!'

Looking back now, I think that Karpov sensed danger as early as 1978, when at the age of only fifteen I qualified for the top league of the Soviet Union. Nothing like this had ever happened before. I was not yet even an international master. This must have set alarm bells ringing for the champion, although he was engrossed in his contest with Korchnoi and seemed to have nothing else on his mind. But many people noticed that Karpov had suddenly stopped mentioning my name in interviews when the subject of promising young players came up.

At that time I still naïvely supposed that all problems were solved only at the chessboard, in an honest sporting contest. I never imagined that I would soon be drawn into a game without rules. The first time I felt something was wrong was at the so-called Tournament of the Generations – the match tournament of the USSR national teams held in Moscow in February 1981.

There were four teams: the first and second national teams, a veterans' team and a youth team. Of the eight players in the first national team, half were world champions of various years, including the reigning champion: Karpov, Spassky, Petrosyan and Tal. The veterans were pinning their hopes on the former world champion Smyslov and on Bronstein, the challenger who must have come closest to a world title without actually winning it. He tied with Botvinnik in 1951 after being ahead two games from the end. Actually, I have always had the feeling that it is simply given to some and not to others, that if you are destined to become champion, you will. If not, like Bronstein, Keres, Larsen and Korchnoi, then that's destiny too.

I naturally expected that I would play a number one board for the youth team, and so did most of the other players. But the Federation officials suddenly began to insist that either Psakhis, who had just become national champion, or Yusupov should be first board. But by that time I had already one of the highest ratings in the country – higher than Smyslov and Petrosyan, and better even than Tal's. So what was the problem?

The problem, I now realise, was simple. Karpov, who as world champion was number one board for the USSR first team, wanted to avoid playing me. There was no other explanation. In the end we demanded a democratic vote to decide who should head the team. The officials didn't like it, but they had no choice. In the event I won by five votes to three. So it was that Karpov and I faced each other over the chessboard.

A few days before the match, Karpov had won his seventh 'Oscar', a prize for the best chess player of the year, awarded annually by the International Association of Chess Journalists. In a poll, I had been named world third. Our paths were rapidly converging – the world champion and the world junior champion. Flohr wrote at the time: 'There is no doubt that in the near future Karpov and Kasparov will be playing each other often. Many believe that sooner or later they will be fighting it out at the highest level.'

In the match tournament we played two games, both of them richly creative with a keen thematic development, and both lasting five hours. When a correspondent asked me after the first game why I had rejected the draw offered by the world champion at the fifteenth move, I replied: 'I never hear the audience, but at that point I suddenly noticed how many people had come to see this match. I realised that I didn't have the right to disappoint their hopes – no, not hopes of victory, but of an uncompromising contest.'

My second game with Karpov kept the spectators on the edge of their seats too. When it ended, they rushed out into the arena – the event was being held at the Palace of Weight-lifting of the Central Army Sports Club – oblivious of the fact that play was still in progress at the other tables. Both games ended in a draw, but in both the champion had a hard time. Moreover, I had succeeded in gaining victory in a contest of strength among the top players, winning more points than anyone else at the number one board. Karpov could hardly have been left in any doubt that in me he had a dangerous opponent.

But why was there such keen interest on the part of the spectators? Above all, it was because they were sure that this match was a prelude to our future struggle for the world championship. There was also the contrast between our styles of play. Karpov was born with a strong positional sense, with an instinctive understanding of the board and how to play the pieces. But as a rule, he prefers to steer clear of complications. He says of himself: 'Risky play in the style of chess musketeers appeals to those who like sharp conflicts, but it is not to my taste. I attempt to assess my possibilities soberly, and not to rack my brains.' Karpov vividly represents the sporting, competitive style, whereas I am an investigative player. I derive great pleasure from seeking out new theoretical continuations and spending hours at home on analysis. I love complex combinations and am ruthless in breaking my own fixed patterns, avoiding the temptation to solve problems by purely technical means.

In making such generalisations, however, we should always remember Petrosyan's words of warning that 'Every grand-master is a rather complicated individual, and the impression people have of him does not always correspond with reality. Tal is not only "sacrifices", Fischer was not only an "electronic computer", and Petrosyan is not only "cautious".' That is why I'm convinced that in the most important area of all, Karpov and I share the same objective: we both believe that chess is first and foremost a struggle, a fight, in which the opponent has to be laid low.

Botvinnik says Karpov's style is more like Capablanca's,

whereas I am more like Alekhine. This is not simply a speculative conclusion: in his younger days Botvinnik played with both of these great old champions.

Capablanca's strength was in the cool precision of his judgement, invariably choosing the right option, no matter how intricate or imperilled his position. Botvinnik also played with Lasker, who was world champion for no less than twenty-seven years. He was a real fighter, who turned each game into a war of nerves, a psychological contest against his opponent. He used to say: 'My view is that chess is played by real people with different styles and different personalities. When you fight them you have to take account of their strengths and weaknesses – you can't be guided simply by general theoretical propositions or conclusions.'

Botvinnik told me that once Lasker threw out a clock that was fast, saying: 'I will not suffer liars. It's a clock's business to tell the right time!'

Yes, grandmasters sometimes seem eccentric, even not of this world. But we should remember what Spassky said: that all great chess players are difficult characters. This difficulty arises because a strong personality is meeting another strong personality in a game where each is seeking psychological superiority as part of the tactics for victory. In such a clash, there are bound to be sparks.

Botvinnik wrote in 1981: 'Karpov calculates variations very well. But this is not where his main strength lies. He is far superior to Kasparov in his positional understanding of chess. Karpov displayed a fine understanding of the positional principles of the game from an early age. When it comes to the skill of placing the pieces on the board, Karpov has no equal. His pieces are usually invulnerable, while the pieces of his opponent are subjected to continuous pressure. In this respect, Karpov's style is much better than that of Petrosyan who, once he has achieved an absolutely secure position, waits patiently for his opponent to make a mistake. Karpov does not wait; he plays actively.'

When that was written, Karpov was at the height of his

fame and had held the world title for six years. He was about thirty years of age, while I was still only seventeen.

Before our marathon, which began three years later, we met over the board only once more. This was also in 1981, at the Moscow Stars' Tournament, held at the magnificent International Trade Centre. Fate decreed that our game should be played in the final round; but it decided nothing, since Karpov was already assured of overall victory. At the eighteenth move we agreed to a draw. I played well until my birthday, which fell just in the middle of the tournament, but then lost my footing: I failed to press home a winning position against Andersson and lost to Petrosyan. In the end I shared 2-4th place with Polugayevsky and Smyslov.

While Karpov was preparing for his next skirmish with Korchnoi, which was to take place in Merano at the end of the year, I did well at the world youth teams championship at Graz in Austria, with the best individual result: eight wins and two draws.

The American chess master Eric Schiller had watched me closely throughout the tournament, and I quote a few of his live sketches so that the reader can get an idea of how someone else saw me at the time.

It was at this event that I became aware of one of Garik's superstitions. Like Samson, he seems to think that shaving may bring bad results, and therefore after his draw with Kouatly (for which he was clean-shaven) he began to assume a more bohemian visage. Then he started winning again, finishing the tournament with a stunning ninety per cent score against a field which was of good international calibre.

The two most impressive games were against the British player Speelman and the American Fedorowicz. In the Fedorowicz game he revealed an essential element of his style. As John fell deeper into time pressure, and his pieces began to wander to the queenside, Garik decided to 'worry' him a bit on the clock. The tactic succeeded admirably.

Garik's preparation just before the onset of the game is intense. Arriving early at the board, he plunges into deep concentration and starts to get his juices flowing. The face which was calm and peaceful only moments before becomes creased with tension. Sitting down opposite him, one can literally feel the pressure. He is, quite simply, frightening to play against.

Away from the board, it is quite another matter. He enjoys 'blitz', although he is quickly bored when faced by weak opposition. The consensus among some of our finest American blitz players was that he is simply astounding. Garry told me that there is really only one interesting blitz opponent for him – Karpov. His confidence is immense, but never touches on arrogance. And he still worships at the shrine of Fischer. We share an 'illness', both being slightly claustrophobic. Large gatherings make Garry uncomfortable. Garry is an excellent teacher. He gave a lecture in Graz, in which some Third World participants had their games analysed afterwards. His exposition of the Botvinnik training method was superb, and the practical advice proved useful. In fact, my own play improved noticeably in the next few months – and all I did was act as interpreter!

Kasparov's literary style is a sharp contrast to Fischer's, and his general educational level is much higher. An avid reader, Garry's suitcase is never without reading matter of a very high standard.

It is true that I always carried books with me everywhere: histories, memoirs, little volumes of the poetry of my beloved Lermontov . . . I was always eager to learn more about the countries I was visiting. I remember how at the Escorial, the residence of the Spanish kings, I followed a habit formed at school and started prompting the guide. Thanks to a naturally good memory I remembered every date I read in a book. Later I learned to wear my learning more lightly, as they say, but as a boy I couldn't keep quiet. It wasn't showing off: I just couldn't wait to share the things I knew with everyone around.

When I was sixteen or seventeen, I had great fun mixing with the local boys. Bold and unprejudiced, they were kids of the streets. They welcomed me as one of their own, and had a simple admiration for me. They wanted nothing from me except my company, and that was endearing. They listened eagerly to my stories about the writers and actors and other celebrities I had met. With a certain scorn for accepted standards, they bowed to a cult of justice and unwritten code of honour all their own. They created around them an atmosphere of sincerity and freedom from constraint. Incidentally, I already noticed then that I found it easy to get along with high-ranking officials and with the kids from the streets, but not with the people in between.

When I recall the now distant days of my youth, I can see that the notions I had of everything in life outside of chess were pretty hazy. What did my life consist of? An endless succession of planes, cities, hotel rooms, tournaments . . . It's usually problems that one remembers, and my problems were connected with the chessboard. Of course I felt that I was becoming famous, and I won't pretend I didn't like it, though I did begin to avoid crowded places. My friend Vadim Minasian complained that we couldn't just stroll about in Baku as we used to: people would constantly stop us, either for a chat, or to offer congratulations, or to wish me luck. Then the same thing started happening in other towns too. The way one feels about being famous usually changes with time. At first it's nice, then it begins to be irritating, then you take it calmly, and finally it becomes part of everyday life and you simply cease to notice it.

My next overseas excursion in 1981 was to Tilburg in Holland, where the tournament organisers always got together a strong list of competitors. Up till then I'd been helped greatly by the factor of surprise: no one could believe that the young boy sitting opposite them could pose a serious threat. Also, my games were not very well known to overseas players. But now the situation had changed. My name had gone before me on the circuit. They were getting ready for me. What's more, most of the top grandmasters turned out to be fiendishly inventive. Later I came to understand how useful and, above all, how timely my 'failure' at that tournament was. It became a stage in my chess development. But what I experienced in Tilburg at the time was something like shock. I wasn't used to losing.

In principle my performance could not really be called a failure. The general opinion was that for an eighteen-year-old to share 6-8th place among a company of distinguished grandmasters (I won three games, lost three and drew five) was a creditable result. Yet to me, it was a disappointment, the ruin of my hopes. But the main thing that upset me and my trainers was my inability to make the most of the advantages that I gained. The grandmasters were cleverer than I in working their way out of difficult spots, especially in the end-game. Deep down I knew I could beat them, but, as ever, my strongest opponent was myself.

In the second round I played Portisch, who achieved a draw in a situation that I never thought possible. In my game with Spassky I had an even bigger shock in store: I missed at least two opportunities to win, and in the end lost against the clock. To Petrosyan I sacrificed a pawn, gained a promising position, but at the crucial moment failed to find the right continuation of the attack. The vastly experienced Tigran Vartanovich, whose play was actually more like that of a boa constrictor than the tiger suggested by his name, hung on and finally beat me. Later, that bitter experience helped me to pay him back, by beating him in Bugojno and Niksic.

My only consolation was a win against Andersson, which I still regard as one of the best games of my life. Petrosyan, who always supported me even when it was not altogether the fashionable thing to do, wrote: 'Kasparov's appearance on the international scene has had much the same impact on Western chess players as the appearance of Karpov once had. With neither of them can you usually get anywhere by basing your game on general propositions . . . The ability to marshal his reserve forces patiently before going in for the final thrust is one of the secrets of Kasparov's success . . . One can only admire the way all his pieces, except perhaps his king, take part in the attack, and at the same time his opponent has absolutely no possibility of forcing the exchange of any of them.'

At the end of the game, Andersson exclaimed: 'Never again will I play against Kasparov!', and stopped the clock. But of course we met over the board again and again.

All the same, for me it was a bad tournament. Although I played certain games very well, my overall results were not too encouraging. I was still inexperienced, was going all out to win, and the grandmasters punished me for being over-reckless. It was a sobering experience which showed me that in chess I still had a lot to learn and master. I realised that I needed more experience against overseas grandmasters. I needed to harden my game so as to be able to carry my schemes through to their logical conclusion in battles against the top tournament players. My trainers and I agreed that that was the chief lesson of Tilburg.

Inexperience may not have been the only thing that affected my game. I had, too, a suppressed feeling of inner turmoil. Before leaving for the tournament I had been to see my grandfather in hospital. He had just had a serious operation, but was already feeling better. Our parting was, as usual, very warm and of few words; grandfather never liked more words than were absolutely necessary. I left him in the hope that we'd be seeing each other at home in a month's time. But the crisis came suddenly. While I was away playing my first game, he was already dead. They didn't tell me straightaway. My mother said on the telephone that grandfather was still in hospital with 'complications of some sort'. Why was I so uneasy? It was more than ten years since my father had died, and I somehow didn't think that I would once again have to feel the bitterness and pain of losing someone close.

It had become a tradition that when I came back from a tournament my mother and I would go to the Jewish cemetery where Father was buried. On that October day in 1981 I was driven to the Armenian cemetery. For a long time I was convulsed by sobs. My mother did not try to comfort me: she knew that her son was now saying goodbye both to grandfather and to childhood. It was a long time before I could get used to there only being one man left in the house. Grandmother suggested I should take grandfather's place at table, but I still can't do it.

The chess world was still excited by Karpov's resounding victory in Merano, and a fresh series of qualifying competitions had already begun. For Soviet players, the selection process began with the top league of the 49th USSR championship (Frunze, December 1981). Many of the experts, Botvinnik among them, thought the likeliest challenger for the world title in that series would be Belyavsky, Psakhis or myself. All three were taking part in that championship, which incidentally had the youngest competitors in the whole history of Soviet chess up until that time. Not surprisingly, one of its two winners also became the youngest national champion.

According to the writer Chingiz Aytmatov, who is a great lover of chess: 'All the players fought as if this were the tournament of their lives.'

At the championship, new continuations of well-known theoretical positions were tested in battle. The classical approach to chess is that black's prime task in the opening is to achieve equality. But many active-style players have never restricted themselves to such a pragmatic approach to opening problems. There are now systems in which black tries to take the initiative from the outset, thereby challenging white's traditional privilege in the opening, the right to seize the advantage. Botvinnik used to say that the situation was rather like a dance in which the lady takes the initiative and starts leading her partner.

And here, as in so much else, it was Botvinnik who undertook the first researches. He often used opening lines which theory had discarded, relying on his profound analysis and understanding of the fine points of his chosen continuation. He won more than a few brilliant victories using these 'bad' systems, and one of them justly bears the name of its creator. Even when compared with the most recent, highly complex counter-attack variations, Botvinnik's variation of the Slav Defence stands in a class of its own for the acuteness and intricacy of the positions to which it gives rise. For a long while the abundance of possible dangers scared white off it, but in recent years the theory of the system has taken great strides forward.

It so happened that at the Frunze championship I got involved in a theoretical discussion precisely about Botvinnik's system. It involved my games with Gennady Timoschenko and Iosif Dorfman (both of whom subsequently became my trainers). I have to say that in chess, winning the game doesn't always settle a theoretical argument. It can happen, after all, that your opponent may simply overlook something in his preliminary calculations, and your next opponent may analyse the critical position more deeply and refute the whole idea entirely. That was the situation that arose after the end of my game with Timoschenko, in which I sacrificed a knight and achieved a spectacular win.

The debates began as soon as the round was over. Was the sacrifice of the piece correct? Couldn't black have played more strongly? Almost all the players in the championship analysed the critical position that arose at the thirtieth move. In the end, most of them came to the conclusion that given the right continuation, black could have won. Sveshnikov proclaimed for all to hear that he would prove this when he and I met in the second to last round. Returning to my hotel, it took me a long time to calm down. I went through the variations over and over again until finally, at two in the morning, I found the winning continuation.

Next morning, to everyone's surprise, I used the Botvinnik variation again. The spectators watched in astonisment as Dorfman and I managed to complete thirty moves in forty minutes, such was our hurry to get to the crunch. Dorfman was sure he was going to win, and I also had faith in my analytical calculations. My thirty-first move came as a surprise

to my opponent, and my thirty-fifth underlined the helpless-
ness of the black pieces, which were unable to come to the aid
of their king.

But perhaps Sveshnikov would find another answer? I never
found out, because the Chelyabinsk grandmaster evidently
decided that discretion was the better part of valour and
avoided the Botvinnik system when we met.

Going into the final round, Psakhis led me by half a point
(our game at the beginning of the tournament had ended in
my defeat; altogether I lost just two games during the championship). He was clearly in the better position for the further
reason that he was playing white against Agzamov, while I
was about to play black against Tukmanov, who only needed
a draw for a bronze medal. But final rounds do not always
obey the laws of logic.

For me it was a clear case of all or nothing. I therefore settled
for my trusty weapon, the Old Indian Defence. The system
chosen by Tukmanov did not hold out much promise for him
with white, but it did have the advantage of severely limiting
active counterplay by black (see Appendix A: Illustrative
Games). Something had to be done. Of course I realised that
there was serious risk involved in trying to get away from the
continuations sanctified by theory, but the alternative was that
I'd have had to give up any thought of the championship title.

At the seventh move I sacrificed a pawn, achieving lively
play of the pieces in return. Tukmanov could have achieved a
draw by means of numerous exchanges, but chose not to. It
became obvious that my opponent had got carried away by
the excitement of the battle and, in his desire to punish me for
my adventurous opening, had forgotten the sporting problem
before him. This played into my hands, since it gave me a
chance to seize the initiative.

Realising that I'd burnt all my bridges and that the fate of
the game was going to be decided in open battle, I sacrificed
another pawn. This diverted the white rook, which exposed
an unexpected flaw in his first rank. The white pieces were

bunched up on the queenside, while in the meantime black had begun creeping up on the enemy king.

I felt Tukmanov was not aware of the imminent danger, and at first glance white did seem to have things under control. But only at first glance. The tremendous potential energy stored in the black forces suddenly began to burst forth. Belatedly, Tukmanov started rushing his pieces back, but they merely became fresh targets for my men.

Had I wanted to, I could have forced a striking draw, and in any other situation such a draw would have given me enormous creative satisfaction. But on this day, I would take any risk to avoid a draw. Then, when the danger had become plain and the black pieces had seized all the key positions, Tukmanov lost his nerve. A defeat for white was basically a foregone conclusion, but the abundance of threats and time pressure led Tukmanov to make a blunder which lost him the game in a single move.

The scales wavered for a long time in the Psakhis–Agzamov game. At one point Psakhis even seemed close to victory, but resilient defence by his opponent smashed all his hopes of launching an attack. Psakhis decided not to let the bird in the hand escape and offered a draw, but to his surprise it was declined. In the end it was a draw anyway.

It was a dramatic race in which Psakhis and I took it in turns to lead over the whole distance and then finally crossed the finishing line together, having broken away from our closest pursuers by two and a half points. We were both presented with gold medals as champions of the USSR.

My matches with the Soviet grandmasters were a good education. I not only learnt a lot, but also let them know that I was someone to be reckoned with. Encouraging too was the rapid improvement in my results in the national championships: I had moved from ninth place to third, and now to first.

The question on everyone's lips was who would be the challenger in 1984. In my bones I felt it could be me. But ever since Tilburg I knew that I wouldn't get through the knockout competitions unless I gained experience of playing in top-class overseas tournaments.

The following year, 1982, was a very important one for my chess development. Out of the list of forthcoming tournaments (I received a personal invitation from the organisers of each of them) there were three that had the most interesting competitors – London, Turin and Bugojno. After weighing all the pros and cons, my trainers and I picked the tournament in Yugoslavia. Of course I knew I'd need permission from the USSR Chess Federation and the Sports Committee, but I assumed this would be little more than a formality. After all, what reason could there be to refuse a young grandmaster who was, moreover, a USSR champion?

However, Krogius, the head of the chess department in the USSR Sports Committee, had his own way of looking at things. He offered me a mediocre tournament in Dortmund (category 9, I think). This was humiliating to a player of my standard, as he must have known. I had, after all, a much higher international rating than the players who had got permission to take part in major tournaments with no trouble at all.

I was mystified. Why was this happening to me? What had I done wrong? I had the feeling that I had landed in a world of bureaucratic obstruction, and that is precisely what had happened. What I didn't yet understand was that something like a cold war had begun against me.

When I asked Krogius what it all meant, he replied with disarming frankness and no particular sign of the personal animosity towards me that was to emerge later: 'We've got one world champion, we don't need another.'

FIVE

Long Live the King!

I had always known that Karpov held a very powerful position in the Soviet chess system, but not that he ruled it like a king. It was really not surprising: he had restored Soviet pride after the defeat of Boris Spassky at Reykjavik in 1972 at the hands of Robert Fischer, the first Westerner since the war to win the world title. Botvinnik, Smyslov, Tal, Petrosyan, Spassky – we had been totally dominant in the world of chess until the triumphal procession was interrupted by Fischer. Spassky's defeat had been felt as a great blow in the Soviet Union, especially coming from an American and in the full glare of international publicity.

After Reykjavik the chess officials were accused of connivance, and the leading grandmasters of complacency. There were a host of other reproaches and mutual recriminations, and it was decided that a firmer attitude and tighter discipline were needed. The general feeling was that our distinguished grandmasters had gone a little soft playing against each other all the time, and that they needed tougher overseas experience. The main hopes were pinned on Karpov, who had been coming on fast and had brought the world junior title back to the USSR after a long break. The young favourite suddenly found all doors opening easily to him and permission for travel to prestigious overseas tournaments readily granted. Nothing was too much for the great white hope of Soviet chess! It should be remembered that Soviet officials can also suffer themselves when their national players do badly. Fischer's victories caused problems for many of our chess functionaries, because it was thought that there had been serious errors of training that should be corrected. No one could accept that it was simply Fischer's genius that was causing the trouble.

Once it had recovered from the shock of Spassky's defeat, the chess establishment immediately saw a number of advantages in giving centre stage to the young champion from the Urals. Karpov offered hope of success against Fischer. Furthermore it was clear that unlike Spassky, this disciplined, dependable and rather conformist workhorse wouldn't rock the boat. Henceforth the chess officials would throw in their lot with this rising star. Karpov, incidentally, was the 'satellite' who launched the former cosmonaut Vitaly Sevastyanov into his new orbit as chairman of the USSR Chess Federation.

Karpov rapidly justified the hopes that had been placed in him by winning several tournaments abroad and filling the gap left in world chess by the ghost of Bobby Fischer. In 1973, together with Korchnoi, he won the interzonal tournament in Leningrad. He then went on to defeat Polugayevsky, Spassky and Korchnoi in candidates matches, after which a match with Fischer was in prospect.

The match, however, never took place. The world champion's conditions were not accepted, although, despite the quite understandable resistance of the Soviet Chess Federation, there had been a good chance that they would be. An extraordinary congress of FIDE in March 1975 had approved Fischer's formula of an open-ended match to ten victories, and it was only his other demand – that in the event of a 9-9 draw, the champion would retain his title – that was rejected by thirty-five votes to thirty-two (with three abstentions).

The challenger also rejected that demand, since to become world champion he'd have had to win by at least two points (as Alekhine once did against Capablanca, but in a match to six victories).

'My conscience is absolutely clear,' Karpov wrote later in his book *In Distant Baguio* (Moscow, 1981). 'I did everything I could to enable the match to take place, and accepted all the conditions dictated by the International Chess Federation, but Fischer refused . . . The overall predictions for the game were not in my favour. It was virtually taken for granted that Fischer would win. But I thought that I too had quite a good chance of winning, and I worked hard day after day to increase that chance.'

Would the historic world championship match ever have come about if FIDE had accepted Fischer's last condition too? It's very doubtful. And the reason is not just that Fischer had become a recluse. 'There's no point in fretting about it now,' Karpov said soon after the congress. 'The time to worry was before the extraordinary congress, when I might have thought that absolutely all of Fischer's demands would be accepted. If that had happened, it simply wouldn't have been morally right for me to play the match. But when I heard that the congress had not danced to Fischer's tune, my mind was immediately put at rest. It was clear that either the match would go ahead, or else I was world champion there and then.'

There is further testimony in the book by Karpov and Roshal, *Ninth File* (Moscow, 1978): 'It is a great pity that the match didn't take place. But I am not to blame that it didn't, because there are principles from which I cannot deviate. Fischer – and this is his fault entirely – turned out to be someone who wasn't satisfied with partial gains and wanted, to put it harshly, simply to ride roughshod over everyone. And what was the point? After all, they had already conceded him almost everything. Who knows what other demands he would have put forward if they had gone on meeting his wishes to the bitter end.'

And so there was a different historic day, 24 April 1975, when the FIDE president Max Euwe crowned Karpov with the laurel wreath of the world champion. It was a ceremony of great splendour. The Hall of Columns in the House of Unions was full to overflowing, the stage was a mass of flowers, and the exploding flash-bulbs competed in brilliance with the sparkling crystal chandeliers. The speeches of congratulation flowed in an unending stream.

At the press conference which followed, the new world

champion gave this answer to a question about the possibility of a contest with Fischer: 'Since the ex-champion's right to a return match was abolished long ago and no one has revived it, I cannot play a match with Fischer for the world title.' But he declared that he was still willing to play with him *unofficially* and on different conditions (some thirteen years later, in an interview with the West German magazine *Der Spiegel*, Karpov was to say: 'In 1975 Fischer was a slightly stronger player. I'd say my chances then were forty to sixty . . . Later I won a whole number of tournaments. In 1976 I was very strong and by then I was certainly playing better than Fischer').

In the event, Karpov never did meet the 'chess legend' over the board. However, to gain the title by default brought no satisfaction either to him or the true lovers of chess in our country. I've always felt that Karpov had something of a complex about this. This is why he took part in such an enormous number of international tournaments, more than any other world champion. It was as if he was demonstrating to the world his right to wear the crown. He appeared at Portoroz-Ljubljana and Milan in 1975; Skopje, Amsterdam and Montilla in 1976; and Bad Lauterberg, Las Palmas, London and Tilburg in 1977. Not since Alekhine had the chess world seen such a triumphal march from one victory to the next.

Time began working for Karpov. He was just the man for a system which elevated to the skies everything that helped to affirm its own ideological fetishes, even in sport. By that time chess had begun to loom larger in the politicisation of sport. The British grandmaster Michael Stean remarked: 'Karpov's widespread popularity in the Soviet Union is not difficult to understand. He looks like one of the masses and so the masses find it easy to identify with him.' Karpov wasn't a Jew like Botvinnik and Tal, or an Armenian like Petrosyan. He was a Russian from the depth of the provinces. Karpov himself is also at pains to emphasise his 'proletarian' origin. All this has probably played a decisive part in creating the Karpov cult.

Some Western journalists have suggested that the fact my father was a Jew has been a reason for my conflicts with the

Soviet chess authorities. I don't think so. I am Russian by culture and education. My mother tongue is Russian, and certainly not Armenian or Azerbaijani. I studied Russian literature at school, and my view of life and of the world has been shaped by the Russian classics. One thing is certain: having been brought up in a family of mixed nationalities, I have not cultivated any specific, purely national traits of conduct.

I think all the difficulties I've had to contend with have had to do, not with my nationality, but with a struggle against forces of a different kind. Probably if I'd been obliging and more amenable to the establishment, things would have gone differently for me.

They say a man is lucky in his friends. He can also be lucky in his enemies. It was a piece of great historical fortune for Karpov that his leading challenger for many years was Korch-noi. 'Renegade', 'traitor', 'betrayer', 'deserter' – the Soviet press rewarded him with all the names under the sun after he defected to the West. No wonder such huge political import-ance was attached to beating Korchnoi. Karpov's victories in Baguio (1978) and Merano (1981) created a special halo for him in our society and enabled him to become not just a chess champion, but a symbol of the Soviet system. It suited the top sports officials too, who imagined themselves to be engaged not in sport, but in big-time politics. Under the banner of fighting a 'political enemy' they could count on the very highest support and whatever help they required from the State.

The history of the struggle for the world title is created not only by the champions, but also by those who have given them a serious challenge. Among the grandmasters who in their heyday posed a threat to the chess throne, an unbiased chronicler would list first and foremost, of course, Chigorin, Tarrasch, Rubinstein, Bogoljubow, Bronstein, Keres . . . But not one of these 'runners-up' had such a tough struggle away from the chessboard as Viktor Korchnoi.

As early as 1974, during his first contest against Karpov, it became obvious that the sympathies of the establishment were wholly on Karpov's side. This angered Korchnoi, who said in his post-match interviews for the foreign press that pressure had been put on him in the course of the match. In addition, he accused the sporting authorities of having provided Karpov with the best-qualified trainers and better facilities for preparation. But Korchnoi was a voice crying in the wilderness: he had no one to defend him.

In July 1976, after a tournament in Amsterdam, Korchnoi cut off his relations with the system by seeking political asylum in the West. Korchnoi's defection plunged Soviet officialdom into a state of shock. Of course, chess players had left the country before him, but they had gone officially. That someone should simply stay behind in the West – and that it should be a grandmaster of his standard – was quite beyond their comprehension. Korchnoi was disqualified and stripped of all his titles, and a wave of censure rolled through the pages of our newspapers and magazines.

At international tournaments, Soviet chess players had to support the boycott of Korchnoi imposed by the USSR Chess Federation. FIDE, however, demanded that in official competitions for the world championship play-off they would play with Korchnoi, or else be counted as having lost. There was no choice. When Petrosyan, Polugayevsky and Spassky met Korchnoi in candidates matches, they didn't exchange a single word with him. Even a draw had to be offered through a go-between. Despite this 'triple shielding force' of former compatriots, Korchnoi once again became Karpov's opponent, just as he had four years earlier.

It came as a most unpleasant surprise. Korchnoi at forty-seven suddenly started playing as never before – tough, aggressive chess. His move to the West seemed to have imbued him with new strength and energy. To recall briefly his career, he had been national youth champion in 1947. After that he won the title of USSR champion no less than four times and was several times a challenger for the world title. But it was regarded as common knowledge that Korchnoi was long past his best.

Many years before, in 1957, the chess master Lev Abramov wrote: 'Many very highly qualified chess players have shared with me their impressions of Korchnoi's play and have admitted (as I must too) that at times they do not understand it. Sometimes his play is exceedingly profound, rich in content and far-sighted. We must ask, however, whether this striving to depart from the laws of positional play has not become for Korchnoi an end in itself. Does he not sometimes ignore possibilities of simple resolution of problems of the chessboard?'

Korchnoi replied that he broke the rules for the sake of chess itself: 'Emanuel Lasker once remarked that when the opponents are equally matched the games are seldom interesting and usually end in a draw. The chess player who does not like draws – and I am one of them – must somehow destroy this equilibrium. Either he sacrifices something in order to seize the initiative, or he allows his opponent to attack, in the hope of exploiting, as compensation, the weaknesses that this gives rise to in his opponent's position.'

This counter-attacking philosophy was well suited to Korchnoi's character. During the match in Baguio one commentator wrote: 'His will to win and his energy are quite phenomenal. When he sits down to play, everything else is forgotten. He must defeat the man opposite. He must win at all costs.'

In 1978 the chess world waited frantically for the match in the distant Philippines to begin. By July, when it was scheduled to start, the hullabaloo had reached its climax. But the hopes that the long-awaited match between Karpov and Korchnoi would prove to be the greatest chess contest in history were not realised, though without doubt it has gone down in history as one of the strangest. I had to admit that the Baguio match was of a very high standard, and that Karpov at times played brilliantly, although I cannot say the same for the match in Merano. Unfortunately, the match has been remembered not so much for the quality of the chess as the craziness of the whole event.

The very choice of venue was bizarre. Baguio is situated 250 kilometres from the Philippine capital, Manila, and is 1,500 metres above sea-level. Sometimes the town would vanish beneath a dense fog, because the match was being held in the rainy season, and the rains caused the players some discomfort. Both must have asked themselves many times how on earth this particular place had come to be chosen for the match, since each of them had both expressed a preference for other cities: Korchnoi had put Baguio second on his list, and Karpov had named it as a 'reserve'.

The man to answer that question would have been the extraordinarily active and infinitely cunning Filipino, Florencio Campomanes, who enjoyed the protection of the dictator Marcos. This was his debut on the world chess scene. He had established good relations with Sevastyanov and Baturinsky, the head of Karpov's delegation. And it paid off. It was at Baguio that Campo, as he became known, made his big bid for the top job in the world of chess by getting into the good books of the Soviet officials and Karpov. Campomanes got his reward four years later in Lucerne, when with crucial Soviet support he was elected President of FIDE.

There was no shortage of conflicts at the match. There was, for example, the famous 'yoghurt affair'. The 'yoghurt' was a nourishing fruit-flavoured mixture formulated specially for Karpov at the Moscow Institute of Nutrition. After the second game, P. Leeuwerik, the lady in charge of the Korchnoi delegation, protested against Karpov being handed a glass of yoghurt while play was in progress. She wrote to the chief arbiter, Lothar Schmid: 'It is clear that a cunningly arranged distribution of edible items to one player could convey a tiny coded message.' And although, according to Karpov, the mixture 'could only have two shades of colour, depending on how much acid was in the glass', Schmid still requested that Karpov be given the drink always at the same time. He added the remark that 'Even a banana skin could be a code, but no one had any suspicions of the salted fish that Fischer ate in his match with Spassky.' Be that as it may, the affair put Korchnoi off balance.

Then came the 'problem of Dr Zukhar', Karpov's psychologist, who had been staring at Korchnoi from his seat in the fourth row (the first three being reserved for the guests of honour).

Was the professor trying to hypnotise the challenger? Just in case, Korchnoi demanded that Zukhar should go and sit further away from the stage. He also demanded a one-way mirror between the players and the spectators. There was already a wooden partition under the chess table in case the players tried to kick each other. In the end they arrived at a compromise: Karpov agreed that Zukhar should move to the back, on condition that Korchnoi took off his enormous mirror-glasses, which were interfering with Karpov's vision, and that he withdrew his demand for a one-way mirror. On the day of the last game, however, Zukhar returned to the fourth row, and Korchnoi accused Karpov of breaking their gentlemen's agreement.

Next there was the 'parapsychologists affair', when Korchnoi invited two members of the Ananda Marga sect to attend the hall to help him with his thought processes. It soon emerged that they had been convicted by a Philippine court for the attempted assassination of an Indian diplomat, and were released on bail pending an appeal. After long altercations, statements and discussions, they were banned from the hall.

The reason I have gone in such detail into aspects of the match unassociated with chess is that it is interesting to trace how Karpov behaved in a conflict situation, particularly since at the time he was at the peak of his fame.

Another point of interest is that it was in Baguio that the *entente cordiale* between Karpov and Campomanes, which had far-reaching consequences for the world of chess, was formed. But let's not jump the gun. Back to Baguio.

Korchnoi, then, in an apparently hopeless situation (after

twenty-seven games Karpov was leading 5-2, and they were playing for six wins), managed to turn the tide and level the score. That was on 13 October. 'Having, at that point lost two games and allowed my opponent to come right up close to me on points,' Karpov recalled in his book *In Distant Baguio*, 'I was still, quite honestly, not really very worried. I knew that my time would come sooner or later and that I would take myself in hand and be able to deliver the coup de grace. But when I was beaten in game thirty-one, it really got to me, both because the score was now 5-5, and because I had committed an incredible oversight in one move. I had still not lost my faith in final victory, but you can imagine my feelings, first of all reaching 5-1, then getting 5-2 and then sinking down to 5-5 . . . I had every reason to lose my head.'

Years later a sensational report appeared in *Der Spiegel*. It appeared that on the very day he lost game thirty-one, Karpov had signed a contract with a company called Novag in Hong Kong to advertise a chess computer. One can only admire the composure and presence of mind of our champion in 'not losing his head' at the most tragic moment of the match. The go-between in the deal was Karpov's business partner, the West German TV journalist Helmut Jungwirt. Here is what the ex-president of the German Chess Alliance, Alfred Kinzel, told a *Moscow News* correspondent in September 1988: 'Jungwirt met Karpov when he was presenting the TV programme *Put the Champion in Check*, in which West German viewers played against Anatoly Karpov. While reporting the match in Baguio, Jungwirt frequently flew to Hong Kong where he met Peter Auge, the owner of a computer company. They hit on a plan to use the name of the world champion in their advertising. Jungwirt reported to the boss of Novag that Karpov had accepted the offer on condition that he was paid a commission for each computer sold.'

The moment chosen for the signing of the contract seems surprising. Jungwirt said later that Karpov, fearing persecution in his own country if he were defeated by the emigre Korchnoi, was intending to defect to the USA, and had a Pan-Am ticket to Los Angeles waiting for him at Manila airport. On 30 November 1988 a Hamburg court pronounced Jungwirt's 'revelations' to be a flight of fancy. Kinzel, who incidentally was one of Karpov's business agents, had earlier said the same thing: 'My opinion is that Jungwirt made the whole thing up. Even in court he was still making up fairy tales.'

Now everything depended on who would win the next victory. It was at this point that rumours started circulating that the Soviet delegation, out of concern for Karpov's state of health, had suggested stopping the match at 5-5, Karpov, of course, retaining the world title. At the time, the denial of these rumours seemed to me convincing, but over the years doubts have arisen. The then President of FIDE, Max Euwe, told Raymond Keene, one of Korchnoi's seconds, that the match should be stopped at an even score. He put this forward as if it were his own idea, but it's quite feasible that it had been suggested to him, as it was to another FIDE President, Campomanes, seven years later, when he stopped my first match with Karpov in a smiliar situation and under the same pretext.

What happened next in Baguio? '. . . Vitaly Ivanovich Sevastyanov came to the rescue,' Karpov wrote. 'A live wire, energetic, always the heart and soul of the party, a person in whose company it was simply shameful to be depressed . . . Vitaly Ivanovich was always, off his own bat, either sitting down with me to play cards, or teaching me a new game of patience or making me get out of the car and take a walk at night . . . And at a decisive moment in the contest it was he who insisted on the need (many of us were in two minds) to take a break from chess – not in order to spend the time-out in the usual surroundings we had all had enough of, yet again analysing the position at the chessboard, but for a change of scene. We were to take a trip to Manila, where the world basketball championship was drawing to a close. It was a bold and risky decision. A five-hour drive along a mountain road – to say nothing of the return journey – was not the sort of thing anyone had previously recommended on the day before the most crucial game. But the particular situation called for a particular approach. Taking a creatively bold decision, as I learnt on that occasion, is of the utmost importance in an emergency.'

'Meanwhile in Baguio,' Karpov continues, 'quite different passions were raging. Just an hour or so after we left, Florencio Campomanes, the chief organiser of the match and FIDE vice-president, called a sudden press conference on the continued interference by the members of the Ananda Marga sect.' Campomanes demanded that Korchnoi should observe the proprieties and show respect for the people who had created superb conditions for him in the Philippines: 'We do not want lovers of the game to associate the world championship match in their minds with persons who are tainted with crime.'

Then came the finale. It was described by the press spokesman for the Karpov delegation in Baguio, Alexander Roshal, in his book *Ninth File*. 'On the stage in the evening of 17 October, when game thirty-two, which was to prove decisive, was being played, we saw at the chess table the familiar and well-loved figure of the champion . . . On the following day, when the match arbiter, the Czechoslovak grandmaster M. Filip, announced that Korchnoi had conceded game thirty-two without resuming it, the world champion, with a weary smile, "gave permission" for his victory to be reported back home. The chairman of the USSR Chess Federation, USSR Pilot-Cosmonaut V. Sevastyanov, said: "Well, Tolya, this is your finest hour" . . .'

On that same day Anatoly sent off a telegram to Moscow:

To Comrade Leonid Ilyich BREZHNEV

Esteemed Leonid Ilyich,
I am happy to report that the world chess championship match has
ended in our victory. Please accept, dear Leonid Ilyich, my
heartfelt gratitude for the fatherly concern and consideration you
have shown me and my delegation during the preparation period
and the match itself. I assure the Central Committee of the CPSU,
the Presidium of the USSR Supreme Soviet, the Soviet

Government and you personally, Leonid Ilyich, that I shall devote every effort in the future to increasing the glory of the Soviet school of chess.

World Champion Anatoly KARPOV
Baguio, Philippines, 18 October 1978

That is how the book ends. It begins with Brezhnev's telegram of congratulations:

To Comrade Anatoly Yevgenyevich KARPOV
Baguio, Philippines

Dear Anatoly Yevgenyevich,
I was very glad to receive your telegram. I congratulate you warmly and cordially on your victory in a crucial and difficult match. Our whole country is proud that in a strenuous and persistent struggle you displayed consummate skill, inflexible will and courage – in a word, the qualities that make up our Soviet character. I am confident that you will in the future redouble your creative efforts and make a great contribution to the treasure-house of the art of chess. I wish you good health, happiness and brilliant victories to the glory of our great Homeland.

L. Brezhnev

When Karpov returned from Baguio, he was ceremonially received by Brezhnev, and Anatoly Yevgenyevich remembers this as one of the 'high spots' of his life. Karpov was presented at the Kremlin with the order of the Labour Red Banner, after which Brezhnev left him with the words, 'The crown is yours: make sure you hold on to it!' Brezhnev could hardly have expected his words to be interpreted literally, but the officials took them perfectly seriously.

Karpov's victory was important in every respect. It finally erased the memory of Reykjavik and restored the prestige of Soviet chess. The splendour of the victory was further enhanced by the important fact that he had beaten the 'defector', and this deflated the latter's criticism of the Soviet authorities. As it turned out, both Fischer and Korchnoi had, despite themselves, done Karpov an enormous favour. One had ceded the world title to him without a fight, while the other had helped make him into a political figure.

The authorities were of course grateful to the Chess Federation for upholding the nation's honour, and the chess officials, in turn, were bound to feel gratitude to their hero, Karpov. Many backs deserved to be scratched, but none so much as the champion himself, and he was rewarded like no one else. He was granted a mass of privileges, including, probably, freedom of action abroad.

Take that secret contract between Karpov and Novag. It was only much later, when it emerged that Jungwirt had kept some half-a-million dollars which should have been paid to Karpov, that the details of the contract became public knowledge. Had the authorities helped Karpov with the deal? Or had they simply turned a blind eye to it, as they may have done to his foreign currency accounts in Western banks? Or did he get up to all these things behind their backs? These questions remain unanswered. What is beyond doubt is that Karpov was later assisted in his attempt to get his hands on his 'rightful' money. And it wasn't the Soviet officials who helped him in this (in 1983–4), but Campomanes and Kinzel (the same Kinzel who, with Campomanes, acted against me in February 1985). Their private investigation was successful: on 30 August Jungwirt finally admitted in conversation with Kinzel (a former police chief, incidentally) that he had been receiving money for Karpov. A week later Kinzel took up his duties as chairman of the appeals jury for my first match with Karpov.

By late 1981, when Karpov was again due to play Korchnoi – this time at a match in Merano – the champion was at the centre of an unparalleled patriotic campaign, given the best coaches and all the help that the State apparatus could provide. As had happened three years before, Korchnoi defeated Petrosyan and Polugayevsky in the candidates matches, and then beat Hübner in the final duel.

The atmosphere of suspicion surrounding the match in

Merano can be gauged from the fact that the Soviet delegation, including Karpov, went there several weeks beforehand to check the drinking water, the climate and the noise and radiation levels, or at least so it was claimed by the chairman of the organising committee in an interview with the Swiss magazine *Chess Press*.

By this time the politics of the match had become more important than the chess itself. Eloquent proof of this is given by something that Sevastyanov wrote in an article entitled 'The Karpov We Love', which *Literaturnaya Gazeta* published in December 1981: 'In Merano he [i.e. Karpov] was not only defending his title . . . He was defending the honour and dignity of our country and our system. The contrast between this citizen of the land of the Soviets and his embittered and confused opponent staggered even the journalists of the bourgeois press, whose bosses had hardly sent them to Merano for the purpose of being fair and objective. It was not just the difference between two people. Or rather it was more than the difference between two people: it was the difference between the world of lies and money-making and the world of a radiant future.'

Korchnoi took advantage of the pre-match situation to start a campaign to get his family, who were still in Leningrad, out of the country. He was especially worried about his son. According to an article entitled 'Challenger's False Move', published in the newspaper *Sovietsky Sport* just before the match in Merano, 'his son first of all dropped out of college, thus forfeiting his right to postponement of military service, and then pointedly refused to obey the law on universal conscription. He evaded the draft into the army, and was eventually convicted by a Soviet court in accordance with the law . . .'

The two opponents found themselves in totally different circumstances. Whereas Korchnoi was ill-prepared (one thing that must have affected him was his lack of participation in major tournaments, from which he was barred because of the boycott by Soviet players), Karpov had received help from all our best grandmasters. We'd been obliged to furnish him with information about our opening lines and variations and reveal all our professional secrets. We were given clearly to understand that this was our patriotic duty, since the 'traitor' had to be routed at all costs.

Many of the grandmasters meticulously did what was demanded of them. I, however, refused, saying there was no need for it, as Korchnoi's defeat was a foregone conclusion anyway. (And indeed, there was no struggle in Merano as such; Karpov won 6-2.) What is clear is that Karpov was being offered a far from unwelcome opportunity to extract all the new ideas that the Soviet grandmasters had.

So Karpov continued to rule as king of chess. As befits a reigning monarch, he was surrounded by a large retinue. His was the power to decide who should go abroad and who should not. All chess players found themselves divided into 'travellers' and 'non-travellers' and the principle by which they were divided was no secret.

You will recall what Krogius, the head of the chess department of the USSR Sports committee said to me: 'We've got one world champion, we don't need another.' Those words are a monument to the old regime, and not just in chess. Karpov should remain champion until the end of the century, so why change anything or let anything develop? That attitude was not considered immoral, nor was it basically directed against me personally. I was just fated to be the unlucky one who wasn't permitted to become champion because he turned up at the wrong time.

It was 1982, and a new series of knockout contests for the world championship had begun. I needed experience of overseas tournaments, especially now that the Moscow interzonal was imminent. I have no doubt that if anyone had been able to keep me out of it, they would have, despite the fact that I was now one of the world's top five players.

Ivonin, a deputy chairman of the Sports Committee and one of Karpov's highly influential supporters, had the temerity to say, in Baku of all places, that 'the Sports Committee will do everything in its power to prevent a Kasparov–Karpov encounter in this cycle.'

As mentioned before, I had invitations from Bugojno, Turin and London, but instead I'd been offered a second-class tournament in Dortmund. I decided to fight. But what weapon could a young man of eighteen wield against the formidable power of the world champion? It was like David and Goliath. I looked around for a sling.

The First Secretary of the Azerbaijan Communist Party at the time was Geidar Aliev. He had congratulated me warmly on my victory in the USSR championship and chatted with me, asking about my studies at the Institute. He said how much he approved of my active involvement in Komsomol life in Baku and the promotion of chess in the republic. Soon I was invited to speak at a congress of the Azerbaijan Komsomol. Sevastynov and Ivonin unexpectedly turned up at the congress. I don't know who had invited them, or whether they had been invited at all, but since they were here I decided to take the opportunity and appeal directly to the leadership of the Chess Federation and the Sports Committee, and at the same time to Aliev.

The result exceeded all my expectations. They gave me permission to take part in the super-tournament in Bugojno. Now that I had overcome all the problems, I had to get as much as I could out of playing the best overseas grandmasters.

Later on, too, when things got difficult, I had occasion to ask Aliev for help, and he assisted me as much as he could. There are certain people now who try to use this fact to accuse me of dishonesty. How can Kasparov tell us, they say, that he's been persecuted for years by the *apparatchiks*, if he himself enjoyed the protection of someone who figured prominently in the 'era of stagnation'? I have to admit that without the support of influential Party leaders, I could never have fought my way through to the world championship. But not once did I use that help to the detriment of anyone else.

I often wonder about the reasons that prompted Aliev to pay me so much attention. Because whereas the help I was to receive in the future from Alexander Yakovlev and Stepan Shalayev was largely due to the changes that were taking place in the country, Aliev – as one of Brezhnev's old guard – should logically have been expected to take a different line. The best explanation is that natural pride in the achievements of someone from his own part of the world, and the opportunity to bring glory to his native Baku, must have played a part. But could such emotional considerations have outweighed the danger of a confrontation with that section of the establishment whose idol was Karpov? It could be that in supporting me Aliev was testing the water to see how real were his chances of winning the power struggle, knowing full well the opposition he was up against. Be that as it may, Aliev's timely intervention enabled me to set about preparing to storm the chess Olympus.

The tournament in Bugojno brought together a whole constellation of stars: Spassky, Petrosyan, Hübner, Larsen, Polugayevsky, Gligoric, Andersson, Ljubojevic, Timman, Kavalek, Najdorf, Ivanovic and Ivkov. The even quality of the players promised a sustained struggle. But there was no particular struggle for first place. The stiff pace that I set from the start was too much for my partners.

I was glad to discover that the errors and lack of confidence that had dogged me in Tilburg had disappeared. I lost not a single game and won the tournament by one and a half points over Ljubojevic and Polugayevsky. My hardest game was with Timman: from a losing position, I managed to entangle my opponent in ghastly complications and avoid defeat. I had another fighting draw with Spassky. On the other hand, my game with Petrosyan showed how much I had grown in experience since the previous year. It brought this comment from Botvinnik: 'Kasparov succeeded in playing a refined positional game against Petrosyan. Although Petrosyan is famed for his positional understanding, in this game he got into trouble at the very opening. Making simple moves, without resorting to combinations or positional sacrifices,

Kasparov, by about the fifteenth move, had placed his distinguished opponent in a hopeless position.'

I am more proud of that game than of many of the chess fireworks that usually delight the fans. Having gained an overwhelming position, I had just started to weigh up the best forcing continuation when I suddenly remembered a conversation I'd had with Spassky the previous day: 'Remember, Petrosyan is a tactician with enormous understanding of position and a sixth sense. Don't deal any direct blows and try not to sacrifice anything. In the worst positions it's difficult to defend yourself against Petrosyan without counter-play. So squeeze him, squeeze, but whatever you do, don't rush.' I looked at the position again. 'Squeeze him, squeeze' was still ringing in my ears. My next five moves were not too brilliant, but still just about the most difficult of my life. Each of them improved the situation just a fraction, without creating any visible threat. For four moves Petrosyan held out, but on the fifth he faltered, and I switched into a winning end-game.

In an interview, Botvinnik made this comment on the tournament: 'While I thought previously that Kasparov could not become a rival to Karpov until the next series, after Bugojno I'm inclined to think it may happen sooner.'

After that, the journalists began to assail me with the question: was this 'my' series, or 'not mine'? A difficult question. If I gave a definite answer one way or the other, I risked seeming not quite honest. If I said it was mine, they'd think me conceited. If I said it wasn't, they would decide I was discounting any hope at all for the next three years. But that wasn't so!

Now it was time to prepare for the major event of the year, the interzonal tournament in Moscow. But first I had to pass my end-of-term exams. I was, as I said, a student at the Institute of Foreign Languages in Baku, where I was majoring in English. Time was short, so I had to rely on my 'chess' memory. It didn't let me down. A good memory, by the way, is an absolute must for a chess player. He has to remember thousands of games, and a multitude of openings and theoretical positions.

There is an interesting story about Fischer's memory. He once telephoned the Icelandic grandmaster Fridrik Olafsson, but there was no one at home except his small daughter. Fischer didn't know a word of Icelandic, and she didn't know a word of English. Fischer memorised parrot-fashion everything the little girl said, rang up an Icelander he knew and asked him to translate. Imagine Olafsson's surprise when Fischer telephoned exactly at the time his daughter had told him to.

Once *Der Spiegel* decided to test me. They showed me five positions and asked me to say what games they were from. It took me just a few seconds. I remember the games to this day: Karpov–Miles (Oslo, 1984); Botvinnik–Fischer (Varna, 1962); Hübner–Timman (Linares, 1985) – I mistook Timman for Ljubojevic in this one; Alekhine–Capablanca (Buenos Aires, 1927); and Sokolov–Agzamov (Riga, 1985).

Then they asked me what I thought of the phenomenal memory demonstrated by the famous American champion Harry Pillsburg. One of his spectacular turns was this: on each of fifty numbered sheets of paper five words were written, then the sheets were thrown into a cylinder. They pulled them out one by one and gave the number, and Pillsburg would recite the words from memory. I said I wouldn't do it, because I thought it was bad for you. Many years ago the coach Alexander Aslanov did a rather similar trick for me and some other schoolchildren. We wrote down thirty nouns and numbered them, after which Aslanov looked at the list. First he matched the nouns with the numbers, and then vice versa. He could memorise 150 words in succession from the dictionary and reel them off by heart. Afterwards, though, he was a bit confused . . .

I spent the two summer months before the interzonal, as usual, in Zagulba, a little village by the Caspian, forty kilometres north of Baku. Nowhere can I work so well and fruitfully as here. That's why I'm so attached to Zagulba. I live there both summer and winter, and also in the early spring, when the beach is deserted and I can be alone.

My team then comprised Alexander Nikitin (my regular trainer), Alexander Shakarov and Yevgeny Vladimirov. Naturally we spent the mornings on the beach. We would swim and play football, crazy beach football like no other game on earth. I would not join in straight away, but after a run: three kilometres barefoot along the seashore on wet sand which made running difficult. The same thing every morning . . . People who think preparing for competitions means just working at chess are wrong. Without physical exercise you couldn't take the strain, especially at the top level. After the beach I would always sleep for an hour. My trainers and I began work in the afternoon, after our traditional post-lunch cup of tea. Our best time, we found by experience, was five o'clock. But if we came across some fascinating idea, time would naturally be forgotten . . .

The Moscow interzonal was the last of three tournaments to decide who should go on to the candidates matches. Ribli and Smyslov had already been victorious in Las Palmas, Portisch and Torre in Toluca; while Korchnoi and Hübner, as finalists in the previous series, were exempt from the knock-out competitions. Now they were all waiting for news from Moscow.

Not everything went smoothly for me as the tournament progressed. After a good start came a series of draws. This drew criticism from some newspaper journalists, who took me to task for being over-cautious. Yes, I was trying to avoid risks, the course was short and losing just one single game could have made it highly difficult to achieve my main aim. Having studied what had happened at the two other interzonal tournaments I came to the conclusion that the most important thing was to pace myself. In Las Palmas and Toluca victory had gone not to the player who had begun with a flourish, only to spend all his time afterwards thinking about how not to fritter away his lead, but to the one who kept back his strength for the final dash.

As this was the first time I had taken part in an interzonal, I was naturally nervous. It showed in my playing. But a well-chosen tournament strategy helped me to overcome both nerves and inexperience. Above all, I tried to control my emotions, so as not to get carried away, not to get into time trouble. I did feel the lack of time now and then, but not once was I under serious time pressure. There were practically no adjournments, either.

Every tournament has its key moments. In Moscow the high points for me were my games with Tal and Andersson, though both ended in draws. Why do I single them out? In the game with Tal I used a new scheme which took him by surprise. At the beginning things were going well for me, but when all I had to do was to strike a simple combinative blow, I succumbed to the temptation of another, more spectacular continuation and wound up by putting the initiative into the hands of Tal. Fortunately, everything still turned out well for me in the end. Nevertheless, I got a shock. I had made an error in the very tactical complications, where I felt in my element. I tried to forget the game, to distract myself somehow. But I couldn't rid myself of the thought of how badly I had miscalculated. Then on the next day, after I sacrificed a piece to Belyavsky, the alarming feeling never left me that I might make another mistake. That feeling of constraint also affected my play in the following rounds.

Then came my game with Andersson. I got into a bad position. What should I do? My instinct for self-preservation was activated: instead of nervously running about the stage, I simply sat at the chess table and looked imperturbably at my opponent. Only very recently, at the tournament in Bugojno, self-possession had saved me in a game with Timman, when I suddenly lost my rook. He was obviously waiting for me to resign. But I went on playing as if nothing had happened, and caught Timman out in a well-disguised trap.

In my encounter with Andersson, too, a small miracle occurred: I saved myself! That success gave me a great charge of positive emotions and brought me out of my depression.

From that moment, I was in business. And when in the finishing straight I managed to win four games in a row, it became clear that I had paced myself properly. In the end I got ten points out of thirteen (seven wins and six draws), one and a half points ahead of Belyavsky, who came second.

There were many trials ahead, but at least I had planted my feet on the road leading to the world championship. A dream was beginning to come true. I had confidence in my game and my strength, and was superbly prepared. But in my heart I was uneasy: 'What else will they think up?' I realised that there are certain thoughts which you have to drive from your mind if you are not to lose faith in what matters most in life. And still I was unable to shake off the gloomy premonitions. But every time I thought: 'It cannot happen, because it will never happen.' And with that in mind I played chess, and chess only.

But there soon came a time when I had to face reality and I realised that anything, absolutely anything, could happen after all.

SIX

War and Peace

The Swiss town of Lucerne, with its beautiful lake, its snow-capped mountains and its stillness, seems created by nature itself as a haven of peace and repose. No wonder this picturesque spot was chosen as the venue of the 25th Chess Olympiad. Yet ironically, the events that unfolded in Lucerne at that time plunged the chess world into an abyss of endless contention and conflict. For it was there, towards the end of 1982, that the balance of power in world chess was suddenly upset. The future of the game fell into the hands of a man who looked down on chess players and who became, not a president of chess, but a president above chess.

At the time I was still only nineteen and more concerned with chess than the byzantine politics surrounding the board. Only now have I come to realise that it was in Lucerne that most of my troubles began.

Who would have imagined, even just a short while ago, that chess needed such a mighty organisation as the present FIDE? There are just thirty-two pieces on the chessboard, and once they are arranged, what else do you need? A referee perhaps, to ensure that the kind of ploy urged by the sixteenth-century Spanish priest, Ruy Lopez, is not being used: 'Sit your opponent with the sun in his eyes', and so on. All the rest can be settled by gentlemen's agreement.

But now we have an International Chess Federation in charge of everything. It was founded in 1924, and thanks to the efforts of enthusiasts did much to promote the game. But in the pre-war period FIDE did not have the resources or the authority to take charge of organising and holding world championships. Besides, its plans to do so lacked the support of the top grandmasters and the champion himself. It was not until Alexander Alekhine died and the Soviet Chess Federation joined FIDE in 1947 that the situation changed. An orderly system was developed and put into practice for world championship play-offs. The first world champion in a competition held under the auspices of FIDE was Mikhail Botvinnik, who carried off the victory in a candidates match tournament in 1948.

Today FIDE is a powerful bureaucratic structure with a vast administrative apparatus which has its president, secretary-general, secretariat, five regional vice-presidents (one for each continent), executive council and central committee. As one seasoned journalist put it: 'The politics of chess is enormous, proliferating, horrendous. The reason is that chess arouses deep and violent human passions . . . FIDE has come to resemble, almost exactly, the United Nations itself. Squabbles, power blocs, international rivalries, lobbying of votes and behind-the-scenes intrigues – the whole diplomatic way of life is there.'

As in so many cumbersome international organisations, power is concentrated at the centre, around the president, who is at the top of the pyramid, as it were. The voting system cannot guarantee that problems will be settled fairly, since the major chess-playing countries are unable to protect their interests. It's one country, one vote. That rule applies, without exeption, to everything. What's more, once a decision is taken it is binding on all chess federations, and on the world champion. Little countries are able blatantly to dictate to others without the restraining factor, as at the UN, of either a right of veto or a Security Council. In the days of the true democrats such as Max Euwe of Holland or Fridrik Olafsson of Iceland, things were different in FIDE because those presidents did not try to rise above chess; they acted as mediators between the opposing sides and always took into account the interests of the players themselves. Fischer almost drove FIDE into the background, but in a situation of stalemate each of those two presidents displayed, in the name of chess, both firmness and flexibility and – most important of all – objectivity. By contrast, the present FIDE leadership simply disregards the grandmasters, who don't even have a vote in the elections. FIDE's principal interest is not chess at all, but banking operations and election campaigns.

In that autumn of 1982 few people thought the Filipino Florencio Campomanes had a serious chance of taking Olafsson's place. Many people in Lucerne saw him as a comic figure campaigning like an American politician, chasing the votes of the Third World delegates and liberally scattering presents and souvenirs. His 'one of the lads' act helped disguise his business acumen and inordinate vanity. Campomanes bragged about his powerful connections at home: 'When I ask President Marcos for two million dollars, at worst he asks whether I want it straight away or whether he should put a cheque in the post.' His audience knew this was no idle boast, for Campomanes had organised the match in Baguio City at a cost of over a million dollars. As to his own chess abilities he invariably referred to himself as a 'gifted player' who had taken part in five Olympiads.

As the voting started, one delegate was heard to mutter: 'Have you ever seen a man who puts fifty thousand dollars down on black and can countenance the possibility that red might come up?' To give Campomanes his due, the roulette wheel spun as it had been programmed to spin. I remember that after the votes had been counted, but before the result was announced, an episode occurred which struck me as highly symbolic. The chairman of the meeting was handed a note, which he read out in a sombre tone: 'It is with great sorrow that I have to announce the death of President Brezhnev. I ask everyone to stand and honour his memory with a minute's silence.' In the deathly hush that followed, Campomanes's victory was announced. It seemed as if the chess world was mourning, not the departed Brezhnev, but its own future. So in this rather strange way, Campomanes's election and Brezhnev's death have become intertwined in my memory. For me, the former suggested difficult problems in the chess world, while the latter meant hope of changes for the better in my own country.

Even at the time, the programme which Campomanes put forward made me vaguely uneasy. 'I want to propose new paths for the work of FIDE and demonstrate . . . a new philosophy. I feel it is time for a new emphasis. FIDE's motto *Gens una sumus (We are all one family)* must be effective for all federations, even the most remote and underdeveloped . . . In my programme I intend to put the emphasis on the developing countries. What I want to say to them is this: There are no heights that cannot be scaled . . . I cannot say that Olafsson had no wish to help the developing countries, but a man who has been brought up on European culture and has not worked with them from scratch cannot appreciate all the problems.' It was a long-term programme and although, in one of his first interviews as President, Campomanes said he did not intend to stand in the next election in 1986, it was clear that having gained power, he wasn't about to let go of it so easily.

Meanwhile, however, the present was looking pretty good, both for me and for the whole Soviet team, which put up its best performance for several Olympiads. We beat the runners-up, Czechoslovakia, by six and a half points, losing only three games in the entire tournament. I moved up from board six, where I had played in the Malta Olympiad, to board two in Lucerne, behind Karpov. I brought the team the largest number of points, just as I had done two years before, winning six games and drawing five.

I had an exciting game with Korchnoi, who was leading the Swiss team (see Appendix A). Karpov diplomatically avoided the encounter; he was to have played black, and evidently didn't want to risk it. He also thought I would get a bloody nose, as this was my first encounter over the board with Korchnoi. Karpov was trying to put me in an exposed position, but actually he did me a good turn.

For many Western journalists, this was their first sight of me. The writer David Spanier described me like this:

> Medium height, slightly sallow, with a shock of dark fuzzy hair and a white turtle-neck sweater, Kasparov has a look of the West Side rocker, ready for action. He sits nervously at the chessboard, continually shifting around, frowning under thick eyebrows, staring narrow-eyed at the pieces. Or he stomps up and down, waiting for his opponent's move. The players did not shake hands at the start of the game (that was only to be expected) though Kasparov, to his credit, made a half-gesture to do so; it was Korchnoi who refrained. Korchnoi played a Queen's Pawn opening and Kasparov responded with the Modern Benoni, his usual choice. It did not take Kasparov long to set off in a new direction, whether prepared in advance or devised over the board hardly mattered for the fireworks that followed. He left a knight *en prise* for seven moves; he moved his queen into the enemy back rank where it was apparently cut off from safety; he held the spectators, following the game around the board and on television monitors, spellbound. Yet so provocative and complex were his ideas that even the experts could not analyse if or how he was winning. Instead, there was an overwhelming sense of mastery, of inevitable fate, of the passing of the generations.

Yes, it was a memorable skirmish. Later, mind you, Korchnoi, found that he could have made it a draw at the twenty-ninth move . . .

Less fortunate for me was the draw for the candidates matches which was held towards the end of the Olympiad. In fact it was a strange draw altogether. Here is the list of pairings that resulted, with the ratings of the players:

> Hübner (2630) – Smyslov (2565)
> Ribli (2580) – Torre (2535)
> Kasparov (2675) – Belyavsky (2620)
> Korchnoi (2635) – Portisch (2625)

I had said in advance that the most dangerous opponents for me would be Belyavsky and Korchnoi, and now I was to meet them both, in succession. Why? Because after the pairs had been decided, it was simply announced that the winner of the first pair would meet the winner of the second, and the winner of the third would meet the winner of the fourth (though it was perfectly obvious that three of the four players in the top half of the draw were far weaker than those in the bottom half). Had the lots actually been drawn, and if so, why was it done without our taking part? I cannot say what did or did not happen. Portisch was indignant and walked out of the hall, accusing the organisers of cheating. It was bad enough that he had been paired with Korchnoi, but if he won, he'd be playing me or Belyavsky.

Contrary to my expectations, Belyavsky had unexpectedly turned out not to be too difficult an obstacle for me: I beat him in Moscow by six games to three. But it was an uncompromising battle, and it was only my victory with black in game eight which determined its outcome. When I rose at the end of the match to shake Belyavsky's hand, I said to him, bearing in mind the unfortunate draw: 'It's a great pity for me that we met so soon.'

That was in March 1983. My semi-final with Korchnoi was due to be held in August. But where? The choice of venue for the match provoked a crisis, the first of many under the rule of the current FIDE President. Even now I cannot fully understand why the crisis was allowed to go as far as it did. But I know that unless I had taken decisive action at the time, the Soviet Chess Federation and Campomanes would have ruined my chance of a crack at the world title. Let us try and figure out what happened.

Korchnoi and I were invited by three cities: Las Palmas ($25,000), Rotterdam ($100,000) and Pasadena ($100,000). Under FIDE rules, each player had to list them in order of preference. Korchnoi plumped for Rotterdam alone. In my list, which I sent to the Sports Committee in mid-May, I also put Rotterdam first, with Las Palmas second and Pasadena last. But the Sports Committee suggested that I change the cities round. They explained that Las Palmas was not going to be selected anyway, but that it was politically important to support it. I attached no importance to this, and, since Rotterdam was on both lists, I agreed. It was a wrong move. What I didn't know at the time (but the Soviet sporting authorities must have known) was that if the opinions of the players differ in any way, the President has the right to choose any city at his own discretion, duly considering all the circumstances. Little did I know what far-reaching consequences this seemingly innocent castling, and Campomanes's right *to consider all the circumstances*, would have.

The President chose Pasadena. The press immediately began to speculate that Campomanes had a secret plan to draw Fischer, who had gone to settle in Pasadena, out of retirement and finally arrange the long-awaited match between him and Karpov. The reason Campomanes himself gave for his decision was that Pasadena had offered the highest prize money, including a bonus of $40,000 to promote chess in the Third World, a cause that could not fail to warm the Filipino's heart (this money would, according to FIDE's own rules, be left for the President to disburse at his own discretion).

A fortnight later Korchnoi expressed agreement with Campomanes's decision, but the Soviet authorities rejected it out of hand. Further oil was poured on the flames by the President's decision that the other semi-final, between Smyslov and Ribli, would take place at Abu Dhabi in the United Arab Emirates. To agree to this meant placing our renowned veteran in unfavourable conditions in advance, given the hot climate and other exotic delights.

Many people never did understand the real reason for the Soviet objections to Pasadena. The official reason was that the safety of Karpov and of the members of his delegation could not be guaranteed, as Pasadena was closed to Soviet diplomats.

There were those – and I was one of them – who naïvely thought that we simply wanted to put Campomanes in his place because his disregard for the opinion of the players looked unduly provocative. It wasn't difficult to be taken in. Here, for instance, is what Roshal wrote in *Sovietsky Sport* regarding Campomanes's promise to guarantee security by his own personal presence: 'What most likely happened was that after Campomanes achieved his high office, it simply went to his head . . . Come off it, Campomanes! In a place where the security of the US President isn't guaranteed, and where even Soviet diplomats, who are very seldom allowed to go there, are attacked, your "personal presence" isn't going to solve all the problems.' Meanwhile, the Soviet swimmer Vladimir Salnikov was setting new records in the swimming pools of Los Angeles . . .

My personal acquaintance with the politics surrounding the match began on 12 July.

The previous day, I had received a phone call in Baku saying that Campomanes was flying in to Moscow, and that I had to go there for negotiations. Just before the meeting with Campomanes, I had a conversation in the propaganda department of the CPSU Central Committee with Stukalin, the head of the department, in the presence of a KGB general. There I was told that we were a great country and would not allow anyone to dictate conditions to us; there would be no match in America, a split in FIDE did not frighten us, and even if they declared Korchnoi world champion, so what? We would give him that pleasure, hold a knock-out series of our own, and actively involve Karpov in boycotting Campomanes's decisions. The country's prestige, they said, was at stake. In the end I was forced to refuse to play in Pasadena. Anyway, I was sure everything would eventually settle down. At that point I had no idea that I was being made the victim of an intrigue.

The meeting with Campomanes took place at the Sports Committee at 9 p.m. on that same day. The talks with the President were conducted by Gramov, the chairman of the

Sports Committee, in the presence of Ivonin, Krogius, Karpov, Smyslov and myself.

The talks lasted an hour and a half. Gramov put the pressure on, but Campomanes fought back and wouldn't give in, and by the end almost everyone there was raising his voice. I remember I said to Campomanes: 'Mr President, by your decision you have disregarded the right of the candidates to choose the venue of the match.' He replied: 'Yes, that's right, but why didn't you put Rotterdam first?'

I think it was then that I began to understand a few things.

Towards the end of the talks, our side quietly came up with a new proposal: that the Smyslov–Ribli match would be held at the scheduled time and place – Abu Dhabi – but that a match in Pasadena would take place only on the following conditions:

1. The complete security of the Soviet team must be guaranteed.
2. Soviet diplomats accredited in the USA must be allowed to enter Pasadena during the period of the match.
3. No demonstrations of any kind were to be permitted during the match.

Campomanes said that he was unable to settle these points immediately. He was given telex facilities to contact the organisers. Everyone seemed to revive somewhat, and even cheer up – except me. I was bewildered. Just a few hours ago, they'd been speaking to me about boycotting both matches and about the need to take a firm stand. Now suddenly they'd decided to play the match in Abu Dhabi as arranged, while my match with Korchnoi was left hanging in the air pending the fulfilment of unfulfillable conditions.

I returned home at about 1 a.m. shattered and dispirited. I said to my mother: 'I don't understand a thing, but I think I've been betrayed.' I had a bad night, and in the morning we heard that Campomanes had flown off to Tunis without telephoning anyone. A telex was sent after him, reiterating the proposals that had been made at the meeting.

Two days later Campomanes said at a press conference in Tunis: 'If Kasparov does not turn up for the match on the appointed day, 1 August, he will be counted as having lost.' Then a day after that it emerged that Smyslov had been sent five tickets from Abu Dhabi, with thanks for agreeing to play. I telephoned the place where, just a few days before, I had been guaranteed support. When I asked him what was to become of me now, Stukalin replied: 'As a citizen, you've got to understand that it's in the interests of our country.' And when I asked why was I the only one who had to drop out, he said: 'You're still young, you can afford to wait three years.'

By the evening the situation had changed again. Gramov asked me to come and see him at home. He received me very warmly and told me that in any event the matches would not begin on 1 August, that another telex was being sent, and that the talks with Campomanes were to be published in the press. 'Can I go to Baku?' I asked. 'Of course! Baku isn't Pasadena – we'll always be able to track you down there.' He saw me to the door and took leave of me warmly.

Campomanes did indeed announce that the matches were being put off for five days. But I didn't go to Baku, and spent four days waiting. Still there was no decision.

It was during those days of crisis that I first spoke with Karpov. After the talks at the Sports Committee, the world champion suggested that he and I should discuss the situation in private. The conversation that took place at his home on 15 July was a difficult one for me psychologically. Karpov was at pains to convince me that the main thing now was to avert a split in FIDE – or, as he put it, not to be mated in one move. He went on that we ought not, therefore, to obstruct the holding of the Smyslov–Ribli match, but should launch a campaign together for the match in Pasadena. He advised me to get in touch with Aliev, who was then a member of the Politburo, and promised for his part to arrange a meeting with

Zimyanin, a Secretary of the Communist Party Central Committee.

Because of my inexperience it was difficult for me to make sense of the stratagems being played in the struggle behind the scenes over that match. But at that moment I instinctively smelt danger. I was already aware that the Party Central Committee and KGB considered the match in Pasadena to be a political *faux pas*. The decision to boycott the Los Angeles Olympics had probably already been taken, and Karpov knew this. That is why it was so important to divide the matches between Abu Dhabi and Pasadena. Karpov's promise to find some other way of including me in the candidates cycle in the future if the match with Korchnoi didn't take place after all only increased my suspicions.

From now on I no longer had any doubt that my only chance to continue my battle for the world title was to ensure that the two semi-finals began simultaneously. What could I do? On 21 July I rang Aliev and told him the gist of the matter. He reassured me that the match would take place. Only then did I go back to Baku.

The situation then took a U-turn. The first thing that had to be done was to find a decent pretext for bringing the two semi-finals together so that a boycott of the FIDE President's decision would be more effective. As a result of the changed situation, the UAE Chess Federation issued a statement. Here is an extract from the report in *Sovietsky Sport*:

On 31 July the UAE Chess Federation withdrew its offer, having satisfied itself that the President's decision had not been agreed with the match players. On 4 August, F. Campomanes, in a virtual admission that the choice he made on 1 July was unsound, informed the USSR Chess Federation that 'in view of the refusal by the UAE Chess Federation, I tried to find, and have in readiness, a friendly European chess federation willing to organise the Ribli–Smyslov match if Mr Smyslov and you will notify me in writing today that Smyslov will play the match in that friendly chess federation, irrespective of the other conditions which you have already mentioned'. Thus, without naming the federation or disclosing the proposed venue, date and other conditions, F. Campomanes was, in effect issuing an ultimatum and that we should agree, that very day, to his anonymous offer.

No specific offers of any kind followed, however, and the destinies of the two matches were once again merged into one. Now, even if Campomanes had carried out his threat to disqualify me (if I refused to go to Pasadena), he would have had to apply the same sanctions to one of the players in the Smyslov–Ribli match. And that would have wrecked the entire cycle of world championship matches.

So on the one hand there was the FIDE President invoking rules which were vague and in many respects contradictory, and on the other, the authority of the top grandmasters. Which would tip the balance? This was a question to be decided by the whole chess world, certainly not by the leadership of FIDE. After all, the World Chess Federation does not exist for its own sake, and it cannot function properly if it treats chess players as tiresome humble petitioners that it cannot be bothered with.

The crisis had gone too far for either side to be able simply to give in. Along the way, Campomanes had managed to insult his predecessors, Euwe and Olafsson, by saying that, unlike them, he had no intention of yielding to pressure from the Russians.

But how quickly everything changed! Whereas until quite recently, my removal from the cycle had been regarded by the sporting authorities as something quite normal, and no one had been worried about what would happen to me after that, now the USSR Chess Federation began a veritable storming of Campomanes's position, using all the mass news media. *Sovietsky Sport* carried a whole section headed: 'FIDE Chairman's decisions under critical fire'. Various newspapers published statements by Botvinnik, Petrosyan, Chiburdanidze,

Belyavsky, Polugayevsky and a number of foreign grand-masters.

You can imagine the state I was in during the early hours of 7 August. That was the time when, in Pasadena, where it was still 6 August, Korchnoi arrived at the hall of the City College, shook hands with the referee, sat down at the chess table and made the move d2-d4. Then he pressed the button on the clock. According to the *Los Angeles Times*, he spent the next hour pacing about the stage, hands clasped behind his back, with a deadpan expression on his face, as he solemnly went through this farce. And no wonder: he'd been given victory and a quarter of the sum he would have received if the match had taken place. Furthermore, he was told that he was already through to the final.

It was the end of everything. I was finished before I'd begun. Someone asked me recently what would have happened if Korchnoi, having made his move, had informed the referee that he conceded defeat? I don't believe that is a thought that would have occurred to Korchnoi. But it would have put Campomanes in a very difficult position. And it's hard even to imagine what the Soviet press would have said about it.

Interviews, interviews – several of them a day. Everyone wanted to know whether the theatrical performance in Pasadena was the end of the affair. And when I told them it was only the beginning, they advised me to write a letter to the FIDE congress, which was due to be held in Manila in early October.

Three days later the same fate befell Smyslov. The world championship play-off was on the brink of collapse at the semi-finals stage . . .

Meanwhile, the chess public was waiting to hear from the world champion, but he was in no hurry. Only on 8 August did Karpov make a public statement: 'Korchnoi is counted as having won without having played, yet it was not because of whim or illness that his opponent failed to appear for the match. It was the result of circumstances, in other words, for reasons only peripherally connected with chess.' So in Karpov's opinion the crisis had been caused by circumstances only *peripherally* connected with chess! But who knew the causes? And who created them? Was it only those who stood on the periphery of chess? In many people's opinion the purpose of the intrigue begun in May 1983 was to 'do everything possible' to prevent Kasparov from drawing level with Karpov. But the plot-writers behind the scenes were so far from taking the second match seriously (evidently considering neither Smyslov nor Ribli as rivals to Karpov) that they didn't think it necessary to consider all the variations thoroughly. Yes, one disqualified candidate could be justified somehow or other, but two looked like carelessness! So near to the aim, but yet so far . . .

But in that hot August (and, indeed in the critical times which followed) fortune sent me a chance to save myself, as if to test how far I was able to make use of it. It came in the form of a phone call from the famous Yugoslav player, Milunka Lazarevic, who is now an active chess organiser. Milunka was sincerely worried on my behalf. She has a fervent love of chess, and reacts acutely to any injustice done to it.

She told me I was invited to Niksic for a category 15 super-tournament in which all the greatest chess players of our time, except Karpov, would be taking part. It was explained to me later that this was the organisers' way of showing how they felt about the crisis. The tournament was being held to mark the sixtieth birthday of the doyen of Yugoslav grandmasters, Svetozar Gligoric, for whom I had a deep respect. That respect was to be expressed subsequently in my wish that he should be chief arbiter in my matches with Korchnoi in 1983 and Karpov in 1984. Ironically, it was Gligoric who sanctioned the stopping of the match between Karpov and myself on 15 February 1985. It clearly wasn't his decision, but he supported it.

But in August 1983 I was glad to have been invited to such a tournament, and even more glad that I managed to achieve a resounding victory, winning by two clear points from

Larsen. All my training for the match that should have taken place between me and Korchnoi was put to good use to produce my best games in that tournament. The journalists singled out in particular my game with Portisch, for which the USSR Sports Committee awarded me a special prize 'For Creative Achievement in 1983'. However, the tournament has remained in my memory not only for the chess: it was also the first occasion in which I was able to display my organisational skills. It was a matter of saving the matches, and that took some doing: I had to organise a letter from the grandmasters to FIDE and negotiate with Korchnoi.

I did not know at the time whether I had the courage and firmness to stand up for democracy in chess. *Perestroika* – the restructuring of our society – was still to come. There was a struggle ahead of me, and I was told that in that struggle I could be broken. There was also the risk that the struggle itself would break me.

I was strengthened in my resolve after talking with my fellow chess players in Niksic. They were in sympathy with my belief that it was necessary to resist the dictates of Campomanes. Yet still my doubts persisted. Was it worth risking everything that had hitherto given my life purpose? What was more important – to beat Campomanes, or become world champion? And was it not possible to achieve the former by other means, in other words, become champion first, and then, after strengthening my hand, begin the fight?

I asked those taking part in the tournament to sign a letter demanding that the semi-finals be held. The desire to see those matches was universal. It was especially apparent in the brief interviews which kept appearing in the local papers: all the grandmasters without exception said the matches must be held as soon as possible. Here is the text of the document they adopted:

'The participants of the international tournament in Niksic, Yugoslavia, consider it important that the FIDE congress should do everything possible to organise and hold the Kasparov–Korchnoi and Ribli–Smyslov semi-final matches. We are guided by the interests of chess. – B. Spassky, T. Petrosyan, M. Tal, U. Andersson, S. Gligoric, L. Ljubojevic, B. Ivanovic, P. Nikolic, B. Larsen, A. Miles, L. Portisch, G. Sax, Y. Timman, Y. Seirawan.'

This was quite possibly the first petition in chess history to be signed by almost all the world's leading grandmasters. Some of them (Timman, Seirawan, Miles) expressed surprise: 'We'll sign, of course, because you've got to play Korchnoi. But why didn't you go to Pasedena? How could you risk your entire chess career just because they chose the wrong town?'

This display of unanimity by the grandmasters made it clear to FIDE that the chess world did not agree with the President's unsporting decision. There was no doubt any more that the question of whether Smyslov and I would take part in the finals would be decided at the chessboard. The only thing that is unclear is how things would have developed if Korchnoi had exercised his formal right to enter straight into the finals, instead of taking the noble decision that he did to play in the semi-finals. Of course, moral condemnation is a force to be reckoned with, but in my life I have come across people who treat moral condemnation by the chess world like a common cold. Korchnoi was different: he proved by what he did that his criticism of the 'championship on paper' was not just empty words.

Our personal relationship was helped by a lightning tournament in Herceg Novi, on the Adriatic coast, which was held immediately after Niksic. I won this tournament, beating Korchnoi twice. I think Korchnoi appreciated my gesture in appearing with him at that time, when negotiations for the candidates match were still at a crucial stage. We were able to have several frank talks about the coming match, which both of us wanted.

The wheel, then, had begun to turn the other way. The 'miracle' had happened. To complete it, money was needed. The Soviet Federation agreed to a fine of $210,000. Some of the money was paid to Korchnoi as compensation for his cancelled victory, and some went to reimbursing the costs of organising the match in Pasadena and covering FIDE's financial and moral damages. In reality though, not all of the sum was paid out. When passions had cooled, Campomanes suggested to the Soviet Chess Federation that the burden should be lightened. In lieu of part of the money, the Soviet Union held chess seminars for the developing countries (though it must be said that they didn't do much good, as it was mainly sporting officials, rather than actual chess players, who attended). In addition, Korchnoi was given a promise that the boycott of tournaments in which he took part, which the USSR Chess Federation had initiated in 1976, would cease.

That was the price the Soviet authorities had to pay to repair the damage caused by their own machinations over the semifinals. It was the biggest concession by our Federation in the whole history of its relations with FIDE, and Campomanes gleefully seized the opportunity to show the chess world how he'd called us to order. Yes, it was a dramatic moment in the lives of our sporting authorities. They were forced to protect themselves, and laid low in the hope that the wind of change would slacken or even change direction.

The next job was to find a venue for the matches.

A key figure in helping to find a solution this time was Raymond Keene, the British grandmaster who was also Secretary of the FIDE Council of Players. He flew to Moscow to meet the Soviet Federation. He was surprised when Krogius himself, the head of the chess department of the Sports Committee, met him at the airport. A rare honour indeed! But he was even more surprised when they all started falling over one another to recount how they were helping Kasparov. This was something new . . . Keene said he could arrange for both matches to be played at short notice in London, but on condition that the Russians publicly acknowledge that Campomanes had not exceeded his authority as President of FIDE in selecting Pasadena, and that they pay the required compensation. Keene had already squared Campomanes by promising that his publishers would donate a large number of chess books to promote the game in the developing countries. The way to persuade Korchnoi to go along with these arrangements, he said, was to combine a cash inducement with dropping the boycott against him in tournament play.

After a week of discussions, the matter was settled on terms very close to Keene's proposals.

The result was that the matches, which at first had been scattered to various corners of the globe, would now come together at the Great Eastern Hotel in London. Acorn Computers had come in as sponsors with a bid of £75,000, beating offers from Holland, Austria and Yugoslavia. All the publicity given to the bitter controversy in the chess world had created bigger worldwide interest in the outcome.

Another thing that raised my spirits was a trip to Barcelona, where I was presented with my first Oscar, for my results in 1982. In the voting, I got 1021 points against 943 for Karpov. A remarkable feature of that trip was that my mother was able to come with me for the first time. It was rare in those days for any Soviet chess player to be allowed to take a close relative abroad. It was a special sign of trust on the part of the authorities. In my case this was very significant, because there had been persistent rumours that I was going to defect to the West. It may be that deep down my opponents wanted me to defect so that I could be branded a public enemy like Korchnoi and many other Soviet defectors. But I still have bad news for them. I haven't the slightest desire to defect. Of course I could earn more in the West, and day-to-day life would be easier in many ways. But it's only at home, in your own country, that you can derive genuine satisfaction from public and political activities. I think it's extremely difficult for a person to realise his potential if he's cut off from his roots.

The atmosphere for my match with Korchnoi, when we finally reached the chessboard, was far calmer than might have been expected. All passions had been spent in the battles which preceded the match, and now we could concentrate on the chess. My relations with Korchnoi were normal, partly perhaps because in 1976, when he was publicly condemned by the Soviet grandmasters, I was only thirteen years old, and had had nothing to do with it.

In no way did I underestimate Korchnoi as a player. I knew he was a dangerous adversary with a wealth of match experience. He had moreover, already competed in two world championship finals. There were thirty-two years between us, which of course gave me a certain advantage, but Korchnoi still knew many chess tricks. I knew I must not allow him to dictate the match in simple and technical positions, so I devoted a lot of study to the end-game, study which amounted to forty per cent of my total preparation. This is how we worked. My trainers would show me a position from an actual game and ask me to analyse it. Then we'd compare my play with the moves in the book. In this way we studied all the best practical endings over the past twenty-five years. This exercise brought good rewards in the match.

At 4 p.m., then, on 21 November, my white queen's pawn moved two squares forward. This, you will recall, was the one single move which had brought Korchnoi victory in the match in Pasadena. But in London I lost the first game. Korchnoi began it with speed and confidence, whereas I took a long time to consider each move. In the end I was left with half an hour to make twenty-two moves, while Korchnoi had one and a half hours in hand. It was a triumph of experience over hope! I recalled a grim statistic: in all twelve of the previous candidates matches Korchnoi had won; once he had gained a lead in points, he never relinquished it. But at that time not many people knew that thirteen was my lucky number!

The decisive moment came in game six, which after a bitter fight was adjourned in an unclear, but probably drawn position (see Appendix A). When we resumed, Korchnoi, in an attempt to sharpen the game, chose a continuation which was not of the best, and at the 57th move a prosaic looking rook ending emerged which would require a certain precision from white to achieve a draw. Korchnoi needed to swap a rook for a passed pawn in a favourable position, but he made a transposition, missed an opportunity to get me in check and after that his position was hopeless . . .

In an interview at the end of the match, which I won 7-4, Korchnoi admitted: 'After game six I lost faith in my technique and my seconds. The score was equal, but psychologically the match was lost. My pre-match impression of Kasparov as a player with one big punch was wrong. Kasparov is very practical for his age. He takes risks only when he is one hundred per cent sure they are justified.'

But my restrained tactics were a disappointment to some of the British players, who had been expecting combinational fireworks. Harry Golombek wrote in *The Times*: 'There has only been an occasional flash of Kasparov's brilliance. Normally he breathes life and fire into positions.' Raymond Keene said: 'Kasparov has been playing like Karpov, taking opportunities from Korchnoi's mistakes. He is a naturally inventive and ingenious chess player, but he has shown little of his true skill here.' True, Jonathan Speelman commented that 'after the sixth game Garry has turned from a tortured dog to an uncaged lion'. But an assessment which impressed me more was that of the American Robert Byrne: 'The impetuous grandmaster from the Caucasus managed to display remarkable patience and self-possession, showing exceptional psychological stability in a tricky situation. Creatively, too, Kasparov has matured as the battle has progressed. This young player has been able to adapt, curb his imagination and acquire a taste for playing in the simple positions with few pieces, imposed by his rival – though this is something Kasparov has always disliked.' Many people even suggested that I should thank Korchnoi for accelerating my maturity as a player and helping me grasp the subtleties of positional play. And indeed, it would be hard to overestimate the benefit I derived from that match.

All that now stood between me and a match with Karpov was Smyslov. An old campaigner with the wisdom of experience who had been through the crucible of many years fighting Botvinnik, Smyslov had become world champion six years before I was born. A quarter of a century later, he astonished the world by a crushing victory against Zoltan Ribli, a man only half his age.

There was something deeply symbolic in the fact that both the disqualified Soviet grandmasters eventually emerged as victors in the semi-finals. Spice was added to the coming duel by the players themselves, who were totally unalike. One of them reached his sixty-third birthday during the match, while the other was just twenty-one. Before the candidates matches, the remark was often heard: 'Where do they think they're going at their ages?!' Of course each person had his own interpretation of that phrase. The interzonal tournament, the quarter-final and the semi-final were for each of us a victory against time. The age limits were stretching in both directions at once.

Smyslov's great strength had always been his ability to achieve microscopic advantages through innocent looking exchanges and manoeuvres, and in the end-game his virtuosity was unsurpassed. The British press called him 'The Old Master Immortal'. By that time his longevity at chess had begun to rival Lasker's, who was still appearing in tournaments at the age of sixty-eight.

Our match took place in Vilnius in March and April 1984, and ended in an 8.5-4.5 victory for me. My victory was due to successful use of the Tarrasch Defence. I already knew that in a match a player's frame of mind often depends on his play with black: if it goes well, you can afford to try and exploit the advantage of white. On the whole, I felt happier in complicated situations, but my greatest satisfaction came from two end-games in which I was able to secure a slight positional advantage.

At this period in my life I was greatly influenced by meeting Marina Neyelova. Our friendship lasted more than two years, starting with that wonderful evening in Moscow when I saw her as Masha in Chekhov's *Three Sisters*. Marina really understood my problems. She understood the true nature of my struggle, and her support gave me strength. We had many friends in common among artists and writers.

Marina is exceptionally well read and well educated. She has an incisive mind and a fine sense of humour. When I rang her from Vilnius after beating Smyslov and said I was 'only five minutes away from the world title', her dry comment was: 'Are you sure your watch isn't fast?'

It may well be that we got on together so well because of our sense of being exceptional. Her perception of the world was interesting to me, as I hope mine was to her. We understood each other intuitively, without having to spell things out. Being so much in tune helped us to cast a bridge between our brief and infrequent meetings. The gaps between them were filled by long telephone conversations, and for a while that would be enough: I would begin to feel easier and more confident. I was constantly surprised and delighted that we were able to find points of contact in areas that were so very different and remote from each other.

But our occupations – that of a great actress and a prominent sportsman – kept us in orbits which moved further and further apart.

My victories over Belyavsky and Korchnoi – and at the tournament in Niksic – brought me a second Oscar. In the voting I got 984 points against 918 for Karpov. By mid-1984 my rating was better than Karpov's as well: 2715 against 2705.

After my match with Korchnoi, Karpov gave an interview in which he said: 'I don't wish to belittle Kasparov's achievement, but it has to be said that Korchnoi is past it . . . the emperor has no clothes . . . even a young Indian player [Barua] has beaten Korchnoi.' The absurdity of that statement was all too clear when you remembered that just two years before, Karpov had demanded that the authorities mobilise the full might of the Soviet chess organisation to support his fight against Korchnoi. Nor did Korchnoi's tournament appearances bear out the claim that he was 'past it'.

On the subject of my forthcoming match against Smyslov, Karpov drew the traditional comparison that is was 'a contest between youth and daring on the one hand, and common sense and experience on the other,' and added: 'It's like the eternal battle between the raging sea and the solid shore.' As we know, the 'raging sea' usually loses this 'eternal battle', or the world would not have survived. The fact is that Karpov was absolutely sure I would win. When the magazine *Ogonyok* invited its readers to predict the result of the match, it also asked the world champion to do so. Karpov's sealed envelope contained an exact prediction: 8.5-4.5 in Kasparov's favour. Our other grandmasters had no doubt about the outcome either.

Nevertheless, in the Soviet press my chances were deliberately played down. Why? Perhaps someone was afraid of encouraging me too much or, God forbid, boosting my popularity? Of course Karpov himself cherished no illusions. He was well aware that after the failure of the Pasadena operation, he couldn't avoid the match with me. The threat to his title was all too obvious, though he said in the interview that gaining the right to play a world championship match was 'in itself an achievement that few people dare even to dream of'. Karpov is a cool man who can accurately and objectively assess the risks. So, too, could the people around him, whose positions depended on Karpov retaining his title and who wanted him to go on feeling, for as long as possible, that they were his prop. Smyslov had a point when he said to me just before the match in Vilnius: 'Young man, if that business with our semi-finals had happened not in the summer of 1983, but a little earlier, we'd never have met in the finals.'

In many myths and fairy tales the hero has to go through the most frightful ordeals before he finally comes face to face with a monster of incredible power and strength. But the man who has overcome all obstacles is no longer the fool who would once rush in where angels fear to tread. The battles have steeled his mind, and his victories have endowed him with a miraculous power that enables him to stand firm in the final combat. So it is in one of my favourite books, Tolkien's *The Lord of the Rings*, where Sauron first sends out his black riders. So it is, too, in the Russian fairy tale of Kaschei the Immortal. Yet there is an obvious inconsistency of logic here. Even as a child, I used to worry about what would have happened if Kaschei had deigned to go out to meet his uninvited guest when the latter had only just set out, and was still weak and inexperienced. The outcome of the battle would not have been difficult to predict. So why does he wait and give his enemy time to grow strong? I think I now know the answer: it is simply that in ninety-nine cases out of a hundred it is quite enough for Kaschei to send out his henchmen. Only one person in a hundred has a chance of reaching him. In general, however, the inevitability of fate and retribution is far more likely in fairy tales than in life.

When I began my struggle, I knew that I was entering the 'kingdom of Kaschei'. I did not yet know the rules by which the struggle would be fought, but I had already sensed my adversary's power.

SEVEN

Face to Face

It was the summer of 1984 and I was feeling close to the goal I had worked so hard to achieve – the world title. But first I had to go back to London, the scene of my recent victory over Korchnoi, for a match between the USSR and the Rest of the World which was due to be held in June. The first competition of this kind had taken place in Belgrade fourteen years before, and had been dubbed 'the match of the century'. At that time, the USSR had won 20.5-19.5. Not surprisingly this latest contest immediately became 'the return match of the century'. Our team consisted of Karpov, Kasparov, Polugayevsky, Smyslov, Vaganyan, Belyavsky, Tal, Razuvayev, Yusupov and Sokolov, with Romanishin and Tukmakov as reserves. The opposing team comprised Andersson, Timman, Korchnoi, Ljubojevic, Ribli, Seirawan, Nunn, Hübner, Miles and Torre, with reserves Larsen and Chandler.

Unfortunately, Petrosyan was not with us. He had wanted to travel with the team, refusing to believe that his illness was incurable. But his days were already numbered, and two months later Tigran Vartanovich passed away.

The match was being held in a rather unsuitable place – a then rather remote part of the English capital known as Docklands. It was once a peninsula, but numerous canals had turned it into an island bearing the not very euphonious name of Isle of Dogs. But for me it has happy memories. On the Isle of Dogs are the Limehouse Studios, where I played at the time an unusual 'simul' on ten boards using clocks. Only five of my opponents were physically present – the others were 'in vision' by satellite television link to the Intercontinental Hotel in New York. It was the first satellite chess match in history. I won seven games and drew three, evoking the praise of Harry Golombek, the doyen of British chess: 'He was able to produce the most brilliant moves and the most profound ideas without manifesting any signs of undue strain or pressure.' What he wrote about me when my match with Karpov got under way, however, was far less flattering and far more contradictory.

As for the 'return match of the century', the Rest of the World did not succeed in gaining their revenge. The Soviet win was even more clear-cut than in 1970: 21-19. 'Of course the USSR team has every reason to be pleased with the result,' I told a correspondent of the British *Morning Star*. 'Although on the other hand we could have done even better, because in a number of cases our players did not use the advantages they had gained to the full.' That remark was equally true of myself. Despite the promising positions I achieved against Timman, I beat him only once: the other three encounters ended in fighting draws.

My match with Karpov was scheduled to open on 10 September. But four days before we made our first move, the psychological attack on me began. Campomanes said I must put my signature to a new set of match rules, otherwise I would be declared the loser without playing. I was reluctant to give in to such pressure. And I did not agree that the rules intended for the new two-year cycle of the world championship play-off should be introduced now, in this match, which was the last of the old three-year cycle. It wasn't clear what they were up to. One of the new rules gave Campomanes, as FIDE President, *emergency powers* over the match, the meaning of which became all too clear five and a half months later.

In the event, I had no choice but to sign, as the sports officials made clear to Yuri Mamedov, my head of delegation. But it took a great deal of nervous energy out of me just when I needed it most, which was exactly what they intended.

So I didn't start the game in a contented frame of mind. What's more, I knew that I had some formidable obstacles in front of me and felt very hesitant. People said later that I'd started the match very confidently, but in fact that was not the case.

In a way I had beaten my earlier opponents too easily. Now that I needed to give it all I had, I wasn't ready for it. I was like a boxer who has always won by a knock-out in the first few rounds, then in the next match has to go the whole fifteen. Besides, I wasn't really familiar with Karpov's style, whereas he had not only had time to do a thorough job of studying mine, but had been able to bring in the cream of the Soviet grandmasters to help him analyse it.

Before the match I was in no doubt that I would somehow beat even the champion. Unfortunately I was too sure of myself. The 'somehow' didn't turn out, and the battle dragged on for one month after another. The match was open-ended, but I never expected we would come to feel that sense of open-endedness quite so literally.

On 10 September Karpov moved his queen's pawn from e2 to e4, and the longest chess match in history began. The venue was the Hall of Columns in the House of Unions, the same hall where Max Euwe had proclaimed Karpov world champion nine years before.

The match unfolded to a scenario which Cassandra herself probably couldn't have predicted. I learnt later that the magazine *Ogonyok* had run a competition in which readers had to predict the result and length of the match and, if possible, its theme. Needless to say, none of the prizes was claimed. What happened was impossible to predict.

Of the first nine games, I lost four. Imagine – to have lost three games in the previous two years, then four all in one go! All I can say is that I played badly. Though there's a well-known fallacy here. Every loser says he played badly, but the winner for some reason says the opposite: my opponent was strong, but I was stronger. I know this, yet I still insist that I played badly. As a player, Karpov was more cunning and nimbler than me, to say nothing of experience in general and match experience in particular.

* * *

The match as a whole fell into three distinct phases. 'In the first I was somewhat nervous and made rather a lot of mistakes,' I said in a *Tass* interview after the match. 'In the circumstances, the world champion found his game sooner: his much greater match and tournament experience had its effect. At that stage Karpov was playing in his characteristic style, calculating the variations precisely and drawing maximum advantage from each of my blunders. Then came a long series of draws. Here the art of defence came into its own. During this period the battle took on an even, steady rhythm. And finally, the last phase of the match was marked, I think, by richer games from the point of view of the quality of play. The fight became more intense.'

We began the match without sounding each other out, striving to seize the initiative at all costs. I made several gross errors, especially in the second game, which Keene described as 'one of the most violent and tempestuous' he had ever seen. A position arose where I would normally win, but, as Keene put it, 'Kasparov had a black-out.' At the end, after Karpov, in time trouble, overlooked a winning continuation, I was glad to find a perpetual check for a draw.

In the third game I used a dubious innovation in the opening and then, in trying to solve the problems this caused, wrongly sacrificed a pawn. Karpov exploited these errors with surgical precision to give me my first taste of his ice-cold scalpel. At move twenty-seven in game six I had a golden opportunity to win, but let it slip by, and, as one commentator said, 'the remainder of the game was torture for white'. Then in game seven the champion dealt a strong blow against the Tarrasch Defence which had stood me in such good stead in the candidates matches. The pity of it was that I played the game quite well, only to commit an incredible blunder at the end. Another black-out! That was when Vaganyan said: 'Kasparov delivers one blow after another, he attacks, but all he gets out of it are lost positions or at best a draw. It's enough to give him a complex.' Keene said he couldn't see the match going beyond game twelve: 'Kasparov's brilliant career has furnished him with insufficient experience of defeat to surmount the psychological shock of repeated loss,' he said.

Well, I wasn't about to get any complexes, but it certainly wouldn't be a bad idea to think about a change of tactics, otherwise the match could end very quickly and very badly for me. From then on, I began to act with maximum caution, trying to eliminate even the slightest element of risk from my play. It was out of character for me to play in this colourless fashion, but I knew I had no choice. When you are clinging to a life-raft, it's no time to experiment with fancy swimming strokes.

When I cast my mind back now to those dramatic days, I think that one reason for my failure at the outset was my lack of experience of playing at championship level. Even candidates matches are no comparison with a final. Here Karpov was a professional, while I was an amateur. I could only guess at what the battle rules might be at the top level, while Karpov knew them inside out. He was calm and confident of victory; I was merely hoping for success. Before the fight began, I not only lacked the right experience; I did not even have a proper concept of what that experience was. My understanding of everything that concept involved came later, and at enormous cost. It implies that you have the knowledge you need, that you can accurately assess your own potential, that you can tell when the crucial moment of battle has come and draw up the right strategy, and that you have the ability to remain cool and objective during every encounter throughout the entire match.

After my defeat in game nine, it looked as though Keene could be right. I made a blunder on move forty-six, either out of sheer fatigue or carelessness, but whichever it was, I was losing 4-0. It was disaster! Everyone, not surprisingly, had already written me off and had begun to speak of me in the past tense. 'Keene and I had hurried to join the match in the middle, but it seemed we were just in time for the end,' the British grandmaster Speelman lamented. 'Karpov has always played well, but this I hadn't expected. As for Kasparov, he probably lost his nerve. He's still young. His nerves are not good. He hasn't developed an iron will.'

All Karpov had to do, as they say, was wrap up his opponent – me, that is – and put him in a box. But at that point he slipped up and broke the immutable law of battle that you must kill off the enemy. He had decided that I would ripen and fall of my own accord. He had, of course, good reason for thinking so. A four-point lead is pretty solid: I might well fall. And he let up the pressure. I think if Karpov had gone on playing as he did at the beginning of the match, it would have been all over by game twenty. He might have lost a couple of games along the way, but this wouldn't have made any difference to the result. In a *Tass* interview after the match, Karpov admitted: 'Being four points ahead, I wasn't out to push things to extremes either. That may have been where I went wrong – you have to strike while the iron's hot.'

The ease with which Karpov achieved overwhelming superiority in the first few games had had a bad effect on his fighting spirit. I thought it was then that Karpov, intoxicated with success, had set himself the overriding goal of beating me hands down and putting his dangerous rival out of action for a long time. But Roshal later told me that this thought had occurred to Karpov at an earlier stage: 'Once he was leading 2-0, Karpov made up his mind he had to win 6-0. Nothing less would do. So he no longer wanted to take any risks. The important thing was not just to win, but to win 6-0.' He was pitting himself not just against me, but against the ghost of Fischer, who had in his time beaten Taimanov and Larsen in candidates matches with that same score. As it happened, his decision only played into my hands. It was important for me to recover, to regain my composure and confidence. Hence the long run of draws, many of which rightly displeased the fans. Karpov was waiting for me to make a mistake, and I was not yet ready, psychologically, to take the initiative. But it couldn't go on like this for ever.

* * *

The turning-point came in game fifteen. It lasted ninety-three moves, but Karpov never managed to capitalise on his extra pawn. I saw the expression of his face and realised that he was played out . . . We beat all records by drawing, after the ninth game, seventeen times in succession! It's not, of course, the record I am most proud of, but it was certainly one of the hardest to achieve. It took a degree of persistence I didn't then know I possessed. Nor, I suspect, did my trainers. But at least I could go out and play every day: all they could do was wait there and pray that I didn't make any mistakes.

By then, interest in the match was at its height. Despite the snow and the cold, hundreds of people queued up opposite the Hall of Columns in hopes of getting a ticket. They were like spectators trying to get in to an execution, only the victim refused to lie down and die.

Amid the fairly unanimous censure passed on me for the large number of draws, the opinion given by Yuri Averbakh after game twenty-one struck a discordant note: 'There is a lot of talk now about the nature of the match having changed and about the new strategy that the challenger is supposed to be pursuing. Everyone has his own idea about what's happening. Some people think Kasparov now considers himself lucky if he can draw just one more game with the world champion. Many are convinced the challenger is simply using draws to prolong the match so that this fight won't go down as just about the shortest and most unequal match in history. To me, that's hardly likely. Kasparov is still too young to think seriously about history. I think the real idea of these draws from Kasparov's point of view goes roughly like this: even if the match ends in victory for you, as it probably will, it won't be that you'll have won, but that I'll have lost, by walking into the lion's mouth. But you just try and win, now that I'm not squeezing any more out of the position than is due to me. It is, if you like, a kind of revenge on Kasparov's part, his justification both to himself and to public opinion, and even his staking of a claim on the future.'

I knew that if I lost with a nil score, it would be the most crushing defeat in recent chess history. Only Fischer had meted out such punishment, and even then it wasn't in a match for the world title. It still surprises me how I managed to keep my self-composure at all under those circumstances, because I sometimes get depressed over less important things. I can't imagine how I endured such tension for months on end.

My friends did everything they could to raise my spirits. My relatives from Baku – close ones and the not so close – took it in turns to come to Moscow, and all tried to cheer me up, some by telling jokes, others by simply being in the hall to create a 'home ground' atmosphere, and yet others by awkward attempts to distract me from my painful thoughts. The one who succeeded probably better than anyone was my driver, Kolya, a man of inexhaustible folksy humour, to whom I'm greatly attached. When the score reached 0-5, one of my friends from Baku even offered to bet me his car that I would still win the match . . .

It was very hard for my trainers, too, who didn't know what to advise in such a desperate situation. Only later did my mother tell me that some of them even wanted to resign because they felt they were to blame for my lack of success. But she persuaded them to stay on, knowing how much I needed their support.

My mother's role at this time was vital for me. I don't think I could have managed without her. Some people blamed her for my early losses, saying it was her fault that I had been over-confident of success. This is untrue and unfair. Nobody who knows us could possibly think that. My mother plays no part in my preparations for chess: she has too many other different things to take care of! But there can be no doubt that without her, without that selfless help that only a mother is capable of giving, I would not have become champion at the early age I did.

The most important thing is that I can talk to her as I can talk to nobody else. In a crisis you listen to a voice you've learned to trust over many years. Each of us needs someone to confide in, someone to whom you can spill everything that's on your mind without holding anything back or being afraid to call a spade a spade. Then, more often that not, you can see the right solution yourself. My mother says jokingly that she is my stress-absorber.

We usually sat up talking late into the night. And even though everything seemed so impenetrably gloomy and hopeless, there was some tiny ray of hope that was never extinguished. When the score was 0-5 we felt very low, but then I had a win, and there was something to cling to, not much, admittedly, but something real. It is hard to put into words everything that we went through. The winter of 1984 was the time I finally grew up.

'Imagine a man dangling over a precipice, clinging on by one hand, and you'll have a good idea of the situation Kasparov was in after the twenty-seventh game,' Mark Taimanov wrote. 'Basically, one wrong move could have cost him the match. Such was the sword of Damocles that the challenger long had hanging over him – playing none other than the world champion himself! Yet he succeeded in winning one game, and managed in several others to produce a tense situation and dictate the course of the battle.'

There was a man who helped me a great deal at this time. I couldn't name him then because it had to be kept secret, even though he was a well-known figure. His name was Tofik Dadashev. Born in Baku in 1947, he carried out his first psychological experiments when he was only thirteen or fourteen. In the summer of 1964, when he was in Kharkov, he met the famous Wolf Messing. That meeting decided his destiny.

I met Dadashev when I was losing 0-4. He gave me support in what seemed a hopeless situation by convincing me that I would not lose the match even if the score went up to 0-5. Dadashev sort of predicted that score, though it wasn't inevitable.

I, too, am a creature of intuition. I usually have a feeling of what is going to happen. But in this case I had no such feeling.

My mother said that she didn't know how it would all end either, but she simply couldn't believe I would lose. This helped us to hold on when all seemed lost. Of course it was impossible to foresee the end of the match. Who could have imagined the fiasco into which it would be plunged by Campomanes on 15 February 1985, still many months ahead?

But there was someone else, too, whose invisible presence supported me throughout that endless marathon – Vladimir Vysotsky. Half an hour before the beginning of a game I would find a quiet corner, put my headphones on and switch on my cassette player. All forty-eight times his *Horses* chased along the brink of an abyss. Forty-eight times that incredible, unreal vision gave me strength to continue the relentless struggle.

I never saw Vysotsky in the flesh. I was simply too late: our paths were separated by a barrier of time. But there was no barrier that could or ever will stop Vysotsky's voice from breaking out to us.

I don't remember the first time I heard a recording of his songs – it must have been when I was about twelve or thirteen – but I remember nothing so clearly as the strong, sharp impression which that thick knot of emotions made on me when it burst forth from the tape. As I grew up, my view of the world around me broadened and the social significance of Vysotsky's art slowly began to dawn on me. And once I started distinguishing different shades of colour and shook off the familiar black-and-white perception of things that we have in childhood, I made my choice once and for all. From that time on, Vysotsky became my constant companion and inspiration. Each step on the difficult path upward – and taking a step sometimes involved a blind yet unavoidable risk – brought to my mind associations with the world of Vysotsky. Such was his deep insight into the psychology of struggle.

I am certain that the charge we get from Vysotsky's songs is no narrowly specialised stimulant. We all derive extra energy from it, enabling each of us, in our own sphere, to achieve things. You only have to listen, and you begin to understand that behind the sometimes deliberate simplicity of the song there are hidden values which are located in a quite different dimension from, say, chess, sport, or even literature and art. He begins to draw us away into the depths of those universal human feelings and values that live in and around us independently of our will and on which, probably, the universe rests. Some people are not concerned with all this. Others sense something different from what they're used to, and try to shut themselves off from unwanted emotions. The odd person will agree to sacrifice their peace and comfort, and take the first few steps along the hard road, but forsake it when he encounters unforeseen difficulties. Few indeed are those who march forward without a backward glance, obeying the indestructible instinct which prompts us to fight for the triumph of justice.

> See, he's walking the tightrope with no safety net.
> Lean a bit to the left – he'll fall and die.
> Lean a bit to the right – there's still no saving him.
> Yet it matters much to him to go four-quarters of the way.

Despite the colossal inner tension, the match itself took place in what was described at the time as an exceptionally friendly atmosphere. 'Karpov and Kasparov are behaving like perfect gentlemen,' said one observer. When the well-known playwright Leonid Zorin was asked for his feelings about the atmosphere of the match, he said: 'Extremely optimistic. I've long found it depressing that the world of chess has become so thoroughly embittered and that the hostile relations which surface between the games are distorting the image of this chivalrous art. So it's all the more gratifying to see Karpov and Kasparov sitting down after a game to analyse it together. You can see at once that the truth of chess is more precious to them than anything else.' We actually did analyse each game after we'd played it, right there on the stage. My trainers advised against this, fearing that by analysing things together I would allow the experienced Karpov to read my mind. I told them I couldn't refuse. I didn't want to be the first to make a discourteous gesture.

The Times described the scene:

> Looking down past the white pillars and glittering chandeliers to where the two men sit at the chessboard on the red-carpeted stage, one can see how body language expresses the state of mind of the champion and challenger.
>
> Karpov, pale and predatory, sits relaxed and bright-eyed, sometimes resting his chin on his folded hands, sometimes turning to stare nonchalantly at the audience or getting up to disappear behind the curtains, rather like a conjuror. Kasparov, by contrast, sits stolid and square, his athletic and well-built frame apparently helpless in this war of nerves. He stares fixedly at the board, pondering moves for a long time.

But there was one diversion that could not be ignored. It emanated, surprisingly, from *The Times* itself. Even more surprisingly, it was written by Golombek, who made the ludicrous claim that I had been ordered by the Soviet authorities to 'throw' the game and lose to Karpov. 'Perhaps Kasparov has been warned not to play well and has been given to understand that the consequences for him and his family would be disastrous,' he said.

The head of my delegation wrote to FIDE rejecting this nonsense. Campomanes described the story as 'unfounded and absurd'. At last he and I had found something we could agree on.

One could agree with Golombek, too, but only with his statement that 'something abnormal' was happening. It certainly was. Many of my friends couldn't understand either why I was losing virtually without putting up a fight. But it was absurd to attribute any of this to political motives. I have to admit that there was also a degree of truth in Golombek's chess analysis, when he noted that in the early stages I had been attacking without due preparation and that some of my openings were familiar to Karpov. But the reason lay in me myself, in what I was aiming at in the beginning. No one forced me to play that way. Crazy as it may seem, I worked it out for myself.

My losing game twenty-seven interrupted the long sequence of draws, and I was now standing right on the brink of sudden death. Surprisingly, though, I felt a sense of relief: I'd lost the match, there was nothing to lose, so I'd try and hold out to the end. The only thing left for me was to show the world that I could play. Above all, I wanted to prove it for myself.

Meanwhile, the other side were convinced they had it in the bag. The magazine *64-Chess Review* started hinting that I had achieved all my previous successes by chance and that there were other young players with more talent. By coincidence, the editor-in-chief of this magazine happens to be Karpov. His deputy is Roshal, whose main job is to serve as the mouthpiece of the Sports Committee's latest favourite and sing his praises.

The crunch was to come in game thirty-one. That was their plan. Karpov had put on a new suit for the occasion. His whole retinue also turned out in their Sunday best. The USSR Chess Federation had a laurel wreath standing by. On that day, Karpov played the first half of the game really well. He gained a big positional advantage and soon won a pawn. Then something extraordinary happened. He just panicked. I was the one who should have been in a panic, but I was completely calm. 'To make sure, I even took my jacket off.'

Karpov was on the point of winning hands down. It was a standard position and he was a pawn up. But he couldn't take the initiative. He waited for me to lose instead. But it happened differently. I got a chance to hit back, and took it. Karpov's advantage quickly evaporated.

When he got into time difficulties I offered a draw and he agreed. According to eye-witnesses, his hands were trembling and he seemed strangely relieved to accept the draw.

The initiative had just crossed the table between us, I was in no doubt about that. He may have sensed it too.

It was no surprise that I won the next game. It was my first win in the ninety-four days since we started, and my first-ever victory against Karpov since first playing him as a schoolboy, in that 'simul' ten years before.

Then came a most opportune extra time-out, giving him just the chance he needed to recover his composure. The hall was needed for a session of the USSR Academy of Sciences, an arrangement we'd both agreed to in advance. Logically, all the champion had to do now was to change his match strategy, throw off his former caution and put the final squeeze on his opponent. But by now Karpov was unable to change tack. The explanation offered by some commentators, that the force of inertia went on operating, is one that might apply to any number of people, but certainly not to a match-seasoned warrior like Karpov. He was the first to grasp the fact that it wasn't a matter of inertia, or only fatigue, but that his opponent was playing better and better. If he was to complete the match successfully he needed to strain every nerve, and in every game, not just one or two. He had to overcome something in himself and not play against his opponent, as he's fond of saying, but play chess. Karpov couldn't do it.

Incidentally, by conceding an adjourned game without resuming it, Karpov deprived the fans of an opportunity to congratulate me on my victory at the proper time. They did so instead just before the beginning of game thirty-three. The Reuters correspondent, Jon Tisdall, reported: 'The ovation that was planned to mark Kasparov's first win was saved and unveiled today when a long, loud and rhythmic ovation from a standing crowd greeted the challenger's arrival. Karpov's reception was loud and warm, but not nearly so enthusiastic.'

Then there was another time-out, lasting more than a week. The Hall of Columns was required for the lying-in-state of Marshal Ustinov, the Minister of Defence. The length of the match was now causing problems all round. Not only was the building required for other events, some of them booked as long as a year before, but Karpov and I had missed the Chess Olympiad in Salonika. The visas and secondment periods of the people involved in the match were expiring. The prolonged absence from home was even straining some marriages. People began to leave. Even our trainers had tournaments to play. I lost Dorfman for a month while he played in the first league.

The cost of the match was mounting. Pressure was put on us to move it to the Hotel Sport, a long way out of the centre of Moscow. At the beginning of January, at Karpov's suggestion, we wrote to the chairman of the organising committee, Demichev, who was then Minister of Culture and a candidate member of the Politburo, requesting that the venue should not be changed. But all we got was a temporary reprieve. I think the decisive factor was not the letter, but Karpov's personal guarantee that the match would be over by the end of the month. A lecture had been arranged for 29 January at the Polytechnical Museum in Moscow on the outcome of the world championship. I've kept my ticket. But on 30 January, when I won game forty-seven for my second point, it was announced that the move to the Hotel Sport would take place after all.

Keene wrote of game forty-seven: 'Karpov's play was surprisingly feeble and towards the end of the game he turned bright red, a sign of his imminent defeat. Five-two remained a commanding lead, but Karpov has not won a game for two months and must have recalled with apprehension how Korchnoi pulled back from 5-2 in Baguio in 1978.' It wasn't only Karpov who was remembering Baguio – Campomanes, Sevastyanov and Baturinsky were all there too.

It was then, evidently, that the idea occurred to them of bringing the match to a premature end. After his defeat, Karpov got a whole week to recover – a luxury that never came my way in the first phase when I so badly needed it – and even then, he lost again in game forty-eight (see Appendix A). Between then and 15 February, when Campomanes made his 'move' (which I describe in the next chapter), there was another week of time-out.

People began to say that towards the end of the match the quality of the games had fallen off considerably, from which it followed that the world champion was evidently unwell, and my victories the result of luck. Careful analysis does not bear this out. Of course Karpov's play was far from perfect, but surely no one would venture to say that he made more errors at the end of the match than at the beginning.

The people around Karpov couldn't understand what was happening. Because he had beaten me so easily in the early games, they could only assume that he must be unwell to be losing at the end. To them, if Karpov was losing he must be sick, so they must protect him, and incidentally, of course, themselves.

I think Keene came closest to the truth when he wrote the following:

What is one to make of all this? Karpov has always suffered, in my opinion, from the stigma of a champion who won by default (against Fischer in 1975). That he should be allowed to duck out of a critical situation by the intervention of a *deus ex machina*, in the form of the FIDE President, can do his reputation nothing but damage. He would have been much wiser to play on and risk the consequences. As for Kasparov, after a highly shaky start, he has produced what is, almost certainly, the most impressive rearguard action of any sportsman in any discipline in the history of recorded sport. Remember that the first player to six games wins the match. From games 1–9, Kasparov went down to four losses and five draws. He seemed annihilated and no one came to his rescue at this point. From then on, displaying remarkable tenacity and maturity, he held Karpov at bay in the long war of attrition from games 10–26. The public may have seen these games as tedious draws, but they were an important part of Kasparov's process of mental reconstruction. Losing game 27 made Kasparov's position desperate, but his opponent's inability to deliver a knock-out blow permitted Kasparov to complete his psychological repairs and ultimately take over the initiative. Indeed, Kasparov won convincingly in the extended 39-game match, from games 10–48, by three games to one with thirty-five draws.

Kasparov had the knife at his throat for four months, yet he never gave up and at the end his chances may even have been superior. He was certainly playing much better chess, and many observers will now prefer to regard his claims to be the legitimate world champion as more valid than Karpov's.

Many people were disappointed at the number of drawn games, and as a chess player I regret it too. But as a sportsman I say it arose out of the unique situation in the match. I have no guilty conscience about it. It is unlikely ever to happen again.

People fondly remember the days of Fischer and say he played to win everything. Karpov wants to win only as much as he needs to. I belong somewhere in the middle. Deep down I am a maximalist too. But I haven't got Fischer's decisiveness. Of course I regret that, but it can't be helped.

Unfortunately, the scandal in which the match ended has obscured the fact that, as chess, it was exceedingly rich. That wealth of content has never been professionally studied by the experts. I'm sure that future chess historians will consider the fruits of that five-month contest between the world's two strongest players, and will discover that our open-ended match marked a point at which modern chess set out in a new direction.

When I won two victories in a row, the ground beneath the champion's feet trembled. The chess authorities were suddenly faced with the frightening prospect that I might conceivably win. The 'corpse' had not merely come to life: it was scrambling to its feet. Was the unthinkable about to happen? They couldn't risk the possibility.

The chessboard was not set aside. It was irrelevant. Another war was beginning. As ever, Vysotsky had the right words for the occasion:

> Decide who you are – a coward
> Or the chosen one of fate,
> And try the taste
> Of a real fight.

EIGHT

Campo's Circus

Who will remember in ten or twenty years' time why our match was stopped? And if they do remember, who will they consider to have come off worst? Karpov, of course! They took two points away from him, and then his world title as well! Who will remember that FIDE President Campomanes was a close friend of Karpov, which he publicly admitted at his famous press conference (the only thing that may stick is the catchy name invented by Spassky – 'Karpomanes')? Will they remember that the entire bureaucratic apparatus was on the champion's side? Will they remember the unqualified support that the USSR Sports Committee and the presidium of the USSR Chess Federation gave Karpov then in his battle against his compatriot for the world crown? No, they won't. They won't remember because few people knew what was actually happening: *glasnost* had not yet arrived.

Luckily, chess is objective, and the strongest person is decided at the board. The well-planned blows of fate this time did not reach their target, although not for lack of trying by the people who inspired them, who to this day feel unscathed and invulnerable. Campomanes, for example, while campaigning for re-election in 1986, boldly declared that his decision to end the match had been one of the greatest achievements of his term as President.

So that nothing like this should ever happen again, I have decided to tell the world exactly what went on behind the scenes at our match.

My first win simply dampened the triumphant mood in my opponent's camp, but my second win, immediately followed by a third, radically changed the match situation. Neither Karpov nor the people backing him were prepared for such a change. A 'general mobilisation' was urgently called – Campomanes flew in to Moscow. Something was about to happen!

Botvinnik made a witty analysis of the situation that arose after game forty-eight: 'There are three possibilities of how the match will end. The first, and least likely, is that Karpov will after all win the single game he needs and will remain champion. The second, and more likely, is that Kasparov will win another three games and become the champion. And the third possibility is that the match will simply be stopped. The third possibility is the most likely, because the second possibility is more likely than the first.' Botvinnik turned out to be right.

But how did it happen, and what were the motives of the people behind it? We will probably never know the full story because most of the negotiations took place without me, and the main characters undoubtedly have an interest in keeping it all quiet.

On 31 January, the day after the score reached 5-2, Gramov, the Chairman of the Sports Committee, expressed concern – according to Campomanes – at the players' state of health and asked if a way could be found to stop the match. That was the same day that the question of transferring the match from the Hall of Columns to the Hotel Sport was finally decided.

On 1 February our next game, the forty-eighth, did not take place: I was informed in writing that it had been postponed to 4 February. The organisers said the reason for this technical time-out was because the hall was not ready. It emerged, however, that no steps had actually been taken to get it ready. On the night of 1 February Campomanes tried to arrange a meeting between the two players, but Mamedov, the head of our delegation, refused to involve me in these negotiations. Nevertheless, Campomanes insisted on holding a meeting that same night, which was attended by the heads of the two delegations, Gligoric, the chief arbiter of the match, and Kinzel, chairman of the appeals jury.

Campomanes's proposal, which had allegedly been approved by Karpov, was as folows: 'To limit the match to a further eight games; if no result as prescribed by the regulations is achieved during this time, the match will end. Karpov will remain the champion, but a new match will be held this September starting with a score of nil-nil.' A few hours later Campomanes flew off to Dubai leaving the negotiations to Kinzel.

I couldn't accept the proposal. Even a child could see how absurd it was. For me to clinch the match I would need to win every other game, and there had only been eight wins in the previous forty-seven games. At the same time there would come a certain point after which Karpov would be in a no-lose situation. Given these circumstances I asked a natural question: 'If the rules are being changed anyway, then why do we need to play extra games?'

These words of mine were subsequently quoted in FIDE documents and in Karpov's statements as evidence that I had been the one to call for the match to be ended. At the time, though, they were simply used to delay the next game.

Yes, I was ready to take part in negotiations, but I wanted to be accepted as an equal partner in them: a natural desire to emerge from a difficult situation with dignity. The score was not in my favour, but my playing had not deteriorated. Four-nil – that was in the early part of the match. But then in two and a half months Karpov had not won a single game.

I asked that 'fateful' question of mine on 3 February. Gligoric told me that Karpov would give his answer by noon the next day. But that time came and went, and there was no answer. Naïvely, I assumed that meant game forty-eight would go ahead. But no: the organisers sent me a letter saying that the game had been postponed yet again, from 4 to 6 February, this time giving no explanation whatever. Then I realised that what they were doing was giving the champion an opportunity to recover after his defeat, while trying meanwhile to entangle me in a web of negotiations.

On 4 February Gligoric handed me the following conditions from Karpov:

1. Kasparov acknowledges himself beaten in the match.
2. A new match will begin in September with the score at nil-nil. If Kasparov wins by three points or less, he will become world champion until 1 January 1986 since he will have failed to show outright superiority over Karpov in the two matches. The title will then revert to Karpov, and Kasparov will play in candidates matches.
3. If Kasparov wins the match by four or more points, he will become the world champion and will promise to defend his title in 1986 in a match tournament of three players (against Karpov and the winner of the candidates cycle).

When I categorically refused to discuss such conditions, Gligoric advised me to 'think it all over thoroughly and, on mature reflection, agree to it'.

That same evening Kinzel took up the cause. He came to my hotel and also began trying to persuade me to accept Karpov's conditions. So FIDE, in the person of Kinzel (standing in for the President while he was away), expressed its readiness to discuss the conditions seriously, despite the fact they were a flagrant violation of the FIDE rules for a world championship match.

I asked Kinzel if he didn't think the conditions were an insult. He asked me to think it over, dropping a hint that the next match might be held abroad, where the prize money would be much higher. I told him that money could not compensate for injustice.

Kinzel then said something surprising: 'No separate negotiations between you and Karpov will be allowed. Everything has to take place with the consent of the World Chess Federation.' To which I replied: 'I shall expect Karpov at the chessboard in the Hotel Sport, where we can resolve all our problems under FIDE rules. We don't need any Campomanes or Kinzel for that. All we need is a board with sixteen white and sixteen black pieces.'

This artificially created break had disrupted the flow of the match. On 6 February Karpov, evidently not yet having had enough rest, called a time-out. I felt compelled to write to Demichev:

To Comrade P. N. Demichev,
Candidate member of the CPSU Central Committee,
USSR Minister of Culture,
Chairman of the world chess championship match organising
committee
6 February 1985

Dear Petr Nilovich,
On 31 January 1985, the day after game forty-seven, which took place in the Hall of Columns at the House of Unions, I was informed in writing that the match would subsequently be continued on 1 February 1986, in the conference room of the Hotel Sport. I agreed to this, even though in an earlier letter to you dated 6 January 1985 both players in the match had pointed out the drawbacks of that location.

The organisers, however, did not take the trouble to get the room in the Hotel Sport ready by 1 February for the next game, the forty-eighth, to be held, and on 31 January I received a letter telling me that it had been postponed to 4 February.

For inexplicable reasons, the game did not take place on the appointed day, and six hours before the start of the game I received yet another letter from the organising committee informing me that game forty-eight had been postponed once again to 6 February 1986.

As a result, there was an artificial break of a week in the match which has brought a certain disruption to the flow of the contest.

All this leads me to believe that the match organisers are giving the world champion an opportunity to recover after his defeat in game forty-seven. Further evidence of this is the time-out which Anatoly Karpov called on 6 February.

At the same time, I should like to inform you that after game forty-seven, FIDE President Mr F. Campomanes and his authorised representative Mr Kinzel (West Berlin) put forward

conditions for ending the match which they had agreed with the
world champion, but which were unacceptable to me.

I am writing to you, therefore, to ask for your assistance in
creating normal conditions for the match to be held in accordance
with the existing rules.
Yours sincerely,

G. KASPAROV

Two days later I had a telephone conversation with Demichev.
He told me that Karpov's and my state of health were causing
alarm and that a long break would be good for both of us.
Then Demichev added that the game should be played honestly and that it was wrong 'to hit a man when he is down',
meaning Karpov. I found this a surprising thing for him to
say. After all, at that point I was losing 2-5.

Finally, after a week's break, game forty-eight was held on
8 February in the conference room of the Hotel Sport. It wasn't
the same sumptuous surroundings as the Hall of Columns,
but I had pleasant memories of the place. It was there that I
won the interzonal tournament in 1982 and a match against
Belyavsky in 1983. I crossed my fingers that fortune would not
forsake me this time either. For the first time in five months I
went into the game feeling inwardly calm. The game was
adjourned, and the next day, when it was completed, I
notched up my third victory.

Naturally, that game brought embarrassment to my
opponents. I won it in good style, which destroyed their
argument that we were both too exhausted to play good chess.
Moreover, as the British grandmaster John Nunn pointed out,
forty-eight games is not at all an unusual number for two
grandmasters to play over a period of five months. As far as
the quality of our playing was concerned, it's interesting to
read Gligoric's contradictory evidence (*Radio Revue*, 3 March
1985). In reply to the question: 'In Moscow, while you were
commenting on the last two games, you said that the champion was making crude mistakes, and that this could only be

due to his greater physical exhaustion and lack of concentration. What else could you say about this?', he answered: 'Yes, that's what I said, and can now add the following about the last game, the forty-eighth. Kasparov played an excellent game, and there was nothing the world champion could do about it. Nevertheless, both players are tired and have lost weight, although it is more noticeable in Karpov.'

It later emerged that on the day I won the last game, Gligoric telephoned Campomanes in Dubai asking him to return urgently to Moscow. When Campomanes put the phone down, he turned to Keene and said: 'Karpov cannot continue . . .' So there can be no question at all as to how this whole crisis arose. There has been debate as to whether it was Gligoric who actually made this call, and if so, on whose behalf he was acting. Gligoric could not deny that it was he who made the call because this can be confirmed by independent witnesses. He said later he was acting on Kinzel's behalf.

I was naturally far from delighted that Gligoric, whose duty it was as chief arbiter to be neutral, should have initiated dubious moves unassociated with chess itself in the interests of just one of the players. I later made my own views plain to Gligoric in an open letter after he published his own distorted view of events. It deeply saddened me that Gligoric was being used in the dirty game played by Campomanes. This is what I wrote: 'The chess world is going through hard times. A battle is going on for the purity of the ideals of chess. It is hard to believe that such a renowned player as you finds himself in this battle on the side of people who are using chess for their own personal gain. Campomanes and company have absolutely no interest in the art of the game, but you are a true chess player, and I am sure that you are not indifferent to what happens to the game. This is not the right company for you, Grandmaster.'

The day 10 February was a Sunday, and we had a chance to discuss the situation calmly. There were hopes now which had not existed before: I was now on form, while my opponent seemed to have lost his. We spent a long time deliberating on what strategy to follow now, and finally decided to call a time-out on 11 February, so as to be able to prepare properly for game forty-nine. It was my turn to play black, and it was vital not to lose the initiative. In addition, I needed to get used to my new standing in the match: 5-3.

I often wondered later what would have happened if I hadn't called a time-out at that point. Would the game have gone ahead? And if not, then who would have called it off? Kinzel? The organisers? In any event, Campomanes was at that time still in mid-air on his way back from Dubai . . . (Gligoric's opinion on the subject, which he gave to the Zagreb newspaper *Vjesnik* on 19 February, makes interesting reading: 'If Kasparov had not called a time-out, game forty-nine would have been played and the situation could have become even more complicated.')

As soon as he arrived back in Moscow, Campomanes, on the night of 11/12 February, handed the leaders of my delegation fresh proposals, which again mentioned the need to limit the number of games, this time to a total of sixty. What is noteworthy is that at this point he still did not have any intention of immediately stopping the match.

Mamedov replied that he was not going to have me disturbed until game forty-nine was over, particularly as the new proposals essentially contained all the demands that Karpov had previously put forward.

On the morning of 13 February, the day the game was supposed to take place, I was told that this time a time-out had been called by the President himself. No official explanations were given, and Campomanes told Mamedov that he had declared a break at the request of the Soviet Chess Federation in order to find an acceptable way of ending the match.

As soon as I learnt of this latest postponement, I called Demichev. He told me candidly that the reason for the break was Karpov's unsatisfactory state of health (although he still had one more time-out that he could call), of which he,

Demichev, had been informed that morning by Gramov. Demichev once again started talking of sporting ethics, the nervous and physical exhaustion of the players, and the need to call a friendly end to the match. Quoting expert opinion, he pointed out that I had not used my advantage in game forty-eight in the best way that I could, and that this was indicative of the fact I was exhausted. It's difficult to convey the amazement I felt at this, because I thought I had played the game very well, and chess commentators were unanimous in calling it my best creative achievement in the match.

An hour later I received a telephone call from Gramov, who told me that responsibility for the match lay with FIDE and that all disputes should be resolved with Campomanes. 'But why did the President call a time-out?' I asked. 'That was his own personal decision. No one asked him to.' It was becoming more like a game of ping-pong.

Campomanes came to our hotel only on 14 February, at noon, accompanied by Gligoric. No longer was there any talk about playing sixty games. Campomanes began saying how exhausted the players, arbiters and organisers were. When I objected, he suddenly brought out a letter signed by Sevastyanov.

It was the first time I had seen the letter. No one, of course, had bothered to tell me about it before.

USSR CHESS FEDERATION

Mr F. Campomanes   *13 February 1985*

Dear Mr Campomanes,
In view of the unprecedented duration of the world championship match between A. Karpov and G. Kasparov, which has been going on for more than five months and in which forty-eight games have already been played (in other words, two complete matches under the old rules), the USSR Chess Federation, concerned over the players' state of health, requests that a three-month break be declared. It will be recalled that the agreement on the open-ended match between Fischer and Karpov in 1976 provided for a break

after four months of play. That provision was included on the basis of medical opinion. The Karpov–Kasparov match, as noted above, has been going on for a longer period of time.

We would also point out that the proposal to call a break does not run counter to the FIDE statutes or the match regulations and will, we believe, be met by the world chess community with satisfaction.

An affirmative decision by you on this matter will promote the interests of the creative development of chess.
Yours sincerely,

V.I. SEVASTYANOV
USSR Pilot-Cosmonaut,
Twice Hero of the Soviet Union,
Chairman of the USSR Chess Federation

The vice-chairman of the Federation at the time was Baturinsky, the head of Karpov's team, and its official press spokesman was Roshal. Needless to say, no one asked for my agreement to the letter or even inquired about my health. Sevastyanov himself never once exchanged words with me throughout the whole match. I was informed after the event, and even then not by my own countrymen!

I replied that I did not consider Sevastyanov competent to draw conclusions about my health and stated firmly that I could see only two ways of ending the match: either Karpov would concede the match to me if he was unable to go on playing, or we would continue playing to the bitter end in full accordance with the existing rules. Campomanes, however, said there was a third way: 'That I myself take the decision.'

What exactly the President meant by that I was to find out that same evening, when Mamedov was summoned at around midnight and officially informed that the match was to be ended. The FIDE President's decision was to be announced at a press conference the following day. I, of course, was not invited. I rang Gligoric three times to ask him what all this was about. He promised to ask Kinzel. Then he rang back and reported Kinzel as saying that Campomanes had every right to take such a decision. 'OK,' I said, 'let me have this officially, in writing.' He got in touch again with Kinzel, who replied that the President wasn't obliged to explain his position on paper. At this point the Yugoslav grandmaster complained: 'You know, I'm acting as no more than a commissionaire in this matter.'

I was racked by doubts as to whether to attend the press conference or not. I was just twenty-one years old, and the bureaucratic brick wall before me seemed insuperable (the country was going through troubled times – the last days of Chernenko's rule) . . . Officials from the Sports Committee were reassuring, saying I had nothing to worry about.

But suddenly I had a strange feeling. I said to my mother: 'I think we should go to this press conference. I feel uncomfortable about something. I can't explain it, but I think we should go.' Mamedov had been warned: 'Stop Kasparov from going, otherwise there may be a major row. There are over a hundred cameramen at the Hotel Sport.' My mother advised against it, saying I would only find it frustrating, better just let them get on with it. But then she had a telephone call from Rhona Petrosyan: 'I think your son should go to the press conference,' she said. 'If he doesn't, he'll never forgive himself.'

So I went with my coaches – Nikitin, Timoschenko and Dorfman – to the press conference, arriving five minutes before it started. Karpov wasn't there, and they clearly hadn't expected me either. Krogius came up to me and suggested that I sit in the front row, but I refused. I didn't want anyone to think that we were taking an official part in this 'event'. There were about three hundred people from the world press and television in the hall, with floodlights and television cables strewn everywhere.

The cameras started to roll as soon as I arrived. They recorded the bewilderment caused by my appearance among the press conference organisers, including some highly revealing details such as someone peeping through the curtains to make sure the bad news was true, that I was actually there.

My appearance seemed to throw Campomanes into confusion. It took another twenty minutes or so for the press conference to begin.

Eventually the platform party filed into their seats on the stage. The huge banner with the FIDE motto *Gens una sumus* did nothing but mock the proceedings. Campomanes was clearly lacking his usual confidence, his eyes shifting uneasily around the room. The President was obviously under acute strain. You can see this clearly on the video. Sitting alongside him were Gligoric, Averbakh, Mikenas, Krogius, Kinzel and Sevastyanov, plus two deputy chairmen of the USSR Sports Committee, Rusak and Gavrilin, and a Foreign Ministry spokesman, who conducted the press conference.

To understand the bizarre events that followed it is important to know the precise words used by Campomanes, so that the reader can see for himself the pile of evasions and lies that Campo put together. I reproduce below a direct transcript of the tape, deliberately unedited and in the original English.

CAMPOMANES: Good afternoon, ladies and gentlemen of the press and broadcast media. First of all, I apologise for the delay. This reminds me of the time I had been elected President in Lucerne in 1982. The day after, I was supposed to name the Secretary General and as is normal in these matters there were many options. When I got to my seat in the conference hall to make my announcement, up until I was before the microphone I did not know whom I was going to choose – Mr Clues of Wales, Mr Keene of England, Mr Kazic of Yugoslavia or Professor Lim Kok Ann of Singapore. No one believed me when I said I didn't know what to do – whom to choose – up until that final moment, and I suppose many of you will be good doubting Thomases when I also tell you to this very moment, I do not know. This match, this current world chess championship match, has been an unusual competition which created unusual problems demanding special solutions. Whereas in accordance with FIDE statutes the President is empowered to take decisions in between congresses and whereas under the match regulations the President is personally and officially responsible for the entire match, and, further, is empowered to take the final decision on all questions affecting the match as a whole, I therefore declare that the match is ended without decision. A new match shall be played from scratch – zero-zero – starting 1 September 1985.

QUESTIONER: Whose consent?

CAMPOMANES: The two players' consent. The next FIDE Congress in August shall determine further necessary match provisions – the winner of that match will be the champion for the period 1985–6. Thank you.

There was a great deal of shuffling and noise in the audience at this news. The video tape shows my trainers and myself discussing what we had heard and laughing. After a few moments' confusion at Campomanes's statement, the floodgates opened and questions came pouring out.

QUESTIONER: What are the reasons for the early ending of the match?

CAMPOMANES: I think there was a glimpse in the statement. This has been a match that beat the record of all other matches – the greatest number of games, the greatest number of draws, more than five months' duration. It has exhausted the physical, if not the psychological, resources not only of the participants but all those connected with the match, however distant that connection might be. I for one have not been fully able to perform my functions and fulfil my other duties as President of FIDE because this has hovered over all my activities.

QUESTIONER: Is Mr Karpov unable to continue the match?

CAMPOMANES (*smiling*): I wish you had the possibility of tracking me down during the last hour then you would have found a ready answer to that question . . . (*long pause*).

QUESTIONER: Well, sir, if you don't answer the question . . .

CAMPOMANES: Just a minute, sir, I have not finished. Mr

Karpov is well and appealed to me to continue with the match till the very end on Monday. I left him no longer than twenty-five minutes ago and I just told one of my colleagues here behind me that I make this decision despite him. As all of you know very well, or have suspected, or have accused, that I am a very good friend of Mr Karpov – you are right – but that has nothing to do with what I feel is best for chess in the world. I denied his request. I don't need witnesses for this, but I have witnesses – let that be clear. Mr Karpov was ready twenty-five minutes ago and told me to please not play today 'cause Mr Kasparov and he are psychologically unprepared for today 'cause of all this brouhaha. He asked to start playing Monday, to the better or bitter end and that is what I meant when I told you on the podium that that was not what I was going to do.

QUESTIONER: What was the challenger's response?

CAMPOMANES: I have conferred with the challenger – I treat them as equal participants in this match – I am certain he is not happy about the decisions either, but it is the challenge in accordance with the regulations for the President to take a decision as best he knows – to the dismay, maybe, of many of those involved, but decision he must take. He cannot be expected to please everybody or anybody but he must take a decision. And now I understand without abrogation to myself the wisdom of Solomon – how he felt when he held that baby in his hands. Thank you.

QUESTIONER: In your own words, Mr Campomanes, both the champion and the challenger want to play. Can you tell us by what right are you taking the decision? Explain a bit more. What are the special circumstances?

CAMPOMANES: Thank you, Mr Doder, I think I so much in so many words, replied to you yesterday and I repeated it on the podium. The right is clear. The reasons – first we are thinking of the two best players of the world. We are thinking of chess as a sport in the eyes of the world. We are thinking of the well-being of all those connected with the match in Moscow and elsewhere, and other considerations bordering on this theme. I quote Mr Mydans who was trying to get hold of me yesterday I understand but I was not around. In your report iń the *New York Times*, 29 January, you yourself said that this was becoming not a test of chess skill, but a matter of physical endurance. I recall when the score was 5-0 and so many games had been played everybody was saying when will this end and then more draws happened and then Mr Kasparov won a game and then more draws – everybody was knocking at the door saying let's end this match and now that we end the match you ask me why. I think the question answers itself.

QUESTIONER: I have two questions. Thank you for calling the position of the two players regarding the decision. Could you tell us please how the Soviet Federation reacted to this proposal? And how can the ending of the game, when both players want to play, benefit the sport?

CAMPOMANES: I'll only answer one of your questions – the other has been answered. The USSR Chess Federation agrees with my decision.

QUESTIONER (Richard Owen, Moscow Correspondent of *The Times*): Mr Campomanes, I just wonder how you respond to suggestions from qualified commentators such as Raymond Keene that if Mr Karpov is unable to stand the pressure after six months he should have resigned his title given that chess is not only a matter of skill and moves but also of psychological pressure and a matter of endurance over a period of time – and also given that Mr Kasparov doesn't look like a man who is psychologically or physically shattered? (*laughter from the audience*)

CAMPOMANES: First of all, you quote from Mr Keene. What is the date of that thinking?

OWEN: He made this remark in my newspaper, *The Times*, two days ago.

CAMPOMANES: I was with Mr Keene four and a half days ago in Dubai and we had thrown this back and forward over good red wine and then I was on the phone again with him two nights ago – he's back in England. And Mr Keene is a grandmaster of England, your second, and he is entitled to this opinion and that's what makes FIDE such a jolly family – we agree to disagree.

QUESTIONER (*Tass*): What is the most efficient regulation system of the match?

CAMPOMANES: That's a good question (*laughter from the audience*). If I may remind your memory, your good servant was the organiser for the Philippine Chess Federation of the 1978 World Championship match. At the time we thought it was such a long match and I can assure you I can understand here how the organising committee here feels – because I thought at the end of 93 days I was ready to collapse and now this is more than 150 days. But the regulations served that championship, the regulations served the championship in Merano, but as I keep telling my close associates the fact that it has lasted this long is not the fault of the regulations. The regulations may be well and good, but happily – I say happily – the excellence of the players has reached such a level that they have discovered the secret of how to draw, to minimise to the barest of minimums the risk of losing. It is the excellence of present-day chess. If there is anyone one can fault it is the particular excellence that has contributed to the length of the match – forty draws, unheard of in previous matches. So the regulations being the product of human considerations cannot expect to fulfil all situations. That is why there is present in these regulations that somebody has to be personally and officially responsible to look at the events from all standpoints, and hope to goodness he makes the right decision.

QUESTIONER (*Sovietsky Sport*): How does he explain the situation that has arisen during the match, for clarification – but you have made an assessment of the match?

CAMPOMANES (*after consulting a Soviet official for further clarification*): Ah yes! Thank you very much, it is a good question. We have reached a juncture where we have technically two times the size of the match of the previous regulation – twenty-four games. This is forty-eight games, it is a good juncture to pause and give thought. That is why I saw the need to take action, because from here on what do you use – seventy-two games? Anything can happen when the match lasts that long, I don't envy the press people themselves. I remember the first days and all the bustle of activity in the press centre. Before I went to Dubai I visited the press centre. It didn't look like the local morgue (*he laughs*) but there were very much fewer people in the press centre. You do get tired yourselves.

QUESTIONER: You said that the players have discovered the secret of how to draw, but you arrived here just when Mr Kasparov seemed to have discovered the secret of how to win. Doesn't this give the impression that you came at the last moment to save Mr Karpov?

CAMPOMANES: Saving him from himself? No. I have been giving thought to this much earlier. From the point of the thirty-second game I began thinking of this. I recall Baguio was thirty-two games and I needed more input and I had been called away on trips requiring my attention. All of this began to gel when we were talking very much about this in Athens and I had received all kinds of telephone calls from chess leaders all round the world. Twenty-four times two is forty-eight. This is an excellent juncture to take stock independent of what you call the trend of the match – because like all trends doing the stockmarket, which goes up and down, you never know when it will take a nose dive.

QUESTIONER: I just want to know how you feel personally about the decision that both players say they want to continue the match?

CAMPOMANES: Yes, lady. My decision was taken equally for both players. You can't expect to please everybody, or even anybody. Up till that moment I didn't know. I have to live with myself and I sleep very well.

QUESTIONER (*Sovietsky Sport*): Another question about the regulations. So far twenty-nine matches have been played, the biggest one of thirty-four games. The system seemed to be appropriate – all the chess public approved of that system. Why was that system changed? And what system do you consider the most optimal?

CAMPOMANES: I believe I alluded to that indirectly earlier. Any regulation is used – it is the proof of the pudding that counts. When it is applied, given the circumstances, some regulations function well and others falter or fail, and moreover this is the prerogative eventually of the conference of FIDE to which I must defer. They formulate the regulations, starting with the committees and end with a unanimous vote or a show of hands. Regulations are only regulations. People make them; circumstances affect them.

QUESTIONER: I would like to ask just one question, which you alluded to earlier. There have been more specific reports on some of the wire services recently that Mr Karpov was on the verge of a psychological breakdown (*at this point Campomanes smiled and rose*), that he was exhausted and so forth. Would you address yourself to those – that he was in a hospital bed?

CAMPOMANES (*standing and taking the microphone*): You asked the question at the very right time – Mr Karpov is there behind you, now, just arrived.

At this point, the world champion appeared in the hall. Had he been in the building all the time, hiding in the wings somewhere? Or, more likely, had he been alerted to my presence by telephone before the press conference started and set off post-haste? From the back of the hall Karpov could be heard to say: 'I want to make a statement', after which he made his way to the stage.

Some of the audience gave him a noisy welcome. You could hear people questioning him as he walked down the gangway: 'How are you, Mr Karpov? OK? That's good.' The audience was buzzing in anticipation of the entertainment that would come next. When he reached the platform, Gligoric gave up his seat and Karpov shook hands with the smiling Campomanes and the man from the Foreign Ministry. Then he sat down next to Campomanes and took the microphone.

KARPOV: I must tell you, as we Russians say, the rumours about my death were a bit exaggerated.

CAMPOMANES: Anatoly, I just told them about that.

KARPOV: And I consider that we can and we ought to continue the match – and the proposal to end it, and to start from scratch, I do not agree with such a decision. I consider that on Monday we should start, or rather resume and continue, our match. I think Kasparov would second my proposal and there should be no problem at all (*applause*).

CAMPOMANES (*smiling*): Gentlemen, now you know what I told you earlier was true. I have a verification right here in the friend – in the person – of the world champion. I have mentioned this to you and now Mr Kasparov will know that I now told you the truth.

KARPOV: I think we should invite Kasparov here (*motioning with his hand*).

FOREIGN MINISTRY SPOKESMAN: But the decision is taken.

CAMPOMANES: Garry, you want to come and say your piece?

There was a hubbub on the left side of the audience and shouts of 'Let Kasparov give his comment'. Then a lone but clear voice from the group where Roshal sat said: 'If his mother lets him.' I started to speak from the audience, but many of them could not hear me because there was no microphone, so I set off for the podium. As I was going up the steps, I heard Campomanes saying to Karpov (and this is recorded on the tape):

CAMPOMANES: I told them exactly what you told me to tell them.

KASPAROV: We . . . we, but I don't accept this.

People said afterwards I was very pale with anxiety and had sweat on my upper lip. In fact, I was pale, not with anxiety, but with anger at the whole crowd of them. When I finally reached the podium I had to wait for the applause to die down. Campomanes, having heard what Karpov had to say, was now talking to Sevastyanov.

KASPAROV: I want to ask Mr President one question – what all that show is for? Mr President, I shall explain what I mean. You said you have come here twenty-five minutes after your talk with the champion and he was against breaking the match. You knew my point of view too, that I was also objecting to ending or suspending the match with technical time-outs. Nevertheless, you came here and declared your point of view that, despite all those objections, the game is ended. What do we need it for? Twenty-five minutes ago you were speaking with Karpov and now suddenly such a divergence. Will you tell us, or at least me?

CAMPOMANES: I personally believe that what I was doing was in the best interests. But the players are only one part of this situation. Now, however . . . (after some hesitation) however, I am in a very happy position right now. I am in a position that I couldn't have wished for better. If the two players are willing to play to the very end (laughter from audience) I will consider in a conversation with the two of them alone because I have long demanded this situation to happen and I have not been able to get it, because Mr Karpov is not available, Mr Kasparov is not available, and I tried to get them. As a matter of fact, as late as last night I tried to get them together, but Mr Kasparov is sleeping – Mr Karpov has been often times in accordance with the meeting schedule. Now we have it. Now I want to talk with both of you (applause). Let's have ten minutes inside.

With this, Karpov and Campomanes stood up. Campomanes held out his hands in a gesture to the audience. He loves theatricality and histrionics. But I had not yet finished. Now it was my move.

KASPAROV: Give me the floor. I want to make known my declaration. The President's profession is to speak. My trade is to play chess. That is why I am not going to compete with him on the podium. I don't intend to demand a continuation because I'm convinced I shall win very easily because the champion feels unwell. He's here, he can proceed, we can see it. But for the first time in five months I have certain chances, let's say about twenty-five per cent or thirty per cent and now they are trying to deprive me of those chances by the numerous delays – and let those who delayed the match be responsible. The match should continue – I have been speaking about it two weeks ago – without time-outs, without intervals, but it is being prolonged. With each delay his chances are growing while mine are diminishing (*applause*).

At this point the Foreign Ministry spokesman leaned forward and said: 'The press conference is over.' This was greeted with a roar of laughter, so after a few seconds' thought he added uncertainly: 'If President Campomanes considers it appropriate to continue . . .'

CAMPOMANES: If Mr Kasparov refuses to have a huddle with me I cannot change the decision. With me and Mr Karpov – as clear as that. The decision stands if the two do not sit down and talk about it and shake on it. (*Karpov, who had started to walk out for the expected talk, began to walk back.*)
KARPOV: I can make my own statement.
CAMPOMANES: (*to Karpov*). You play today?
KARPOV: No.
CAMPOMANES: Monday?
KARPOV: Monday.
FOREIGN MINISTRY SPOKESMAN: It's better to have a rest.
KARPOV: I think we can make a sort of break now for everybody to calm down (*applause*). And after the interval announce the final decision.
CAMPOMANES: A break of ten minutes.

The break, in fact, went on for one hour and thirty-eight minutes, during which the foreign journalists were in a quandary over what story to file. If they sent a report based on

Campomanes's announcement that the match had been cancelled, they knew they might have to change it later. They began to get restless as the 'time-out' went on indefinitely.

Campomanes, Karpov, Rusak, Gavrilin, Kinzel, Sevastyanov and Mamedov went off to another room. I went up to the hotel room where one of the members of my delegation was staying, but was followed soon afterwards by Averbakh and Chmykhov, the hotel manager, who tried to persuade me to go to the meeting. Finally I agreed.

Once inside the room where the meeting was being held, I quickly found that we were not there to decide anything at all. Everything had been decided already. Even Karpov, who had stated in the hall that he wanted to continue, was now simply demanding a return match in the event that he lost. Sevastyanov immediately supported Karpov's demand and Campomanes raised no objection. *The question of continuing the match wasn't even raised!* I repeated that it was against the rules to stop the match unless Karpov resigned. Campomanes said that I would have the right to state my own position at the FIDE congress. My question: 'And what are my chances of success in appealing to the congress if my own Federation supports only Karpov?', needed no answer.

Karpov and I were asked to sign an official document saying that we agreed with the President's decision. For more than an hour they tried to talk me into signing that piece of paper. The tones in which they spoke were rude and short-tempered. But I wouldn't put my signature to their 'historic' document!

It was clear that Karpov had no great desire to sign, and only did so after Sevastyanov clapped him on the shoulder and said: 'Come on, Tolya, sign it. It's a good piece of paper.' At the same time, though, Karpov didn't forget to add the condition about his right to a return match.

Let us hear what Roshal had to say, four years later, while addressing a gathering in the Polytechnical Museum:

And what was going on behind the scenes? Karpov, the poor soldier, the loyal soldier of the organisations above him (well, not a soldier – maybe a colonel or a general – but he would still never go against any Party or Government decisions) was being urged: 'Sign it, Tolya, sign it . . . The match has to be ended: it's already been announced. And the people above have already said the match is finished, it's over. The decision has been taken. Campomanes isn't going to get into trouble, but you . . .' Tolya said: 'All right, but on one condition. You have to make sure I have a return match, because the cycle calls for one. Whether you change things, whether it's unlimited or limited, that doesn't concern me. In this cycle I have the right to a return match. Whatever else you do, there must be a return match.'

But what kind of return match? For some reason everyone was forgetting about the fact that in the event of defeat in an open-ended match, the world champion had the right to a similarly open-ended return match, which I imagine at that time was the last thing Karpov would have wanted. By signing that piece of paper, he was guaranteeing himself retention of the title if a limited match was drawn, and a return match consisting of twenty-four games if he lost.

Later Karpov said he had signed the document because he thought I was going to sign it too. But I'm sure that if he hadn't wanted the match to end, it wouldn't have. Three years later Baturinsky was to write: '. . . I am the one who is morally responsible for not having been able to dispel Karpov's doubts and persuade him to continue the match' (*Sovietsky Sport*, 28 January 1988). What's more, it subsequently emerged that just a few hours after the match was ended, Baturinsky, on Karpov's instructions, gave Campomanes official proposals for arranging the new match in September 1985.

Yet another important piece of evidence from 'the other side' was given by Roshal when he said in the film *The Thirteenth*: 'Karpov, as world champion, the then all-powerful world champion, ahead on points, could have thumped his fist on the table and said: "Stop!" [in other words, stop trying to end the match!]. But he didn't do it.'

That concurs with the opinion given by the Yugoslav

grandmaster Borislav Ivkov in the newspaper *Borba* in March 1985: 'Karpov, ahead on points, agreed to the match being ended as it was – in other words, it was the decision that he wanted, it was to his advantage . . . Campomanes, who had come under the very strong influence of Karpov, was doing everything he could to block Kasparov's path. During their match, while Karpov was well in the lead, Campomanes was not terribly bothered by the fact that the match was too long, inhumane and exhausting. It was only when Kasparov started to win that Campomanes decided the match was doing them no good . . . Kasparov wanted to play to the finish and become world champion, although just one defeat would have put him back into the ranks of challenger. But if Karpov had believed himself capable of winning that last single game, the match wouldn't have been ended by the President's decision!'

None of this, however, prevented Karpov three years later from coming out in his magazine (*64-Chess Review*, No. 9, 1988) with the following statement, designed only for the most ill-informed readers: '. . . As regards the ending of the 1985 match in Moscow, I should like to quote just one statement by the head of Kasparov's delegation which was never published in the Soviet press. Speaking on behalf of Kasparov, Mamedov said: "Kasparov does not wish to continue the match. Kasparov agrees with the FIDE President's decision to consider the match ended. Kasparov is ready to play a new match in September. Moscow, 25 February 1985." No official protest was made by Kasparov. There was, it's true, a highly dramatic scene played out for the media, but after that, when the question of resuming the match arose, the above statement was made after a week's meditation. But it's understandable: after all, Kasparov was trying to save a match in which I was two points ahead. But even that is not the point I'm trying to make now. Kasparov, as we have seen, agreed with the FIDE President's decision to consider the match ended and thereby lost any moral right to launch the intolerably harsh attacks that he subsequently did.'

In reply to this, Mamedov wrote a letter to the editor of *64* describing what actually did happen at the time (No. 20, 1988): '. . . In the early hours of 24 February I received a phone call from Gligoric, the chief arbiter of the match, who was in Yugoslavia. He said that Campomanes wanted to know what Kasparov's reaction was to Karpov's proposal to resume the match. It became clear to us that if there was agreement, the much-desired long break would come about, because the arbiters and trainers had all gone home, and arranging the second half of the match would have required just the amount of time that Karpov needed. It was for this reason that it has been decided to make the following statement . . . Such is the actual picture of events at that time. The stress in Karpov's text on the word "agreed" with regard to Kasparov is absurd, because on 15 February 1985 Karpov endorsed with his own signature the FIDE President's decision to end the match, while Kasparov did not . . . And I had to work hard to get Kasparov to accept the situation and abide by the decision, otherwise there would have been no one to play against.'

The time has come, however, to return to the press conference. An hour and a half later Campomanes at last declared the final verdict.

CAMPOMANES: This is more than just Solomonic dilemma, it is a Gordian knot put on top of it. The world champion accepts the decision of the President and the challenger abides by the decision of the President. In the course of the meeting I have appreciated the thinking of the world champion who feels very strongly that he deserves, or has a right to, a return match after the new match. I have appreciated likewise the strong wish of the challenger that the provisions for the next match be ascertained fully since he felt that leaving it hanging in congress or for the decision of the FIDE Congress in September, in August, is not the most suitable arrangement for him. The Congress of FIDE shall take place in Graz, Austria, and will end before the match begins. It may be the same day the match begins. I have committed myself to the two players to make this known to Congress and I add on my own, not only to Congress, but to the leadership of the 122 Federations of FIDE, that in accepting on the part of the world champion and abiding on the part of the Challenger to this decision they have made fully known their thinking on these matters. I thank you.

Coming down straight after this into the lobby, I was asked by several reporters to comment on the President's decision. This is what I said:

One thing that is obvious is that the International Federation proved to be absolutely incapable of handling something like world championships. Instead of taking care of the organisation of the match, they are talking about popularising chess. You may remember that it is not the first problem; the semi-finals were nearly disrupted and were normalised by a miracle. Instead of a two-year cycle that the President is talking about, we now have a four-year cycle, as the match is postponed until 1985. The champion keeps his title and for some reason the *status quo* is preserved. Moreover, the champion now demands a return match, and the grounds for it are also quite obscure. I don't know if he really means it when he says he wants to go on playing, but I just keep thinking it looks very much like a well-rehearsed play where everyone knows his part. I've said many times before that I want to play the match, that I want to go on and that I am in very good health. For two weeks people tried to convince me of the opposite and urged me to finish the match on whatever grounds. Many of you probably know about the proposals made when the score was still 5-2 and 5-3. As for the technical time-outs and the President's time-out, which are being taken now and stopping the game, well, in my opinion, those who can think logically will see what happened and why the match finished under such unusual circumstances.

This is unacceptable to the chess world and should not be allowed to go on. FIDE rules should not contain an exceptional clause allowing the President to determine the outcome of the match. But why should we play at all if the President can take the decision at any moment? Saying that the match was too long is absurd. It was already too long at the forty-sixth game when the score was 5-1, but no one had any misgivings about the psychological condition of the players. It all started when the score went 5-2 and then 5-3. I think you see what I mean. This is all I wanted to say. I repeat that I am absolutely healthy and am ready to go on playing.

When I returned home to Baku to brood on that dramatic climax, I decided to write down my own analysis of events. I completed it on 15 March, exactly one month after the press conference. Yet even now, looking back on those events of four years ago, I would not change a single word in it. I present it exactly as I wrote it at the time. The starting point of my analysis was that in trying to assess that decision to end the match, the thing to keep in mind is the immortal question first posed by the ancients: '*Cui bono*' – who profits by it?

On 15 February, FIDE President Campomanes announced that the world chess championship was over 'without a final result'. According to him, a new match would begin in September with the score nil-nil. The encounter which had lasted five months was basically annulled. This unprecedented move, going against all the normal practices of chess competition, naturally caused much controversy in the world of chess and gave rise to all kinds of rumours and distortions. Many issues involved in stopping this match, as well as organising another, remain unresolved. Chess fans and experts are still in ignorance, although the official documents and the known facts, as well as what happened after the match, are enough to say where and how the outcome of the match was decided. A. Karpov described the situation immediately before Campomanes's announcement, as he saw it, in an interview he gave to *Tass* on 3 March: 'Even after the thirtieth game it was being said that the match proved to be too long, that everyone, including referees, organisers and spectators, was tired, that the players' health is in danger and that the problem should be solved . . .' Thus we learn that as far back as the beginning of December – after the thirtieth game – it was being said. But where and by whom was it being said? Did you notice the strange jumble of 'referees, organisers, spectators, players'? I, for one, heard about the possibility of finishing the match early only on 1 February – that is, after the forty-seventh game, when the score was 5-2.

The role of mediators was played first by the chief arbiter, Grandmaster Gligoric, and later by head of the appeal jury, Herr Kinzel. Their peace mission proved unsuccessful. It was then that someone began spreading the rumour that both players were not feeling very well and concern for the world's best two players was often expressed. As for me, from 1 February right through until the end of the match I kept saying to all the officials that I felt fine and that the match should continue.

With hindsight, Karpov thought the game should have continued too: 'The schedule of a match is law and there shouldn't have been any other outcome apart from continuing the match,' he told *Tass* in the same interview. This is where one can quote clause 6.32 of the world championships rules: '*A match should continue until it is won by one of the players as specified in clause 6.21 or until it is stopped under the conditions of clause 6.22.*' To make it even more clear, let us look at those clauses. 6.21: '*The player who wins six games, not counting drawn games, becomes world champion. The number of games is unlimited.*' 6.22: '*If a player stops participating in the match or if the appeal jury states that he lost, the match is over. The opponent of that player becomes world champion.*'

In this context the FIDE President's reference to the unlimited powers allegedly granted to him by clause 6.11

seems strange, to say the least. It says: *'The FIDE President represents the Federation and has a right to take final decisions on all issues concerning the match in general. In the supervision of the match he consults and cooperates with the referees and organisers.'* As clause 6.32 defines very clearly the possible ways of finishing the match, any deviation from it amounts to breaking the rules. It is absurd for the President to use one clause of the rules to annul another. Unfortunately, reporters didn't really know those details and Mr Campomanes's comment, 'It should be clear', produced no reaction.

It would, however, be naïve to assume that Campomanes himself – who always demanded that the rules be observed – did not realise that his move was actually against the rules. What made the FIDE President resort to this? Let us try to analyse the situation independently and find out the reasons for it, as it is unlikely that we shall ever find out much about the negotiations that were going on between 1 and 15 February. Let me remind you that only one game was played in the meantime.

The document that could throw some light on the matter is the letter from the head of the Soviet Chess Federation, V. I. Sevastyanov, to the President of FIDE dated 13 January. In the letter he expresses, on behalf of the Chess Federation of the USSR, concern about the players' health and suggests a three-month break. The suggestion is made on the grounds that it does not go against the rules. This is quite true – but just because there is no mention of it in the rules at all. 'Can you make a trip to the moon during the match?' Botvinnik said after reading the letter. 'It does not go against the rules either.'

The main argument, however, is the agreement between Karpov and Fischer of 1976 on the unlimited duration of matches, which envisages a break after four months (our four months, incidentally, were over on 10 January). It has to be said that this does not concern the world championship of 1975, but an official commercial match which Campomanes was trying to organise. And I might also add that in all the interviews given at the time, and in his book *In Distant Baguio*, Karpov always denied the existence of any concrete agreement on the above-mentioned match.

It is also important to consider the information given by Campomanes in his answers to some of the questions asked at the press conference. For example, 'I left Karpov literally twenty-five minutes before coming here.' Negotiations behind the scenes, excluding one of the participants, were going on until the very last moment. Even more interesting is the comment, 'If you had been with me in the last hour or so, you would understand everything.' Thus, according to Campomanes, the answer to the puzzle is the position of Karpov. So how did Karpov feel about finishing the match?

Before 15 February he never made it clear. However, at the press conference, after the President announced his decision, he declared that he disagreed and demanded that the match be continued. I also confirmed I was ready to go on playing. This should have surprised Campomanes, who said in the original statement that 'both players agreed'. At this point Karpov himself suggested that a break be announced 'to work out the final decision'. Although logically speaking there was nothing to work out – both players were saying they were willing and ready to continue. However, a meeting of FIDE and Soviet Chess Federation officials boiled down to persuading me to support the President's decision. And all the time Karpov was only saying that he should have a right to a return match if he lost the match in September.

It was at that impromptu discussion that it became absolutely clear to me that my personal readiness to play simply did not matter. The decision had been made. I was in the minority. Campomanes, the Soviet Chess Federation representatives, Karpov himself, all knew that the match was over and that it was only the specific conditions and my 'refusal to cooperate' that made them present it as a discussion.

Announcing the 'final decision', the President was careful

to say how the participants felt: 'Karpov supports the decision, Kasparov will abide by it.' It couldn't have been put any better. One player takes the President's side; the other, with no one to play against, has to reconcile himself to the situation. This could be the end of it, but Karpov's subsequent statements show that, in spite of his support for the President, he had his misgivings about it.

It is interesting to consider in this context Karpov's open letter to Campomanes of 19 February 1985, in which he calls for as early a resumption of the match as possible. His arguments are noteworthy: 'I am sure you were acting in the best interests of chess, but I am convinced that what has transpired is actually to the detriment of chess, to say nothing of my own sporting as well as social reputation, which for many years was considered spotless.' He also refers to the participants' 'readiness to continue the match until a final result is clear, as specified in the rules approved by the FIDE Congress.' (This obscure phrase could have been replaced by a reference to clause 6.32.)

But then we read: 'For me personally, it would be necessary to continue the match in order to prove once again my total commitment to the principles of sports competition.' It seems that the damage to his reputation worries Karpov a lot more than the fact that the rules were obviously broken, though he tries not to show it. It is interesting that, disagreeing with the President as he did, Karpov also explains his stand in terms of the 'interests of chess'. Karpov reminds us that the Soviet Chess Federation did not ask for the match to be stopped altogether, but only to give everyone a break, so that they could rest – in other words, 'It wasn't what we asked, Mr President!'

On the whole, Karpov's letter is a sure try to influence the public opinion that was going against him. He is unlikely to have been seriously considering the possibility of restarting the game. By annulling his 'final decision', Campomanes would have totally discredited himself. But even in this highly improbable case Karpov would have

Defending my world title – I give a press conference in London in July 1986
before the match with Karpov.

My parents.

Right: A game at the Pioneers' Palace, Baku.

Below: Deepest concentration.

My first game against Karpov – a simultaneous when I was twelve.

Another simultaneous – this time against Korchnoi.
It was a draw but I had winning chances.

Three world champions present, past and future: Karpov watches Tal
watching my position in a 1981 game with Karpov.

Below: Tigran Petrosyan (1968).

Right: Mikhail Tal's famous glare (1960).

Victor Korchnoi (1983).

Left: Boris Spassky (1985).

Below: Lev Polugayevsky.

Alexander Belyavsky (1987).

At last the world championship match begins. This picture shows me
concentrating before the first game.

The day of shame, 15 February 1985. I stand at the rostrum, while
Campomanes and Karpov sit next to each other.

World Champion at last – 1985.

won something – several weeks of rest, as opposed to one or two technical time-outs.

The first sentence of the letter is, however, probably the most interesting: 'With reference to our discussions during your last visit to Moscow . . .' That brings to mind Campomanes's remark at the press conference: 'If you had been with me in the last hour or so . . .' So what did – or didn't – the two of them agree on immediately before the press conference of 15 February? We can only guess.

In the interview with *Tass* on 3 March, Karpov looks at Campomanes's actions a bit differently: 'On 15 February, the decision was taken in a hurry and several important considerations were not taken into account.' Well, it is fairly obvious it was a hurried decision. Just compare the President's two statements at the press conference: 'The physical, if not psychological resources of not only the players, but everyone concerned, are exhausted' and 'I thought we should stop and think about the outcome of the competition which could have lasted very long yet' (quoted from *Tass*). Is that logical? The hurry is, however, easily accounted for: forty-eight games seemed to Campomanes to be a very convenient point to stop – twenty-four plus twenty-four, two matches according to old rules. At the press conference he frequently mentioned this so-called argument. And the considerations that were not taken into account were actually the directions that Karpov had given.

To prove this I'll quote what Karpov said at the press conference. This is the way he expressed his disagreement with the President's decision: 'We must continue the match because I don't approve of the proposal to stop it and start again with an even score.' It would be logical to assume that Karpov and Campomanes were negotiating a different option as well, that would have given Karpov all sorts of advantages. For example, he could have been declared the winner; a new match could be started with the score of 5-3, etc. But Campomanes apparently couldn't have met those demands in front of the world press, so he took a decision, the best part of which, according to him, was that it didn't satisfy either player. But remember: Karpov supported it. So how do you explain that? It is easy if we suppose that Karpov wasn't ever going to change his mind. At that point in time stopping the match was more important than losing certain privileges. After all, once you've taken care of the immediate danger of losing the match, if it were to continue you can always get the rest by means of further negotiations behind the scenes. It was half a year until the next match was supposed to start anyway.

With this in mind, one can't help drawing a parallel between the apparent inconsistencies of Karpov's thinking and the subsequent remarks of Campomanes, Gligoric and Kinzel, who were all making so much of their great concern for the players' health. Well, they needn't have worries about my health. Thus we can safely say that the match was ended artificially totally in accordance with Karpov's wishes.

Knowing full well what a dubious position he is in now, Karpov is trying to show that he disagreed with Campomanes. He is, however, very careful in his criticism, avoiding all the dangerous points and emphasising the damage done to his own interests.

My position was always very simple: all arguments should be settled over the chessboard. In his letter to Campomanes, Karpov says something that is certainly true: '. . . he [Kasparov] is displeased because he was *intentionally* [my italics] deprived of the right to compete for the world title.' He couldn't have put it better.

One can't help drawing certain parallels from the history of chess. Exactly ten years ago, amid the controversy over the world championship between Karpov and Fischer, the Soviet Chess Federation demanded, with all its authority, equal rights for both the champion and the challenger. Here is a direct quote from its statement of 13 March 1975: 'The Chess Federation of the USSR has once again to draw the attention of the world sports community to the unhealthy atmosphere building up around the forthcoming world championship . . . One gets the impression that the challenger, who has recently won two gold Oscars, is being put in a humiliating position. Some people would like to see him in a secondary role, meekly going along with the whims of the world champion. The attitude has become more authoritarian. There is absolutely no respect for either the opponent or for sporting traditions . . . *Rules cannot be replaced by playing to lose. FIDE itself should be more independent. Unlawful activities during the world championship have reduced the authority of FIDE, and, whatever the leadership (under M. Euwe) might think, it is now doubtful whether they are suitable for the role.* [My italics again.] The responsibility for all possible consequences lies with those who allow sports competitions to be turned into unprincipled bargaining.' A lot of what was said then is now interesting not only from the point of view of history.

The situation in chess is now very difficult indeed. The President's arbitrary decision, which in practice made chess contests no longer independent of external factors, caused widespread anger. Karpov agrees with that: 'I am sure many fans are dissatisfied with the fact that the contest remained unfinished.' The expectations of the audience were indeed deceived. Therefore I think that before moving on we should assess what has happened. It needs to be done in order to prevent this kind of thing happening again. Public opinion can take decisive action to stop the bargaining traders who have recently been feeling they are above punishment.

I'd like to believe that in the long run the true interests of chess would be considered above the selfish interests of those who want to turn it into a public performance occasionally enhanced by scandals. The sport has managed to overcome serious problems in the past, so let the truth be the winner now too.

It was a vain hope. As in any war, truth was to be the first casualty.

NINE

The Thirteenth!

Everything that happened at the press conference was widely reported by the Western media. Everyone wondered how the Soviet authorities would react to my outspoken remarks about Campomanes. It was inconceivable to them that a Soviet citizen should dare to express public dissent and get away with it. 'For most Soviet public figures,' said the Moscow correspondent of *The Times*, 'such an action would have spelled political and professional disaster.' He thought that 'the challenger has taken the calculated risk that his star status would protect him from official wrath' and concluded that my conduct might just be tolerated on this occasion. 'Despite acute embarrassment and anger on the part of Soviet officials over Garry Kasparov's outburst, chess experts said it was unlikely that he would be persecuted or punished.' I was not so sure.

In the Soviet Union itself few people understood what had really happened, because all the Soviet press reported was the bare facts about the President's decision to stop the match. Chess followers might even have got the impression that this move was made against Karpov's interests, since he was 5-3 ahead. Karpov himself had lent credence to this by writing an open letter to Campomanes demanding that the match be resumed. The absence of reliable information led the sporting officials to expect that the row would be soon forgotten and that this would obviate the need for them to take any decision.

Meanwhile, I was in Baku waiting for the other shoe to drop. But nothing happened. I knew the authorities could not take my public rebellion lying down and would be plotting their revenge. The only thing I didn't know was what form it would take, what it would lead to, or when I could expect to feel the first blow. 'If Kasparov wants to get out of all this in one piece, if he is to survive and flourish, he had better play well,' *The Times* warned.

Observers recalled that in 1974 Korchnoi had been severely punished for far less serious transgressions – expelled from the national team, deprived of his grant and vilified in the press. For a while he was unable to leave the country to take part in foreign competitions. In 1976 something similar had happened to my coach, Nikitin, who had dared to criticise Karpov's actions. A decade before, this had been treated as *lèse-majesté*: how far had Soviet society moved on?

I drew strength from the support I received from my own people in Baku: they knew I had been cheated. And not just in Baku: immediately after the match was stopped, people began writing to me from all over the Soviet Union. But in spite of this moral support, I was far from optimistic. Karpov clearly knew the threat that I posed to his title and the public position that went with it. He knew better than his advisers that my recovery in the match was not merely the consequence of his physical exhaustion, but rather the reverse: his psyche had collapsed because of the improvements in my chess. I therefore had every reason to believe that Karpov would try to avoid a new match altogether. He could do this by provoking me into a situation that would force me to withdraw, perhaps some dispute over the rules, in which he could count on the backing of his friend Campomanes and the Soviet Chess Federation. My realistic conclusion was that, although I could beat Karpov on the chessboard, I could not beat Campomanes. That would require not simply strength, but power. It was frightening.

My only hope was publicity. It was this, at the press conference, that had brought my fight into the open, and onto the front pages of newspapers in virtually every country in the world, except, of course, my own. But opportunities like that only knock once: it was my enemies who had actually handed me the microphone! Ironically, it was someone in Karpov's group of supporters who had first shouted, 'Let Kasparov give his comment', and this had prompted Karpov to say to Campomanes on the platform: 'I think we should invite Kasparov here.' It was then the President himself who had asked: 'Garry, you want to come and say your piece?' They would, of course, have learnt from that mistake, so I could not expect the same courtesies to be extended in future.

Meanwhile, Campomanes had not been idle. He had made a whistle-stop tour of chess federations in the Spanish-speaking world and in the United States, correcting what he termed 'outright distortions of facts' and 'a pattern of disinformation' about the ending of the match in Moscow. He said he had 'managed to disabuse the minds of people who earlier took a critical view because they based their conclusions on reporting that was at variance with the facts'. He even claimed that his own version of events – confounding 'the distorters and maligners' – had invariably been received with wild applause. This had such an effect upon the impressionable President that he seriously intended to immortalise his decision as 'the best he had ever made'. Not everyone, however, was convinced. Keene, for instance, commented after Campomanes had spoken in London: 'He proceeds from the arguable premise that a "decision" was needed at all. In fact, no decision was necessary, since the match was proceeding according to regulations and these should have been allowed to run their course.' Precisely.

Bids were due by the end of April from countries wishing to stage the match in September. There was a strong bid of one million Swiss francs from Marseilles and a lower one from London which reached FIDE's Lucerne headquarters within minutes of the deadline. The executive council of FIDE, meeting in Tunis, offered the players a choice of five different options: France alone; shared between France and USSR;

shared between France and Britain; USSR alone; shared between France, USSR and Britain.

Karpov opted for Moscow. I said I was happy for the match to be played in the Soviet Union, but not Moscow, because that would put Karpov at an immediate advantage. I chose Leningrad and sent my suggestion to the Soviet Chess Federation and FIDE, but neither of them even thought it worthy of serious consideration.

There was no point in asking questions: Karpov wanted to play in Moscow, so Leningrad was out. Karpov said 'Moscow only', so the Soviet Chess Federation said Moscow, so Campomanes also said Moscow – even against the advice of his own executive council.

I think Moscow was also chosen because it would involve them all in fewer problems if it later transpired that the match was not going to take place at all. In that case, there would be no risk of having to make the sort of compensation payments claimed by Pasadena in 1983. And if the match actually did go ahead, they could control it more effectively in Moscow than anywhere else.

I was angry, but not in the least surprised, at this decision. It was just another link in the chain of actions designed to knock me off balance. I registered my disapproval, but not by withdrawing from the match. I had to sit down and play Karpov somewhere! It was possible to win against him even in Moscow, difficult, but it could be done.

By then I was more experienced as regards the true position of the players and the status of the match. To my mind there had been no world champion since the abandoned match in Moscow. The championship was in limbo, as it had been from 1946 to 1948 after the death of Alekhine. The world champion from 1975 to 1984 would be playing the winner of the challenge series in 1982–4 for the right to be called world champion. To say that Karpov was still world champion would mean that he had *retained* his title when in fact, even according to Campomanes, the match had been 'ended without decision'. This was by no means an idle question, and it certainly wasn't a question of pride. It was purely practical. If the new limited-duration match ended in a draw, and Karpov was already regarded as world champion, he would retain his title, as Botvinnik did after draws against the challenges of Bronstein in 1951 and Smyslov in 1954. In other words, Karpov would need only twelve points, whereas I would need twelve and a half. My proposal was that in the event of a draw after twenty-four games, we would play a further six. If we were still level after thirty games, I conceded that Karpov would win the title of world champion, not *retain* it.

There was also the vexed question of a return match. If Karpov was accorded the status of world champion before we started, then he could claim a revenge match if he lost. I was against a return match, since I took the view that seventy-two games should be quite enough to determine who was the better player. Since Campomanes and the Soviet chess authorities had expressed such touching concern for the players' health, I assumed that they would not dare insist on another exhausting competition either. That, however, was an illusion.

For a couple of weeks after 15 February it had been unclear whether Karpov was officially still world champion or not – not that Anatoly Yevgenyevich himself had any doubts: he signed his letter to Campomanes on 19 February 'Anatoly Karpov, World Champion'. The Soviet press referred to us simply as the two grandmasters. But in March the situation changed. First, I gave an interview in which I took care not to give my enemies the slightest pretext for provocations. Then Karpov gave an interview, and everything fell into place: he still regarded himself as champion, and claimed that only he had really wanted to continue our match.

I began to get a strange feeling. Karpov spoke with such conviction that even when you knew the truth, it made you doubt. It was clear to me that Anatoly 'World Champion Karpov' still had some surprises up his sleeve. He was not going to part with his title so easily, and of course he'd be getting a little help from his backers. Karpov had recovered his fitness, and with it his old determination.

The first major problem arose over the awarding of the chess Oscar for 1984. This was an important matter for both of us, because the result would reflect opinion among the chess journalists of the world about our first match. Some people said the prize should go to Karpov, because at the end of the year for which the Oscar was awarded, he had been leading 5-1 against me. Others said no, the match was never concluded, so the points should not count. Besides, Karpov had been the moral loser. As for Campomanes's decision to stop the match, many countries – including Britain, Yugoslavia, West Germany and the USA – had not recognised it. This would be a chance for the journalists to register their protest against Campomanes's behaviour.

The voting had been done after the match was ended, so the journalists were able to form their own view about what might have happened if Campomanes had not intervened. Suppose I had gone on to win 6-5, for example: would the journalists have been expected to ignore that result and think only of Karpov's 5-1 lead at the end of the year? It was obvious that they would have to take account of everything that happened right up to 15 February, even if strictly they were not supposed to do so.

While the world championship match itself was set aside as undecided, our claims to the Oscar were fairly even. Karpov had won two tournaments and I had beaten Smyslov in the challenge final match. I had also won the 1983 Oscar after my match with Korchnoi. I suggested that in these unusual circumstances, the Oscar ceremony should be cancelled, or the two of us withdrawn from consideration, because the question of the world's best player had still to be settled.

Meanwhile, Campomanes was still flitting around the world trying to justify his decision. An Oscar for me would have dealt a serious blow to his prestige, since it would mean that the chess world had accepted my version of events and saw me as a victim of his arbitrary action.

The leadership of the Spanish Chess Federation was strongly pro-Campo, led by one of his chief acolytes, Roman Toran. So both Campomanes and Karpov found themselves invited to Spain on 21 April, just three days before the votes were to be counted.

Two innovations were suddenly introduced to that year's Oscar system. The executive council and the central committee of the FIDE were given votes, and a large group of journalists from the smaller chess federations were allowed to enter at the last moment. When the envelopes were opened, Karpov had won by just thirty votes: 1,390 to my 1,360. First choice on each list got fifteen points, the second twelve, third ten, and so on. There could be no doubt that, but for the changes to the rules, the result would have been different. It was an eloquent fact that the newly enfranchised groups didn't bother to vote at all the following year. Another detail of note is that the award ceremony was shown on Soviet television, which gave Karpov's victory the official seal of approval.

I began to have an uneasy feeling as to whether my match was ever going to take place. Already some sports officials were saying to me bluntly: 'We need a world champion, but one the whole country can be proud of!' I asked them: 'Do you need a world champion – or World Champion Karpov?'

I was determined not to let any crisis occur that would prevent me playing the match. At the same time I had to tell the world everything that was going on, so that my enemies would know that I was not completely powerless and that every false step they took would be recorded for posterity.

I decided to play two matches overseas in preparation for the Karpov encounter, and my opponents and the venues were both carefully chosen with the championship in mind. I would play the West German grandmaster Robert Hübner in Hamburg and the Swedish grandmaster Ulf Andersson in Belgrade. I judged that West Germany and Yugoslavia were ideal places in which to attract publicity, since their own nationals – Kinzel, the German appeals chairman, and Gligoric, the Yugoslav chief arbiter – had become subjects of controversy in their own countries as a result of my attacks over the parts they played in the ending of the Moscow match.

Both Kinzel and Gligoric had assisted Campomanes's attempt to rewrite history by sending personal reports to FIDE, which were then circulated worldwide. In both of them they repeated the lie that the match had been ended 'in accordance with Kasparov's wishes'. The whole world knew the match had ended in a farce. Only a tiny handful of people close to FIDE even tried to defend the President's decision.

You can imagine my feelings, therefore, when Campomanes put both these names forward as officials for the September match, even while they were engaged in a public slanging match with one of the contestants. Gligoric remained unaware that he had simply been a cog in Campomanes's machine, and had even written to me saying: 'After such outbursts on your part, I have ceased to take anything you say seriously.' How could such a person possibly act as a neutral arbiter, and how could Campomanes select him for this role? It was blatant provocation.

Apart from everything else, the correct procedure had not been followed. Wherever possible, an arbiter should be chosen who has the support of both sides. In this case there was one name that appeared on both Karpov's list and my own: Lothar Schmid of West Germany. Campomanes had simply ignored this and chosen Kinzel and Gligoric instead. This was his pointed way of showing gratitude for the support they had given him over his decision on 15 February. The problem over the chief arbiter went on right through the summer, absorbing energy that should have gone into my chess preparation for the match.

The situation was finally defused by Gligoric himself, who withdrew in Belgrade on 25 July in a statement read out by the president of the Yugoslav Chess Federation. Yet on 6 August Lim Kok Ann, the FIDE Secretary-General, announced officially that Gligoric would be chief arbiter. It was only on 19

August, nearly a month after Gligoric's withdrawal, that Campomanes eventually approached Schmid. By this time, as Campomanes knew full well, Schmid could not take on the assignment because of business commitments. The official invitation came too late. Campomanes simply froze him out.

Lists of arbiters then began to appear like mushrooms after rain. The end result was that Campomanes introduced another novel practice in world championship matches: he appointed two chief arbiters – A. Malchev of Bulgaria and V. Mikenas of the Soviet Union – who took it in turns to go onto the stage. What the point of this 'reform' was supposed to be was never made clear. In any case, it was yet another clear breach of the regulations for which the President again claimed emergency powers (in an emergency of his own making). This is just one example of the way simple organisational matters were blown up into formidable problems.

I sent a message to the FIDE congress in Graz to complain about Campomanes: 'He is violating moral principles and written rules daily. I have replied to all letters from the President, but apparently my replies get mysteriously lost. Isn't it strange? His ignoring of all my requests puts me in a handicapped situation. Serving, however – unlike the President – the chess world's best interests, I feel obliged to play even in such conditions. I only hope that the fate of the world championship title will be decided on the chessboard – this time.'

But that letter was written only after the most terrible pre-match ordeal was behind me.

In May, after winning my match against Hübner in Hamburg 4.5-1.5 (three wins and three draws), I gave an interview to *Der Spiegel* in which I decided to tell all, about the whole scandalous role played by Campomanes and Karpov in the ending of the first match, the intrigues that followed and the campaign that had been launched against me on the eve of the second match. The interview was my only chance to let the whole world know what was going on and thereby nip in the bud the attempts to wreck the September match.

I then went on to Belgrade, winning two games and drawing four with Andersson, and making public my dispute with Gligoric in an open letter which was published in full in the Belgrade newspaper *Politika*.

In addition to these two statements in the foreign press, I also made my views known in messages to FIDE, without clearing it beforehand with the USSR Chess Federation. I felt I had no alternative. I was getting no support in the Soviet press. The only help came from Spassky, who was living in France. In an interview with the Dutch magazine *New in Chess*, he said: 'After Karpov had accepted Campo's decision to terminate, which was an incredible thing to do, he found himself in an extremely unpleasant position. He was the only one who had not foreseen that in the ensuing situation he should have taken care of his prestige in the first place. Karpov experienced irreparable bad luck – but it was all his own fault. As far as Campomanes is concerned, by his decision . . . he actually destroyed Karpov.'

I suspected, however, that Karpov was far from being destroyed. My interview in *Der Spiegel* provided him and his friends with just what they had been hoping for. The interview itself, of course, could not have pleased them, but it gave them the chance they had been seeking to have me disqualified. I had failed to rise to the various kinds of provocative bait they had been offering – over the venue, the chief arbiters, the Oscar – but now they must have decided that I had gone too far and had signed my own death warrant. Yet everything I had said was the truth. I would be accused of attacking the Soviet Chess Federation, but what I had attacked was not the Soviet Chess Federation, but the Karpov chess federation.

Karpov must have decided that I was done for, because he gave an interview in July in the Belgrade newspaper *Sport* in which he declared unequivocally that there would be no changes on the Chess Olympus. Usually Karpov is cautious, even evasive, in answering questions, but this time he spoke so categorically that it might appear the new match, as far as he was concerned, was just an empty formality. But then, maybe he knew something that was going to guarantee his championship title would remain impregnable?

It looked as if he really did have grounds for believing that what I said to *Der Spiegel* had scuppered my chances of contesting the world title. In fact, in a way he was right. A special meeting of the USSR Chess Federation had been called for 9 August – three weeks before the beginning of the match – to consider my 'anti-State' behaviour. There was every likelihood that my punishment would be disqualification, and Karpov knew it.

Actually, it was no secret to me either. I turned to my own republic, where the officials agreed without hesitation to help, but it was soon clear that this time I needed even greater political firepower than before. Fortunately, after the April plenum of the Party Central Committee, new leaders had emerged. We turned to Alexander Yakovlev, who had just replaced Stukalin as head of the propaganda department of the Communist Party Central Committee.

When we told Yakovlev what the problem was, he said: 'The match must take place.' Brief and to the point. It was then made utterly clear to the Sports Committee and the Chess Federation that they could not disqualify Kasparov, because he was just as much a citizen of his country as Karpov.

I know – and many officials know – what had been planned for me by Sevastyanov, Baturinsky and Krogius at that meeting. I was to be disqualified and the match cancelled, Karpov was to remain champion, and the decision was to be followed by a campaign of condemnation against me in the Soviet press. All that then was left for the Sports Committee to do would be to simply rubber-stamp the Federation's decision. This was to be the agenda before Yakovlev ruined their carefully planned scenario. Mysteriously, however, no official records can now be found of these proposals. They seem to have vanished into thin air.

I flew to Moscow on the morning of 9 August with Mamedov and Akhundov, the chairman of the Azerbaijani chess federation. We spent quite a few unpleasant minutes. Not until just before the meeting did we hear that it had all been decided differently.

We sat silently while the solemn verdict was delivered. It consisted merely of a recommendation that Soviet grandmasters should not give interviews in the foreign media. That was all.

As my trainer Nikitin said, the whole thing seemed paradoxical to say the least: 'Can you tell me why it was necessary to urgently summon such a high-powered delegation from Azerbaijan to a special session of the presidium of the USSR Chess Federation, something the Federation has never done before, in order to "point out unanimously to the young grandmaster the tactlessness of the things he has been saying" and hand down a decision which none of the grandmasters had any intention of obeying? Incidentally, these "unanimous" strictures came from by no means all of those present. As everyone knows, the invitation for Kasparov to visit West Germany (and, in particular, to give an interview for the first time to *Der Spiegel*) was delivered to the USSR Sports Committee, which sent Kasparov there and assigned a very experienced official to assist him.'

Very revealing also, is a dialogue from the film *The Thirteenth* between me and Roshal:

G.K.: Didn't you get the feeling that the meeting was utterly pointless? That it was incomprehensible why on earth they arranged it?

A.R.: There was certainly some sort of tension in the air. Yes, you felt that what happened next might be something like what happened on 15 February . . . Something similarly dramatic. We discussed it among ourselves – the members of the presidium – we were asking each other: 'Now what? What'll happen?'

G.K.: So you got there, discussed it, found me guilty, as it were. And then what?

A.R.: For me, it was like a harmless firecracker, a blank shot. I thought, 'What have they got us all here together for?' I could see from your expression that you were extremely tense . . .

G.K.: I was just prepared for the worst.

A.R.: Yes, perhaps that's why you were just a tiny bit reverential . . .

G.K.: I simply realised . . .

A.R.: You knew that you'd been perhaps a bit more impulsive than was necessary. Though I personally wouldn't say now that that idea wasn't in the air.

G.K.: Of disqualifying me?

A.R.: You keep using that word. But I don't think . . .

G.K.: All right, it's a strong word. But perhaps there was another, more realistic option, something tried and tested? Let's say the match is played, but before the match there are a number of articles, or a very long piece in *Sovietsky Sport*, in which everything is spelt out and some 'unanimous opinion' is quoted . . . In other words, you think the Chess Federation would probably have taken the decision to have things like that published in *Sovietsky Sport* and other papers?

A.R.: That doesn't require a decision to be taken by the Federation.

G.K.: In other words, things like that could have been published?

A.R.: I wouldn't rule out that . . .

G.K.: And it would have been pretty strong stuff?

A.R.: That would depend on who wrote it.

G.K.: I see. And did they suggest that you write something like that?

A.R.: Well, I, er . . . It's quite possible that, er . . . I was regarded as someone who might write something of the sort. I'm answering with the greatest, er . . . I didn't draft

such an article, but it's not impossible that, er . . . Yes, at
that time I actually . . .
G.K.: . . . could have written it?
A.R.: Yes, I'd have tried to find a way . . .
G.K.: . . . of more or less softening the blow?
A.R.: Not that exactly. A way of being as objective as
possible in that situation. But certainly I would have had to
condemn you!

Up to that moment I was facing moral death, because that is
what disqualification amounts to. When you can't play, you
are dead. But after that April, plenum times had changed in
the Soviet Union and you could no longer get rid of opponents
without allowing them to play a single move.

Finally, on 3 September, after all the political battles, we sat
down at the chessboard on the stage of the Tchaikovsky
Concert Hall. From the organisational point of view, and from
the point of view of pure chess, this match was more up to
standard than the previous one. The course and content of the
battle brought far greater satisfaction to true chess-lovers than
to the FIDE officials.

I was also much better housed than during our last match.
For the whole of that five-month marathon contest I had
stayed at the Hotel Rossiya, right in the centre of Moscow,
whereas Karpov had been given a *dacha* out of town. Although
my mother and friends had done their best to make me feel at
home in the hotel, it wasn't always possible.

This time, thanks to the good offices of Stepan Shalayev,
chairman of the Soviet trade union movement, the trade
unions had provided me with everything I needed in the way
of facilities to prepare for the match, including a magnificent
house in Lenin Prospect. My team soon called it 'the Palace'
and I certainly felt treated like a king. As I joked to them, all I
needed now was a crown to go with it.

I drew white for the first game, which seemed a lucky sign.
Usually in matches at this level the opening games are of an

exploratory nature, as the players size each other up. But this game was different: it could have been regarded as number forty-nine in the series. It had only been a short while since our first match had been brought to an untimely end, and the old impressions had not yet been forgotten. Both of us had, as the legacy from our previous fight, an enormous mass of information which would be digested to determine the line of strategy for the new match. It was only to be expected, therefore, that from the very outset there would be an uncompromising struggle in which each player would try to vindicate his own individual concept.

As if to confirm Karpov's words that 'opening preparation is the strongest aspect of Kasparov's play', I puzzled him in game one by my choice of the Nimzowitsch Defence, something I had almost never done before. It took him an unprecedented fifty minutes to make his first five moves.

Karpov was in difficulties throughout the game and resigned the next day without resumption. I regarded this as my third successive victory, having won the last two games of the previous match. Never before had Karpov lost three games in a row. Nor had he ever lost the opening game in a world championship.

In the preface to his book *The Karpov–Kasparov World Championship Match* (Moscow, 1986), Mark Taimanov wrote: 'It is a well-known fact that the first game always plays a special role. Its outcome and the very nature of the struggle usually determine the mood and creativity of the players, at least in the opening phase. As Karpov has remarked, "He who wins the first game of a world championship match gains a substantial psychological advantage."'

Contrary to this, I was unsettled by the result of game one. I was a little confused. On the one hand, there was the feeling of joy that you have after any victory in an important competition, but on the other I was faced with a new psychological situation; after all, I had spent almost the whole of the previous match hanging on the brink of a precipice, trying to get myself out of trouble. But then Karpov, too, found himself in an unaccustomed role: he was now the one running to catch up. So the second game would have to answer the question of how this would affect our play.

After the opening, I created a maze of complications which, if white played correctly, could have got me into deep trouble. But Karpov failed to find the right path, and by a series of tactical strikes I achieved a won position. Then, under time pressure, I overlooked the continuation that would have clinched it. All the same, from the position we adjourned at I was counting on a win, though my sealed move turned out to be second-rate. Having calculated that however white responded, I would have a clear win, we suddenly discovered, just two hours before the game was to resume, that white in fact had a strong answer. We began frantically searching for other possibilities, but didn't have enough time to find a precise solution.

Returning to the game without any clear idea of how to continue it, I was unable to find my way out of the situation and so lost the initiative. As a result, we drew.

Failures like that are always annoying, and in a world championship match your reactions to everything are doubly acute. Karpov, on the other hand, seemed to have recharged his batteries that evening. Nevertheless, just before game three he called a time-out. The anxiety of the opening games had evidently taken its toll.

This seems to be a good point at which to talk about one phenomenon of world championship matches to which I believe no one has yet drawn attention. All the chess commentators and psychologists keep making great play of the supposedly incontrovertible fact that the challenger has nothing to lose, but everything to gain. They're right; he does have nothing to lose, but he'll still just be the challenger, whereas his opponent is world champion! So however favourable the situation on the board may become, and however deeply you manage to penetrate the secrets of a position, the prestige of the champion and the hypnosis of his title have the most powerful effect on your every decision. This is something I would call the 'champion title' phenomenon.

It might seem that, being one point ahead and having taken the initiative in the first two games, I had good reason to be optimistic about the future, particularly since I had a 'white' week ahead of me (I played white in two of the three games). But the laws of match play are inscrutable. It was to be a black week for me in the fullest sense of the word.

The week began with a quiet draw in game three, but I then suffered two defeats in a row. As the British grandmaster Anthony Miles said, 'Karpov showed a fine ability for finding his opponent's weak points.' His opinion was echoed by Dominic Lawson in the *Financial Times*: 'Karpov is capable of transforming the most minute advantage into a crushing position and he weaves a fine mesh of moves with the relentless care of a spider building a web.'

So in just three days the match situation had changed radically. Karpov had streaked ahead, giving himself into the bargain the highly important psychological boost of a win with black. Given the difficulty of breaking through Karpov's defences, plus the fact that in this match he would have been happy with just a draw, I was faced with a difficult task, something that was already being hinted at in the press. Some people even found it reminiscent of the early part of the previous match. But despite the shock of games four and five, I was far from desperate. Knowing how extensive my pre-match preparation had been, my trainers and I considered my position by no means hopeless. We had no doubt that the strategic line we had chosen was the right one: the shortcomings of my play at the beginning had been all too clearly apparent.

In a nutshell, the task before me was as follows. First, to play as hard as I could to stop Karpov increasing his lead, and second, to weave as many complications as possible in order to regain the initiative and exhaust my opponent. In addition there was the vitally important psychological problem of getting into a calm frame of mind as soon as possible. I can now confidently say that this very considerable task was achieved in the period between games six and ten.

Those five battles ended in draws, all of them tense and absorbing a great deal of nervous energy. The nature of the fight began to change. I used a strong remedy: in all those games I sacrificed a pawn, with black in order not to lose the initiative, and with white in order to gain it. In game nine I sacrificed no less than three pawns, but when the game was resumed I launched such a dangerous attack that Karpov had to part with one of his pieces. The tenth game was an important one in this respect, for I escaped as black with what commentators described as 'a stunning series of sacrifices', which must have left Karpov feeling deeply vexed.

The second half of the match was approaching, and I couldn't help remembering Botvinnik's prediction: 'If, after ten to twelve games, Kasparov stands level or is even losing by one point, he will have a good chance of victory in this match.' A very accurate assessment of the situation at that point in the match was given by the Hungarian grandmaster Andras Adorjan, whom I spoke to on the phone after game ten. After bewailing the opportunities I had missed in games seven, nine and ten, Andras added: 'The main thing is not victory, but the trend of things – and to me it looks good.'

Looking at the next game, number eleven, those words could be called prophetic. I won it in twenty-five moves by a spectacular sacrifice of my Queen, after Karpov had fallen into a simple trap. After the game, some commentators described move 22 – Rcd8 – in highly colourful terms such as 'the blunder of the century', or 'utterly unique in a world championship match', but they were forgetting some other historic blunders in the world championship, including one by Fischer himself in the first game of his match against Spassky.

Of course Karpov's oversight in that game was extraordinary, but it should be remembered that Karpov had been through ten very sustained battles, the last two of which had consumed a vast amount of his nervous energy. Game eleven also shaped up badly for him at first. But after the worst was over, a premature calm seemed to set in, and for that moment of weakness he paid a high price.

In game twelve I startled the experts with a continuation that Averbakh called 'a bolt from the blue'. By sacrificing a pawn I managed to cut through a Gordian knot of problems in a position that one would have thought had been studied inside out. Black in a Sicilian Defence! The journalists weren't far wrong when they said that move d6-d5 was the novelty of the year.

Karpov had no wish to enter the lists unprepared, and opted for exchanges which led to a rapid draw, bringing us all-square at the halfway stage.

On 30 September, *Der Spiegel* published an article entitled 'Tolya's Million', telling the story of Karpov's secret contract with the computer firm Novag, how the middle man – the West German TV journalist Helmut Jungwirt – was charged with misappropriating $446,000 from Karpov, and how Campomanes and Kinzel, at Karpov's request, had been working to recover the cash. Reuters reported that the article had caused Karpov great distress. It quoted Baturinsky, the head of Karpov's delegation, as saying that the strain of it all had 'taken five years off Karpov's life'.

Three years later Karpov gave an interview about Jungwirt's trial to the same magazine under the sensational headline: 'This Affair Cost Me The World Championship Title'! In it he unblushingly declared: 'But for that report [of the trial] in *Der Spiegel*, Kasparov would not have beaten me in 1985 and would not have become world champion. In that sense I don't know who beat me – Kasparov or *Der Spiegel*.' Statements like that are hard to disprove, but even harder to take seriously.

Half the match, then, was behind us. Although it had not been short of dramatic events on the chessboard, there was every indication that the most interesting part was yet to come. Free of the burden of an open-ended match, we both began playing without constraint, striving in each game to seize the initiative as soon as possible. The intensity of the struggle was to increase from game to game, reaching white heat in the fifth hour of the crucial twenty-fourth.

The relatively quiet draw in game fifteen led many people to assume that the match was entering a period of calm. They had seen that after the stormy events of the first five games, only one of the next ten had resulted in a win. It all looked very reminiscent of the series of draws that we had in our first match. But the dominant trend of this phase of the match pointed to the fact that an incredible hidden tension was about to burst into the open at any moment.

It happened in game sixteen, which I still consider now to have been my best creative achievement (see Appendix A). Such games are remembered for a long time, above all by the player himself, who has invested a particle of his soul in a scheme that was realised in a single breath. I had succeeded before in creating beautiful combinations and playing games with an integral strategy, but none of them can compare with this one in the scale of its grand design.

There is another reason why I number this game among my best. The value of every beautifully won game increases in proportion to the strength of your adversary and the level of the competition, and this one was a victory over the world champion in a match for the world crown.

After a burst of creativity such as that, it is not easy to stay on the right emotional wavelength. Moreover, I needed to digest psychologically the change in the match situation. I was once again faced with playing the role of leader, something I had not been allowed to accustom myself to at the beginning of the match. But deep down I was now firmly convinced that I could win the match, and that gave me confidence.

After two comparatively short drawn games I scored a stylish win in the nineteenth, during which something unprecedented happened. In a totally won position I revealed the sealed move by actually playing it on the board, to wild applause from the audience. It was the first time an open sealed move had been made in a world title contest: it is also very rare in grandmaster play.

In his TV chess programme that evening, grandmaster Aleksey Suetin dropped the words 'world champion' and 'challenger' from his vocabulary and replaced them with the neutral 'black' and 'white'. Some people said it was unethical to make an open move, especially if you were in a overwhelming position. Others thought it was a slap in the face to an opponent who could not bring himself to resign in a hopeless situation. Karpov did so only the next morning, in a phone call to one of the chief arbiters.

In his comment on the game, Averbakh said: 'One cannot help being impressed by Kasparov's truly encyclopaedic knowledge of openings. But even more striking is his incessant search in this field, his desire to be at least one step ahead of official theory. Perhaps that is why in the last few games of the match you could see Karpov's tactic of moving away from the standard lines and trying to get off the beaten track . . .'

It was a strategically complete game which gave me creative satisfaction. But what was most important was that winning game nineteen brought me within realistic sight of overall victory, a victory whose significance was difficult even to contemplate. How hard it was to play with the burden of these new feelings suddenly crowding in on me, I was to discover fully in the games that followed.

In game twenty I again made my sealed move on the board. Again the audience went wild, but this time it led to a draw, after a long war of attrition lasting nine hours and eighty-five moves. Even Campomanes's deputy, Raphael Tudela of Venezuela, could not refrain from commenting: 'Kasparov has grown in stature since the last match. There is no question that he is very much in control. His initial weaknesses of too much emotion and youth are gone. On the other hand, Karpov seems to be the victim of some kind of psychological disadvantage. I think the 5-0 score is flashing in his mind continuously.'

After the game, Karpov's situation became catastrophic. As

for me, I was obsessed by the thought that in the remaining four games all I needed was three half-points – three draws. The task did not seem all that difficult. After all, even playing black I was by no means bound to lose: the last time it had happened was six weeks ago!

But the closeness of victory began to cloud my mind. As a result, I missed a win in game twenty-one. A lot of people were surprised that when the game was resumed I agreed to a draw quite quickly, even though I had a tangible advantage. The reason was that after we had resumed the game, I spotted an error in my adjournment analysis. Upset by this, and remembering my two-point lead, I decided not to go on. I had missed a very real chance of winning a twelfth point, and this obvious disappointment affected my frame of mind.

Karpov took his last time-out before game twenty-two, knowing full well that to draw it would be tantamount to losing the match. He succeeded in narrowing the gap in points. In time trouble, I made two impulsive mistakes which cost me the game. I was virtually paralysed in this game by a powerful feeling of responsibility for every decision I had to make. My blunder in the previous game was preying on my mind. This made me over-cautious and led to the time trouble. But to give Karpov his due, he proved that he had nerves of steel at a critical moment in the match.

That defeat dictated my tactics in the next game, the twenty-third, where I needed to guarantee a draw and avoid all risk of losing, which was exactly what I did.

It is good that my mother was taking notes, because I can now go back to those days, my last few days as a challenger. The day before game twenty-four, I said to her: 'Before the first match I thought I was up against a strong chess player. Only a year later have I come to realise that I'm playing against a whole era of chess. And the only way to win is to take everything that is best from the past and make a qualitatively new leap forward, to surpass that era and open up a new one.'

On the morning of 9 November my mother woke me up saying: 'Three years ago today you played one of your best games at the Lucerne Olympiad, remember? You won playing black against Korchnoi and it brought you your first Oscar. It's a good sign.'

So everything was to be decided in the last game (see Appendix A). Its result would decide the fate of the whole seventy-two game marathon that was unrivalled in the history of chess. Such battles, which are of incomparable value to the chess player, have their own laws. When a single move can decide the question, 'to be, or not to be', it is difficult to maintain absolute clarity of mind. It's impossible to dismiss the thought that one incorrect move may prove fatal, because nothing can be corrected afterwards: it's the last game of the match!

In such extreme situations, when the opponents are playing at the limit of their nervous strength, much – if not all – is decided by how psychologically prepared you are, by your mental attitude. Victory goes to the player who proves to be cooler, more calculating and more self-confident.

Of course, Karpov's task in game fourteen was more difficult. Only victory would do. Yet experience of chess competitions shows that playing desperately for victory in the last game is nearly always unsuccessful. But in situations of this kind, the theory of probability can't guarantee you anything; you always risk being the exception that proves the rule.

Deciding my strategy for the decisive battle was a serious problem. Playing with the sole aim of a draw is decidedly fraught with danger, and in any case it goes completely against my view of chess. I therefore threw aside all hesitation and decided not to avoid the continuations that principle demanded: I would go for open combat. I had no doubt that my opponent would come forward.

Karpov remained true to his favourite line against the Sicilian Defence, even though it had so far brought him no joy in the match. In this he may have been influenced by the Sokolov–Ribli game in the candidates tournament in Montpelier while our match was actually taking place. Karpov decided that Sokolov's plan of vigorous attack was in keeping with the spirit of this last, decisive game. We were ready for this, since we too had been studying Sokolov's game and thought it might appeal to Karpov in this situation.

However, when it came to the point, Karpov couldn't bring himself to risk a really aggressive move. He tried to win by not forcing matters. Even at crucial moments he cannot step out of character. He must always play à la Karpov, strengthening his position rather than going for broke. He was evidently unsure, deep down in his own mind, of the correctness of his kingside attack, and therefore couldn't carry it off with courage and conviction. When I replied with rook to e7, a move which looked at first sight to have only a modest aim, he hesitated for a long time. I think he already sensed something. This was, in fact, the most original and the most difficult move of the game, after which the white attack began to peter out.

Not long before that, in the corridor leading to the rest rooms, I had noticed a poster with the inscription: 'Anatoly Yevgenyevich – Congratulations on Your Victory!' This little pre-arranged device, however, had exactly the opposite effect that it was designed to achieve.

I paced around the stage, while Karpov mostly sat calmly at the table. At move thirty-one he spurned the chance of forcing a draw; he needed nothing less than a win. But five moves later he blundered and at move forty-two he froze rigid.

After an agonising wait of several minutes, Karpov at last stretched out his hand to congratulate me on my victory and winning the world title. The thunderous roar from the crowd in that same second finally convinced me that it was true. I had finally made it! I raised both my arms high over my head in triumph.

When I came out onto the street, there was a crowd in the square. More shouts rang out. A reporter asked how I felt. 'Great!' I yelled, as I kept on walking. And it was true. But could there ever be any words to express the feverish excitement I felt at that moment? Not till we were in the car did my trainers and I finally hug each other.

When we got back to our 'palace' I went through room after room for fifteen minutes, just screaming and yelling out of pure animal joy. Victory! I don't expect I shall ever experience such a whirlwind of feeling again. It is enough to have felt it just once in your life. People ask if it was like falling in love. I have to say it was even better than that; you've proved that you're the best in the world, you've finally achieved the target you set yourself many years before, you've overcome every obstacle on the way there, and you know that no one and nothing, no matter what happens in the rest of your life, can take this achievement away, that you have become a part of history. The euphoria continued throughout the night as an endless stream of congratulations and telephone calls poured in.

The closing ceremony of the match took place on 10 November. The gloomy faces of Campomanes, Sevastyanov and Krogius engraved themselves in my memory. What gave the situation its spice was that I was being crowned with the laurel wreath by the very people who had done everything they could to ensure that it would never happen. But even now a lot still depended on them, in particular whether there was going to be a return match.

When I returned to Baku, I gave a little party just for my close relatives and friends. We raised our glasses for one single toast: 'To Kim Moiseyevich Weinstein. How sad he's not with us!'

That match is now part of history. Viewed as sport, and from the creative point of view, it was clearly more interesting than the previous one. Exciting action which kept everyone on tenterhooks till the final minute of the final game, the white heat of battle which scarcely waned, the absence of the lacklustre draws that had marred our open-ended match, the richer armoury of weapons employed by the opponents, the greater range of ideas and the active search for new paths – all these things made the limited match a superior one. The supreme title was being contested by people of different chess ideologies.

Karpov takes a purely sporting approach to chess: for him, chess is a game. His strength lies in a deep knowledge and understanding of his favourite set-ups and in making maximum use of minimum resources in a position. I am a firm adherent of the creative and investigative school of thought based on belief in the unlimited possibilities of chess. For me, chess is, above all, Art. And I think that it is here, in the collision between two diametrically opposed concepts of chess, that the deeper causes of Karpov's defeat lie. Our new match began with a score of 0-0, but it did not begin from scratch. From the forty-eight games we played in the first match, we had both stockpiled invaluable material with which to prepare for our next battle.

Karpov has said everywhere that I learnt a lot from those games, and that is indeed so. But for some reason he failed to appreciate how many useful lessons he could have learnt from them himself, had he made a deep, comprehensive and objective analysis. By the end of the previous match I had already managed to adapt to Karpov's characteristic style of play and had learnt to cover my own vulnerable areas, in other words to fight my opponent on his own territory without suffering any great losses. Nor was that six-month interval wasted. During that time, my trainers and I were able to design a new model of match strategy based first and foremost on the peculiarities of style and taste of my opponent. Many experts put my success in the first game down to the element of surprise. But even later, throughout the entire match, Karpov experienced serious difficulties with that opening. He obviously didn't like the strategic pattern itself, and that is just what we had included in our reckoning.

At the same time, Karpov had not prepared any fundamentally new theoretical ideas for the match, but had confined himself to simply strengthening here and there the variations already encountered in our first match. This was evidently the result of Karpov's dislike of serious analytical work. It brings back to mind his argument with Botvinnik, who always underlined the extreme importance of the investigative approach to chess. Karpov said that Botvinnik's views were hopelessly out of date. It was Karpov's opinion that today the only way a chess player can improve his skill is by constant practice.

Here my comment would be that it was easy for Karpov to take that line. He himself had a large number of highly qualified assistants who kept him regularly supplied with fresh ideas. But I think our combat can be regarded as having settled that theoretical dispute.

Karpov's total composure and superb technique in difficult positions enabled him for a long time to gloss over the deficiencies of his preparation. Nevertheless, in the second half of the match, our strategically sound planning began to bear fruit. When it became obvious that I had the playing edge over him, Karpov contrived, by mobilising his outstanding qualities as a fighter, to avoid serious defeat and even almost save the match.

I hope that the lessons of my matches with Karpov – those relating to chess and, more particularly, the other lessons – will be taken into account when new rules and regulations are drawn up. The main thing is to remember that chess needs laws which do not drag it down to the level of an endless and impersonal sports show, but, on the contrary, protect its status as a noble and elevated art whose purpose is to give people pleasure and enjoyment.

TEN

Back to Earth

World champion! At first, the significance of that title had a paralysing effect and kept me in a state of euphoria. The waves of joy sweeping over me made a level-headed assessment of the situation impossible. A week after the end of the match I gave a talk at the Sovremennik Theatre. I spoke for several hours. It was late, but the people didn't leave until way into the night. My knowledgeable and sensitive audience were enthralled with my simple tale of adventures, misadventures, and the traditional happy ending. It was as though my victory over Karpov had buried all the grief and conflicts of the past and wiped the slate of history clean. I should have known that the past cannot be tamed so easily.

As world champion, I deliberately adopted a conciliatory attitude towards the Chess Federation. I really hoped that we chess players would be able to put our house in order, and was especially concerned that this prospect should not be ruined by any incautious public remarks on my part. 'There is a big difference between the challenger Garry Kasparov and the champion Garry Kasparov,' I told a post-match press conference in Moscow. The Western journalists were quick to notice this change. Possibly they'd been expecting some sensational revelations with which to titillate their readers. If so, they were disappointed. 'Chess Hero Kasparov Buries the Hatchet', said one headline. 'No More Rows, says Kasparov', was another. 'Kasparov refused pointedly to be drawn into fresh attacks against those he had once accused of trying to rob him of victory', said The Times.

And it was true. Now that I'd won the world title, I was determined not to abuse my position in the ways I had accused

Karpov of doing for so many years. My objection had not just been to the fact that too much of his power had been directed against me personally, but to the idea that anyone should set himself up as a chess dictator. I wanted to see democracy in chess, which meant that the champion himself should not throw his weight around.

The changing world political climate presented me with fresh opportunities. Our country had entered a new era in its relations with the West, and it needed people capable of helping to break down the alienation that had existed for so long.

I take that role very seriously, so when I was invited at that time to appear in the popular TV programme *Good Morning America!* I accepted immediately. It was a chance for Americans to see a Soviet personality whose image was totally different from the usual stereotypes. 'Chess is good for connections between peoples and countries,' I said. 'And as a chess player and sportsman I am waiting for the new detente. Detente is the best situation for connections between sport and culture – and I am sure that you're waiting for this too.'

It was obvious to me from an early age that all people are different. And any State system that wants to create a healthy and happy society must reckon with these differences. If people are to get on with each other and work together, they must accept certain differences between them and try to turn them to the advantage of their common purpose. I have always been sure that an intolerant attitude to the opposite point of view inevitably leads to the suppression of civil liberties and the stagnation of society.

Not surprisingly, my honeymoon period with the chess authorities did not last very long. The time-bomb which had been ticking away was the vexed question of a return match.

Return match. The very words sounded strange; twenty-five years had passed since the last such match was held. What, anyway, was the point of giving the world champion the right to a return match? They say it's to ensure that no one is champion by accident. But could the champion of a marathon seventy-two-game contest be accidental?! In this case, a return match went against common sense, elementary logic and, indeed, the laws of chess. Ah, but no: according to the letter of the law, it was quite correct – if you don't count the fact that the laws were changed in the course of the world championship play-off, and that those laws were written and interpreted by those same FIDE officials who had legalised tyranny in the world of chess.

The congress in Graz which ended three days before the start of the match had approved Campomanes's decision to stop the first match and endorsed new rules – or rather, additions to the rules – for the world championship. The idea of the unlimited match, which had been roundly condemned back in 1927 after the Alekhine–Capablanca match and had come back into prominence in 1975 at Fisher's insistence (subsequently supported by Karpov), once again gave way to the traditional twenty-four-game competition.

But for 'some reason' the abolition of the limited match did not mean that the idea of a return match was also abolished. The baby fathered by the old, unlimited contest was successfully abandoned on the doorstep of the new, limited one. Karpov was granted the exclusive right of a return match, exclusive because it did not extend to future champions. This meant that, while retaining the champion's advantage of an unlimited match, Karpov acquired another one, which is the traditional feature of limited matches: in the event of a draw, he remained champion. But even this wasn't enough. As a double indemnity, Karpov reserved another privilege for himself: that he would not be required to begin his fight for the world title from the start of the challenge series – as Smyslov, Tal, Petrosyan and Spassky had done – but would go straight into the super-final. This triple defensive rampart erected around Karpov was far beyond compare with the notorious rampart of dollars that certain champions used to shelter behind in the old days before FIDE.

All these privileges were enshrined in law at the Graz

congress as 'special rules for the 1985 World Championship Match'. The 'special prize' of these rules was stated with cynical frankness: *'Point 6. The match organisers will pay to FIDE a sum equivalent to 24 per cent of the prize money, i.e. a sum corresponding to 24 drawn games.'*

Thus the Soviet Union, as organiser of the 1985 match, paid FIDE twenty-four per cent of the prize money instead of the sixteen per cent that corresponded to the actual number of draws in the match and that was laid down by the basic rules. The difference was 128,000 Swiss francs. Such was the fee that FIDE got from the USSR Sports Committee for its new-fangled special rules.

It was not before long that the grounds for justifying a return match were found. As if nothing had happened, Karpov suddenly awarded himself victory in the first match: 'I won then, with a score of 5-3, and Kasparov has won now. So the score is equal: 8-8!' This line of reasoning – if that is the right word – became quite popular. But it didn't stand up to criticism either. Karpov had won four of the first nine matches out of seventy-two. So by the end of our battle the question of who was the stronger had been settled pretty conclusively!

Karpov said in one of his interviews that I was a meteoric chess genius like Tal. Why pick on Tal, I thought – because he was champion for only one year? Subtly the idea was planted in ways like this that the king had only been temporarily dethroned. In his statements, he kept harking back to the decisive twenty-fourth game of our match. He just couldn't get used to the idea that he'd lost it. He claimed that at one point he had missed an easy win, and that it was more logical for him to gain victory in this game (for 'game', read 'match'!). The implication was that I was just lucky to be the world champion: 'logically', he was still the champion.

For more than a year I had been waiting for Karpov to come up with an analysis of that important game. During that time, many experts, including myself, had studied it down to the last detail. But we all wanted to know what Karpov himself made of it.

That was the reason for my open letter to Karpov, which was published in *64-Chess Review* in February 1987. Here are a few extracts from it:

> *I write to you not as editor-in-chief of 64, but as my old rival with whom I have played many exciting games at the chessboard. Unfortunately, games in world championship matches often go down in history with superficial, spur-of-the-moment annotations written in the heat of battle. This makes it all the more important to have an intelligent annotation that has been produced after a lapse of time, when passions have cooled. Only a detailed analysis based on an impartial approach to the solution of chess problems can provide a complete picture of the contest. It is here that what the players themselves have to say is crucial.*
>
> *I find it regrettable that the statements you made after the match give a distorted picture of events. References to chance or bad luck can scarcely be regarded as a serious argument . . .*
>
> *. . . I should like to draw your attention to the fundamental differences in our chess evaluations. Above all, these relate to the 24th and last game of the 1985 match. You have stated on numerous occasions that you could easily have won that game and thereby changed the course of chess history. For my part, I take the opposite point of view, and have backed it up with proof showing the different variations. Yet you have not once taken the time to give a concrete answer to my objections. I am certain that a contest of ideas between us in print would greatly enhance the popularity of chess in our country and throughout the world . . .*
>
> *I therefore propose that we should engage in an open chess discussion . . . It is my belief that only time and a continuous analytical quest can determine the true value of the games we played and give a true picture of our battle.*

In his reply, Karpov said he was extremely busy before the super-final with Sokolov, and in effect rejected my offer of an open debate in the press. Here is an extract from his letter:

> *You say that my 'statements after the match give a distorted picture of events', and you draw attention to the evaluation of the*

*twenty-fourth game in our 1985 match. I believe this is where the
logical discrepancy lies. You yourself speak of a 'picture of events'.
But the events were such that white missed, in practice (and not
analytically) extremely substantial chances of winning.*

*. . . You must surely agree that the course of play in that
twenty-fourth game of the 1985 match suggests that a victory for
white looked more logical than a win by black.*

So the analytical discussion never took place, and instead
Karpov once again declared categorically that the outcome of
game twenty-four, and therefore the outcome of the whole
match, was wrong. But as we know, history – even chess
history – does not recognise the subjunctive mood.

But let us go back to the return match. On 5 December 1985,
less than a month after losing his title, Karpov demanded his
droit de seigneur, which under the new rules had to be exercised
between 10 February and 21 April 1986. So FIDE was giving
Karpov the right to a return match within the unprecedented
period of just three months. It was the third arbitrary change
to the rules in recent years, all of them to Karpov's advantage.
In all, he was allowed to play ninety-six games to defend his
title, whereas I, now the champion, was given no privileges at
all. Furthermore, if I were to lose, I would face the humiliation
of being the champion with the briefest reign in history.

This was too much. Another storm was clearly building up
and I should have seen it coming long before. But in my
euphoria over the happy ending to the tragi-comedy in August
and my subsequent victory over Karpov, I had failed to see
that defeating Karpov at the chessboard was a necessary but
not a sufficient condition for getting to the roots of the
problem. I had under-rated the difficulty of curing the ills of
the game. Above all, I had under-rated Campomanes. In a
way he had even benefited from my victory, because he could
now claim that the excellence of play in the second match
vindicated his decision to stop the first. Furthermore, by
keeping me constantly engaged in playing chess, he stopped

me playing politics against him. Even after going through hell and high water, the Filipino still landed on his feet.

I cared every bit as much as Karpov about being an active world champion, and had no intention whatever of resting on my laurels, but all the nudging by FIDE for a return match was driving me mad. After all, I hadn't signed up to play solely with Karpov for the rest of my life. The endless encounters between Karpov and myself meant that the schedule for international tournaments was being thrown out in the rest of the world, and many other players were suffering from this. But FIDE seemed to have forgotten that its primary concern was supposed to be the welfare of chess and chess players. It seemed to me that FIDE was obsessed not only with helping Karpov to get his title back, but also with finance, since world championship matches were a chief source of their revenue.

At the same time, my battles with Karpov had stimulated a new interest in chess around the world. I felt I didn't have the right to deceive the hopes of so many chess lovers.

In December I travelled to Hilversum in Holland to play a six-game match with Jan Timman, then ranked as world number three. This was a very unusual thing for a new world champion to do within a month of gaining his crown. It was one thing to play in a tournament, but quite another to put your reputation on the line in this way against a single grandmaster. The world champion could not afford to be beaten in such a contest, whereas the other player had every incentive to win and nothing much to lose.

It was the first time since the days of Lasker that a world chess champion had willingly agreed to contest a challenge with a leading rival without first making that player go through complex financial or qualifying hoops. The prize money, donated by a Catholic radio and television station, was relatively modest for a match at this level. But money wasn't the point of my excursion to Holland. The point was to give the chess public in the West a chance to see the new world champion playing some good chess, which Jan Timman and I duly did. Some of the combinative play was of a high and exciting standard. When I won a spectacular victory in the final game to take the match by four points to two, the stage was stormed by hundreds of fans who wanted to eavesdrop on our post-game analysis.

After the match, I gave a press conference in Amsterdam in which I spoke out openly against the rematch with Karpov. 'This match should not take place,' I said, 'because no one should have so many privileges. The world champion keeps his title in a drawn match, and that should be enough. In future, I will not have a rematch should I lose. According to the decision adopted by the FIDE congress, I must be world champion for one year, for 1986. I was told about the rematch to be given to Karpov only a few days before the opening of the second match in Moscow. I had no time to protest against it.'

I also chose this moment to endorse a rival to Campomanes in the shape of Lincoln Lucena of Brazil, who had agreed to compete for the FIDE Presidency in 1986 together with Raymond Keene. 'In the past few years,' I said, 'there have been a lot of problems in our chess world. During my stay here I have met with people who are prepared to work for more democracy in the world of chess. They want chess players to know what is going on. They want correct rules and they want the wishes of the players to be respected. These are also my feelings. And as world champion I think it my duty to support the people working for these things.' Unfortunately, that press conference was a mistake which was to cost me dearly later on. It was going to need more than goodwill and good intentions to beat Campomanes.

When I got home I received a message of support from the newly formed European Chess Union, which had written the following letter to the Soviet Chess Federation suggesting that the rematch should be cancelled:

The Council of the European Chess Union held a meeting in
Hilversum, Holland, on 22 December 1985 to discuss, among

other things, the question of the planned rematch between Karpov and Kasparov.

We wish to make the following points against the idea of a return match:

1. *It could have a ruinous effect on the players' health (as Campomanes noted when he stopped the 1984 match).*
2. *Such a large number of games between the same two players will lower the importance of chess in the eyes of the public.*
3. *Neither of the players can bring any benefit to chess by participating in other competitions, because they are spending all their time playing against each other.*
4. *No world champion has ever held the title for less than a year before being required to defend it, whereas in this instance the period is just three months.*
5. *The idea of a return match was not put to the Council of Grandmasters for discussion.*
6. *The FIDE congress in Graz only examined the terms of the return match, and did not approve them by a majority of two-thirds of the votes (as required by the FIDE statutes, clause 4.14).*
7. *Kasparov was only notified of the return match two days before the start of the 1985 match. He thus had no opportunity to comment on, or protest against, the decision. Moreover, the FIDE executive council did not inform the congress in Graz of Kasparov's previous protests against a return match.*

In view of the above, the Council of the European Chess Union is of the opinion that the return match should not take place, and respectfully asks the USSR Chess Federation to do everything in its power to cancel it.

R. LITTORIN, *President*

This request was supported by Timman, Larsen and others. Their help could not have come at a better time. 'I am very happy to hear,' I said in my reply, 'that the European Chess Union has been formed to look after the interests of the strongest chess-playing nations. The New Year is normally a time of peace, but sometimes you have to fight to gain that peace. I hope that in the next year we will return to genuine peace in chess and that chess players can then concentrate on creating beautiful games under normal conditions.'

The truth is that this statement of support had been extracted with some difficulty from the European grandmasters. First, they were apprehensive of the despotic power of FIDE. One of them said to me: 'If that's the way they treat the world champion, what will they do to me?' Second, many people at the time saw my fight against the system of dictatorialness and tyranny as a fight for my own interests, and considered the problem of the rematch to be an internal affair between me and Karpov. So despite the support I had from a number of players – Ljubojevic, Seirawan, Najdorf and Short, who said, 'the whole championship cycle stinks' – the grandmasters did not unite firmly enough against it.

In a letter dated 4 January 1986, I called on the Soviet Chess Federation to state its position regarding the return match. In it I said:

The tense situation that has arisen over the return match is the result of the arbitrary interpretation and frequent alteration of the match rules by the President of FIDE. Campomanes's high-handed actions are the subject of strong and well-justified criticism in the world of chess. The European Chess Union, for example, has sent a message to the USSR Chess Federation calling on it to use all its influence to cancel the forthcoming return match. I still do not know our Federation's answer to that message.

I therefore consider that we still have the unprecedented situation whereby the rules are being interpreted in two different ways: one way for Karpov, and another way for everyone else. The only rules that can be considered binding are the standing rules which give no one any special privileges. No one person has the sole right to lay down the rules – neither the President of FIDE, nor the world champion. There is now an obvious need to put matters in order and create proper rules which are fair and permanently in force, and which will be adopted by FIDE as soon as possible.

*In view of the above, I consider Karpov's personal entitlement to
a return match illegal, and I refuse to take part in such a contest.
The right to a limited return match must be accorded to all world
champions, or to none.*

The position of the USSR Chess Federation, however, had
already been decided long before.

In the end I had to agree to play. It was, of course, a concession
on my part, but the threat to strip me of the world title by
administrative measures was by no means an empty one. By
then I was well aware that it's easier to prove yourself right at
the chessboard than in sophistic arguments with chess
officials. Just a short while before, they had been saying that
the open-ended match was stopped because of their concern
over the health of the world's two top chess players. Now
they were pushing just as vigorously for a return match to
begin as soon as possible.

The FIDE headquarters in Lucerne began issuing menacing
statements that I would be stripped of my title if I refused to
play on the stipulated date. Campomanes said that the rules
required me to give a formal undertaking by 7 January, or else
I would be disqualified. As the deadline approached, tension
in the chess world mounted. But when the day came, nothing
happened. In a terse message from Lucerne, Campomanes
was forced to admit that his ultimatum had been based on a
misreading of the rules. The contestants had two weeks from
the announcement of a final venue to make a commitment to
play, and the venue had not yet been decided.

Meanwhile, bids had been in for several weeks from Leningrad and London. Leningrad had bid one million Swiss francs,
while London had offered 800,000 more. Leningrad's million
was partly symbolic anyway: it was of value only to FIDE,
which received its share of the prize money in hard currency.
The players would have to be content with a fixed sum in
roubles.

The British were very keen to host the championship

because it coincided with the centenary of the first world championship match. They had failed in a bid for the 1985 match after Marseilles had bid more money – 1,600,000 Swiss francs (in the end, of course, the match went to Moscow, which had offered the same amount).

Ray Keene was especially concerned at the turn of events over the rematch, because it might mean that London would again be deprived of the chance to host the world championship, in which he and his colleagues had invested a great deal of time and energy. The days leading up to 13 January, the day when Campomanes was due to announce the venue, were very tense for all of us. It turned out that Campomanes had flown to Vienna, where Karpov was playing. It was a strange (though not untypical) move for the FIDE President to make, I thought – consulting the challenger before the champion. After a series of fruitless exchanges, Campomanes announced that no decision had been taken.

The situation had become intolerable, and on 18 January I announced publicly that I refused to play the match. Apart from the issues of principle involved, all these behind-the-scenes negotiations had made it impossible to prepare for any serious chess. Of course, I knew Karpov wouldn't be ready for February either, so why was he pressing for an early rematch? Because he knew that in February I would be without the support of two of my trainers, Dorfman and Timoschenko, who would not be able to go abroad at that time: a month before the rematch was due to start, they had both become 'non-travellers'. What's more, the Army Sports Committee hadn't even given Timoschenko and Vladimirov permission to join me for a training session. In fact from 1983 onwards, whenever they wanted to attend training sessions, they had to get permission from the highest authorities, right up to the USSR Ministry of Defence!

Meanwhile, of course, my announcement delighted Karpov's patrons. Once again, as in the summer of 1985, they had the chance they were looking for to disqualify me. At an urgent session of the Soviet Chess Federation on 21 January,

Sevastyanov said as much: either I agreed to play in February, or March at the latest, or Karpov would be declared the winner. I kept insisting: why did it have to be played so soon? Why should I play two world championship matches in one year, something which had never happened before in the history of chess? The reason they gave was that the FIDE schedule of regional and international tournaments would be disrupted. It was the old ping-pong principle at work again. The Soviet Federation says we must do something because FIDE requires it, then FIDE hits the ball back, saying the Soviet Federation requested this, and we have to respect its wishes because it is the strongest federation in the world, and so on, ad infinitum.

They were carrying on as if nothing in the Soviet Union had changed. But this was 1986, not 1985 or 1983. The time of cynical reprisals was receding into the past. And besides, I was not the only one affected by the situation. Because my battles with Karpov had dragged on for so long, two world championship cycles were overlapping. Other contestants had to be considered – Sokolov, Vaganyan, Timman, Yusupov. I therefore suggested that instead of a rematch with Karpov, he and I should play in a three-way match with the winner among the qualifiers, thereby finishing the two cycles at once and restoring the traditional system of world championship play-offs. Karpov, however, flatly rejected this idea.

On 19 January, with the situation at boiling-point, the following telex from the British Chess Federation was received in Moscow:

It is our view that the reinstatement of a return match would be inadvisable in a two-year world championship cycle. Such a re-introduction would lead to congestion of international tournament schedules. We stress, however, that it is ideally a matter which the players concerned should decide themselves. We take this opportunity to repeat our offer that if the return world championship matches of the current cycle go ahead, then London, the British Chess Federation and the Greater London Council are very willing to stage the first twelve here with the second twelve in Leningrad. It is in our view essential, though, that any problems concerning the staging of the return match should be amicably settled to the mutual satisfaction of both world champion Kasparov and challenger Karpov. It is of extreme importance that no public problems damage the international chess movement and its reputation worldwide. In particular, we would wish to avoid the unseemly default situations which occurred in 1975 and 1983.

This message was intended to clear the air, to offer an alternative solution, and to involve the players themselves in the discussion. I had always maintained that I was ready to negotiate and listen to other points of view, but in this case I felt that a return match was unjust. At the same time, it was now part of the championship rules and therefore a fact I had to learn to live with. I knew I would have to defend my title some time, but it was vital now to have as long a respite as possible.

The search for a compromise was helped by a political factor. The 27th congress of the Soviet Communist Party was due to open in February, so the last thing the sporting authorities wanted was a public scandal, and disqualifying me was certain to cause a scandal that would attract worldwide publicity. In the circumstances Karpov couldn't afford to be seen as the one who rocked the boat. It ceased to be a matter of whether the match would take place, but when.

Karpov and I had an official meeting under the auspices of the USSR Chess Federation on 22 January and hammered out an agreement which presented Campomanes with a *fait accompli*. The key clause, as far as I was concerned, was that there could be no earlier date for the rematch than July.

This is the text of the agreement:

World champion Garry Kasparov and ex-world champion Anatoly Karpov, having examined the complicated situation that was created during the world championship competition and wanting to eliminate differences of opinion and avoid a situation where, in the absence of an agreement, they would have to accept any extraordinary measures decided by FIDE, have agreed the following:

1. The return match between them as foreseen by 1985 FIDE rules will take place.
2. It is to begin in July or August 1986. This postponement from the date set up earlier is necessary for both chess players, in order to rest and restore their strength after having played 72 games against each other in 14 months.
3. Hoping that the wish will meet with the understanding of the leadership of FIDE and the whole chess world, they think a super-final (the match between the winner of the Candidates and the ex-World Champion) will take place in February 1987 and the next world championship match in July or August 1987.
4. Kasparov and Karpov have undertaken the following obligations towards each other: a) neither of them will play a match with the winner of the candidates cycle until the return match between them is over; b) the winner of the return match guarantees the loser that he will not play a world championship match with the winner of the candidates cycle until that player has played a match against the ex-World Champion; c) under all circumstances our position as stated in a) and b) will stay permanent.
5. After examining the bids for the organisation of the return match from the cities of Leningrad and London received by the President of FIDE dated 16 December 1985, Kasparov and Karpov expressed their wish to play the match in Leningrad. If, however, the organisers of either of them withdraw their bids in connection with the changed dates of the match the participants are ready to consider other bids which are made in accordance with FIDE regulations by 1 April 1986 so that the venue, dates of return match and the team of arbiters can be announced a month later.

The document placed on record the shaky balance of power that now existed: I had been unable to prevent the return match that was being foisted on me, but Karpov's absolute rule was coming to an end.

The agreement was signed by Karpov, Sevastyanov and myself and had the unanimous backing of the Soviet Chess Federation. Karpov and I then went to the FIDE headquarters in Lucerne to secure their acceptance of this agreement and to settle on the venue.

At the time, I truly believed in the importance of our mission, thinking that having formed a united front with Karpov I could deal a strong blow against Campomanes. Campomanes did indeed look very gloomy, and he kept complaining of the intolerable high-handedness of the Soviet Chess Federation, which he had to submit to if he was to avoid a split in the chess world. The other leading lights of FIDE starred in their usual role as extras and, to a man, agreed with the President, joining him in loudly expressing displeasure at the Soviet ultimatum. I was enormously proud of my diplomatic victory and felt that a serious crack had appeared in my enemies' alliance. Gavrilin, vice-chairman of the Soviet Sports Committee, who flew into Lucerne on our heels, gave cautious support to Campomanes's attempt to save face by suggesting that the match begin in May; but I, inspired by my success, turned this down flat.

Only later did I realise I'd been rather cleverly bamboozled. The clash between FIDE and the Soviet Chess Federation was more apparent than real, and had arisen because the change in the political situation in the Soviet Union had wrecked the plan of action against me that they had cooked up together. All the details of the forthcoming rematch had in fact been decided at a secret meeting in Zurich airport between Campomanes, Gavrilin and Anderton, an official of the British Chess Federation.

In the end the match was shared between London and Leningrad. Originally, the intention had been to hold the entire match in the Soviet Union, but just in the nick of time FIDE thought up a new rule, according to which no chess federation – in this case the Soviet one – could be the organiser of two world championship matches in succession.

The days I spent in Lucerne were memorable also for the remarkably smooth relations I had with Karpov. An outsider might well have taken us for bosom buddies. We spent all our spare time playing cards with my friend Frederic Friedel, a journalist and computer expert. Even Campomanes, who had seen a few odd things in his time, was flabbergasted by the idyllic picture of us locked in battle over the card table in my hotel room. But the illusions soon vanished when they came up against reality.

On my return home, I heard about the witch-hunt that had started against Dorfman in Lvov and Timoschenko in Novosibirsk. I spent a lot of nervous energy on the business of trying to sort out the problem of my trainers, which involved having to travel to Novosibirsk to negotiate with the military authorities.

In May I was off to Europe again, this time on an extensive tour. I first flew to Basel, where I had a practice match with the British grandmaster Anthony Miles. It was after this match, which I won by five and a half points to a half, that Miles complained: 'I thought I was playing the world champion, not some monster with a hundred eyes!' I then travelled to Barcelona to collect the chess Oscar and went on for a familiarisation visit to London.

After returning to Baku, I immediately locked myself away in my hideout in Zagulba and concentrated entirely on preparing for the match. There was very little time left, but the experience I had gained in the previous matches helped me to highlight what was essential and tackle the main problems. My team of trainers worked exceptionally well; it's difficult now to believe that this was to be our last session together.

ELEVEN

Stab in the Back

Our two delegations arrived in London in July 1986. As before, my match with Karpov was to take place in a novel situation: it was the first match between two top Soviet chess players to be held abroad. This seemed to catch the organisers on the hop. The Soviet flag, for example, appeared over our venue – the Park Lane Hotel – not on day one, but only after we had played the first few games. Our battle site – the Grand Ballroom – was actually underground, on the 'minus-second' floor, and had been chosen by Winston Churchill during the war as a standby location for the House of Commons in case the Palace of Westminster was bombed.

My delegation was headed by the cheery and outgoing Siyavush Yeganov, chief of the Azerbaijani branch of Intourist. In keeping with Caucasian custom, he sent the British Prime Minister, Margaret Thatcher, a present: ethnic tea glasses. In addition to my trainers – Nikitin, Dorfman, Vladimirov and Timoschenko – I brought with me my doctor, Khalid Gasanov, my mother and Viktor Litvinov. Litvinov, who was directly involved in sports administration in Azerbaijan, helped me enormously.

In London I tried not to feed the gossip about the hostility between me and Karpov: we were both now the ambassadors of our country. At a press conference I said: 'My position remains unchanged, but in the months to come, the issue between us will be decided not by words, but by how we play chess.'

Some of the newspapers were categorical: 'This is war! There were no boxing gloves in sight, but that could not disguise the fact that this was a two-man war.' According to

The *Spectator*, 'If looks could kill, one of the greatest world title battles in chess history would have ended before it started yesterday.'

What captured most public interest was the contrast between our personalities. As one commentator wrote: 'Every competitive sport needs heroes with whom the public can identify. Tennis had McEnroe and Borg, then Becker and Lendl; snooker had Alex Higgins and Steve Davis. For ten years the chess world was ruled by the quiet, calm and cautious Karpov. When he was dethroned by the brash and rather temperamental Kasparov, chess the sport suddenly came to life again . . . If the USSR wants to encourage a new image, then Kasparov must be one of its best ambassadors.'

For the opening ceremony, the Grand Ballroom had been transformed into a giant chessboard, decorated at each corner with an enormous rook. Even Margaret Thatcher turned up suitably dressed for the occasion: a black two-piece and a black-and-white chequered blouse. She reminded the audience that she had been presented with a chess set by the Soviet Foreign Minister, Mr Eduard Shevardnadze, during his recent visit to London. 'I give him full marks for diplomacy,' she said. 'The chess set is in fact blue and white' (blue being the colour of her Conservative Party). The Prime Minister listed the qualities necessary to become a leading chess player, including precision of thought, imagination and being in good physical shape. She said these characteristics were also those needed to make a good politician – 'but chess is limited in time,' she added: 'we deal in unfinished business.' The presence of the British Prime Minister at the opening of the match showed that although the world championship play-off was still strictly a Soviet affair, the worldwide prestige of chess had increased considerably.

The level of public interest in chess in Britain impressed us all. Every day there were long queues for tickets. Among the people queuing up, as *The Times* said, were 'bronzed young tourists in garish anoraks, looking for all the world as if they had just fetched up hopefully at a *Jugendherberge*; older men with heavy East European faces that seem to harbour a deep, serious knowledge of the game; then the pin-striped ones and the well-kempt secretaries, clearly truanting from the office.'

The latest technology meant that every move was registered instantly on the monitors, the pieces having been sensitised electronically by a coil inside them which was linked to a computer. This was the brainchild of David Levy and Kevin O'Connell of Intelligent Chess Software and was revolutionising chess as a spectator sport. One commentator wrote: 'The main function of the champion and challenger conducting their private contest on the ballroom stage is to make a move. Instantaneously the move is relayed to thousands of television sets scattered around the hotel. In bars, conference rooms, press offices, lobbies, TV lounges, commentary positions and smoking rooms, the other players immediately begin to work through the zillions of new options that have opened to them . . . Chess is perhaps the only game in the world that cannot attract a single spectator – they all are participants.'

We were living in a spacious house near Kensington Gardens, found for us by Andrew Page, an Englishman with whom I had signed a rather unusual contract just before the London match, and who became my Western manager. I first met him in 1983, when he held talks with me on behalf of the computer firm SciSys. Later, when the contract was due to be renegotiated and the name Kasparov given to the whole range of the firm's chess computers, we discussed working directly together. There were obvious advantages for me in having someone in the West to negotiate for me with Western sponsors and tournament organisers. This was difficult to do from Baku, especially for a young man like me with no business experience. Apart from anything else, it would save me a great deal of time. For taking this sensible step I came in for a lot of flak from the officials, who were beginning to be frightened by my growing independence.

In contrast to the previous match, this one began with a game which passed off quietly and ended in a draw at the twenty-first move. The one thing I would mention about it is that this was the game where I used the Grunfeld Defence for the first time, quite an experiment to venture on in a match at this level. In game three also, this opening enabled me with black to achieve a draw without too much trouble.

Playing white, I was aggressive, although in game two, after gaining a good positional advantage, I got into time trouble and missed a forced win. But my victory in game four was something I could well be proud of – some original playing in the middle-game and confident exploitation of my advantage in the end-game made it for me a rounded work. Alas, the score was immediately equalised: in game five Karpov made a series of strong and confident moves and refuted the extremely risky opening that I had prepared. Game six, where after overactive play in the opening, I had to mount a painstaking defence to save a very bad end-game, formed a sort of prologue to two exciting battles.

In game seven, my 'original' handling of the opening again brought me to the brink of disaster. But Karpov, after obtaining a strategically winning position, instead of attacking on the kingside, switched to another part of the board, thus allowing black to start counterplay. Soon I managed finally to seize the initiative, but, with both of us in time trouble, I failed to find the strongest continuation and the contest ended in a draw. The battle was fought at a very high pitch, but it was still no comparison with what was to happen in the next game.

After sacrificing a pawn immediately after the opening, white gained some rich opportunities for attack, and it might have seemed that black's defensive formations on the kingside would quickly be swept away. But Karpov, displaying enviable tenacity in defence, managed to repulse the first onslaught. White, it's true, could have won the exchange: but then the position would have been simplified and black would have gained quite good positional compensation. I therefore pre-ferred to complicate the play still further, hoping to exploit the fact that my adversary was in imminent danger of exceeding his time limit.

A similar situation had occurred at the start of our first

match, and Karpov, evidently remembering his previous achievements, decided to play to win. But this time the strain of the contest was too much for him. Unable to get his bearings in a rapidly changing situation, he lost the game on time with ten moves to go, something unprecedented in world championship matches. Subsequent analysis showed that at that moment white's threats could no longer have been repulsed. One grandmaster said: 'The time scramble was so exciting I felt a knot in my stomach. The game was quite a mess but Kasparov's nerves were better in complications.'

After this severe knock, Karpov was forced to call a time-out. Yet still he wasn't able to recover completely in time for the next battle. After I had succeeded with black in getting on level terms, he immediately forced a draw by repetition of moves. And in game ten Karpov's imprecise play in a slightly worse end-game gave me a good chance of victory. However, after gliding through the fortieth move, the time control move, I immediately made an error which enabled black to mount a defence.

Although I had no clear way to win, declining to resume the game after the adjournment was an unforgivable psychological concession on my part. In the first place, he would still have had to display a certain precision, and secondly, after that heavy defence, Karpov would have had great difficulty in switching to active play. And after having avoided a tiring resumption of game ten, Karpov put up a real fight in game eleven, offering in the opening a double-edged sacrifice of the exchange. Although game eleven was another draw, it was an exciting game and was awarded the special Save and Prosper prize on the recommendation of leading British grandmasters.

By now there were such crowds queueing for tickets that a huge demonstration board had to be set up in Green Park, across the road in Piccadilly, for the overflow. The *Observer* wrote: 'Kasparov and Karpov are playing the foremost game of pure skill yet devised by the human mind, a game that is in fact beyond the scope of the human mind, well beyond it, an unmasterable game. They are playing this game at a level, at a pitch of complication, they alone can grasp. Towards the end of some of their games, world-famous grandmasters had no idea who was winning.'

Such rapture was premature. It emerged subsequently that in the course of game eleven we had both swapped mistakes which drastically altered the evaluation of the position. In my view, game four had a better claim to be singled out, but by pronouncing game eleven to be the best of those played in London, the British once again emphasised their neutrality. The £10,000 prize (in gold sovereigns) was divided equally between us.

After the turmoil that preceded it, game twelve seemed a bit insipid. White's minimal superiority quickly evaporated, and a draw was recorded at the thirty-fourth move.

So the London half of the match ended with a score of 6.5-5.5 in my favour. On the whole I had no reason to be dissatisfied, either with the score or with my play. The only thing that did bother me was that my extensive pre-match openings preparation had not borne the desired fruit. However, I was pleased with the overall nature of the contest, and couldn't see how Karpov could win in Leningrad with me having a two-point lead.

The match was splendidly organised, largely thanks to the generous financial assistance bequeathed by the Greater London Council before it was 'buried' by the Thatcher government. At the closing ceremony, the former Labour Prime Minister Lord Callaghan referred to this. 'Shakespeare is not always right,' he said, and quoted from Julius Caesar: 'The evil that men do lives after them, the good is oft interred with their bones.'

The prize money for the London half of the match could really have helped a lot of people, because when I heard of the tragedy at Chernobyl I announced that I was willing to donate the foreign currency part of any prize I earned to buy medical supplies for the victims of the explosion at the nuclear reactor. Soon afterwards, Karpov did the same. But our perfectly natural human response didn't meet with any under-standing either at FIDE or the USSR Sports Committee.

First, FIDE demanded flatly that one per cent of the prize money for each draw should go to it, as before. Then it was the turn of the bosses of the Sports Committee to display their financial wizardry. We were presented with the following chain of logical deduction. Since the USSR Council of Ministers had decreed that there should be a prize of 72,000 roubles for the Moscow matches, there was no reason to revise this figure for a return match. As the match had been divided into two halves, the same must be done with the prize money: 36,000 roubles in Leningrad and 36,000 roubles (this time in foreign currency roubles) in London. From this it followed that Kas-parov and Karpov could dispose only of this sum. In other words, out of the 691,000 Swiss francs, which at the official rate of exchange then was 290,000 foreign currency roubles (paid to us by the London organisers in the ratio of five-eighths to the winner and three-eighths to the loser), the USSR Sports Committee paid into the Chernobyl fund only 36,000 foreign currency roubles! There's an obvious difference between 290,000 and 36,000, but still more obvious in this case was the difference between human morality and bureaucratic morality.

A month after the beginning of the match, we left London. As the plane gained height and set course for Leningrad, I glanced down at London's broad river below me and thought: 'All's quiet on the Thames, but what's in store for me on the banks of the Neva?'

Karpov and I were on the same plane, so the two of us played cards with my coaches to pass the time, trying – unsuccessfully, of course – to put chess out of our minds at least for the few hours of the flight. When we landed at Leningrad, it was noticed by the journalists that while I left the airport in an ordinary Volga with a Baku number plate, Karpov was driven off in an official Chaika limousine escorted by a military traffic police vehicle. The local authorities made it clear straight away which of us was the outsider. The organisers, too, went on making sure I didn't forget that I wasn't playing on my home ground.

So from the banks of the thames we had moved to the banks of the Neva. Our team was put up in a three-storey mansion on Kamennyy Island. Karpov settled in nearby, on the same island. For the first time in three matches, the headquarters of the opposing sides were in close proximity to each other, in direct line of vision! That we unexpectedly found ourselves to be neighbours was Karpov's wish: he had declined the out-of-town residence that had been made ready for him.

The match itself was played in the concert hall of the Leningrad Hotel. Sevastyanov, who was taking part in what I thought was his last match as chairman of the Soviet Chess Federation, told the press: 'We hope the second half of the match conducted in Leningrad will be as creative, more interesting as regards the sporting qualities and organised as well as the one carried out in London.' However, not all the members of the press were comfortable there, and some never received their accreditation to cover the match.

The journalist Yuri Rost wrote in *Literaturnaya Gazeta*: 'Technically, the organisation has been perfect. The hall is marvellous, there's lots of light, the chairs are comfortable, press centre equipment is superb, communications perfect. So what is the problem? Only when your pass has been checked a thousand times, only when you leave your notebook, folder, newspaper and what-not at the reception and enter the hall, do you realise what the problem is. You are under suspicion. Most of the audience are not really those who really want to see the match but those who succeeded in getting through. Those who get in have been carefully selected by special personnel, so numerous you get the impression that what is taking place is not a gathering of admirers of two outstanding chess players or lovers of the wisest of sports, but a convention of underworld leaders.'

I wasn't aware of these problems as I sat at the chess table. I just knew that Leningrad was Karpov's kingdom and that I needed to keep my wits about me to prevent him gaining any home advantage.

I found out later how difficult it had been for the head of my team to arrange the catering and see to other routine matters. He even had to write an official letter to the city authorities. Many things, of course, were kept from me, but I can imagine what a worrying time it must have been for the people around me. As the epic story of those three matches in 1984–6 recedes into history, more and more is gradually coming to light about all the various methods that were used in a cold war which could hardly have been waged without official support. We still never cease to wonder how we managed to endure it all and not falter.

In game thirteen, which opened the Leningrad half of the match, Karpov chose the Grunfeld Defence, the same system that was used in game three, only this time he steered clear of rapid simplifications and used a more active plan. Amid the complex manoeuvring, white had the initiative. But then Karpov incautiously allowed play to open up on the kingside, and there was a moment when I could have decided the outcome of the battle with a direct attack on his king. Unfortunately, in the time scramble I made an error, and our painful battle ended in a draw.

The next game is worth looking at in detail. Possibly for the first time in his match career, Karpov decided with black to play to win. This ran counter to his usual strategy of limiting his opponent's possibilities as much as possible. As the arena for the coming battle, Karpov chose, not surprisingly, the Spanish opening, which is rightly considered to be strategically one of the most complex. Skilful handling of the Spanish opening is a good measure of a player's class, and the ability to accomplish it playing either side is the sign of a consummate master. Karpov has to his credit a number of impressive 'Spanish' wins, both with white and with black.

I was happy my opponent made that choice, as I intended to make use of my developments of this opening, which had from time immemorial been regarded as Karpov's territory. Luckily, I didn't get a chance to try out the innovation I'd prepared: Karpov was first to employ strengthening. Luckily, because encountering a new position and being forced to work out its intricacies directly at the chessboard, I in fact played one of my most subtle positional games. The seemingly incomprehensible pendulum-like movement of my rook which predetermined white's superiority must have put Karpov in mind of his own victories in the Spanish game, which have become classics. Confused by the unusual strategic pattern of the contest, the commentators were for a long time unable to evaluate the position correctly. It all became clear only after white's positional advantage was transformed into an ending with an extra pawn. There were then no two ways about it: black was lost. And sure enough, Karpov resigned the next day without resumption.

Before game fifteen I called another time-out. My two-point lead had forced my opponent to try and get the most out of playing with white, and it was obvious that the strength of the Grunfeld Defence would be put to the test yet again. Karpov's aggressive intentions were confirmed by the head of his delegation, Tupikin, who made an appearance at the press centre just before the game started and made the loaded promise: 'Today we begin!'

An odd thing happened before the game began. I, and evidently Karpov too, had been asked to agree to a little ceremony in which Tudela, the FIDE vice-president, was to take part. The ceremony began a couple of minutes before the clocks were due to be started. Campomanes came out onto the stage and introduced Tudela to the audience, after which there were a few words accompanied by beaming smiles, then Karpov and I were presented with commemorative badges from the Venezuelan Chess Federation. It was an absurd, laughable piece of theatre and the game began five or six minutes later than usual. Was this not symptomatic of the fact that in their own minds, the FIDE officials are convinced that chess players, and chess itself, are secondary to themselves?

While the ceremony was going on, I noticed how galling it was to Karpov – he was itching to go into battle!

The novelty that lay in store for me this time was a very aggressive and thoroughgoing variation of the Grunfeld Defence christened in the West as the 'Russian Defence'. Karpov demonstrated an important strengthening in comparison with the famous Botvinnik–Fischer game (Varna, 1962). After long thought, I pulled my knight back to a passive position, which clearly confused Karpov. He failed to find the right plan, after which I succeeded in placing my pieces well and gaining sufficient counterplay. After an intense battle, the draw was a logical result.

Game sixteen, however, was one of my best in the match. The clash of profound strategic plans, the sacrifices and counter-sacrifices, the mass of bewildering variations, all the quintessential features of a fight at the highest pitch of intensity which demands from the opponents all they have: this skirmish had it all. For a long time it seemed that Karpov's position was better. That impression was strengthened after his rook infiltrated my queenside to win my trapped knight. Until move thirty-two, the watching grandmasters were sure I was beaten. It was a surprising turnaround. Faced with innumerable and incalculable variations, Karpov lost control over the position and overstepped the fateful line. When, at the thirty-seventh move, I inflicted a fatal thrust against his king with an exposed pawn, the audience burst into applause. The chief arbiter, Lothar Schmid, waved his arms in the air, urging the spectators to be quiet, and for a while he succeeded. But when I returned to the stage to sign the scoresheet, the crowds erupted again. Karpov left the stage without the traditional handshake.

When I was working on my book *Two Matches*, which was issued by the Fizkultura i Sport publishing house in 1987, I spent two weeks fighting my way through the jungle of variations, and discovered that our play in that game was far from perfect. But I do not think that can detract from the overall impression that it was a mighty battle.

* * *

I was now three points ahead of Karpov and didn't see how I could possibly lose. That is a dangerous attitude, as I was soon to find out.

In game seventeen I was psychologically ill-prepared and the result was a crushing defeat. I should never have tempted fate by repeating the opening of game fifteen, for my opponent had in readiness a serious strengthening which struck me at the board as virtually refuting the whole system. Unable to get into the right frame of mind to put up a stubborn defence, I soon lost. It's interesting that a month later, in Tilburg, the Dutch grandmaster Jan Timman ventured in a game with Karpov to continue the fight using this variation, but white did not succeed in convincingly proving its superiority. The result was a draw.

In the next game I played what observers saw as 'dazzlingly original chess', featuring two moves which astounded the assembled grandmasters. One commentator wrote: 'Typically for Kasparov, the whole board appeared to be in flames.' Although there was one moment when I did not find the strongest continuation of the attack, white still retained the initiative. Despite being short of time, in the heat of battle I rejected an opportunity to force a draw by repetition of moves, and at first my calculation paid off. Three moves from the time control I had an absolutely won position, but in deep time trouble I completely lost my head and adjourned the game in what was now a difficult position for me. After the adjournment Karpov won, but it took two more bad mistakes on my part.

I called a time-out to recover from this battering. Observers were just as baffled as I was. One of them wrote: 'The view here is that after Kasparov's brilliant display of mental pyrotechnics in game sixteen the young champion has fallen prey to a twin evil: overconfidence plus an erroneous belief that the match is effectively over. This may turn out to have been a costly mistake.' I myself worried along the same lines. I wondered if I really deserved this. I asked myself whether what I saw on the board was a punishment for lack of effort in the past.

It's very difficult to play after two consecutive defeats and, to be honest, a little frightening. You think you see pitfalls in the most reliable systems. I'd decided to continue using the Grunfeld Defence, though it would have been more sensible, of course, to change the opening. But this I did only in game twenty-one. In game nineteen I'm pretty certain that even if I'd used a different opening, it wouldn't have affected my opponent's combat readiness. The system I chose gives black, as later experience has shown (notably the match in Seville), sufficient counterplay. But in the few days that I had I couldn't investigate thoroughly all the subtleties of the position. When I came up against the next one of Karpov's innovations, I lost my nerve and embarked on complications that were, objectively, not to my advantage, and in which I also didn't exploit all the chances I had. My recent three-point lead melted away 'like a dream, like morning mist . . .'

It was then that the unforeseen happened: after game nineteen, Vladimirov, who for five years had been my closest assistant, left my team. It was his own decision. This sudden move explained many things which I had previously found inexplicable.

I could take examples at random.

In London I had used the Grunfeld Defence, something that was new for me. I imagined that the factor of surprise would be reinforced by the fact that Karpov had had little practical experience of playing in this opening. But the amazing thing was that on encountering this unexpected opening, not only was Karpov not taken aback, but he struck with great precision smack at the key points my trainers and I had found in our analyses. He successfully avoided all the traps and effectively anticipated all the strikes we had prepared. And as the match went on, I wasn't able to make use of a single serious innovation, although I was no less prepared than in the previous match.

In game five I chose a rare and risky continuation in that same Grunfeld Defence. It took Karpov about twenty minutes to refute the whole scheme. This made me suspicious: Karpov could hardly have prepared himself so thoroughly before the match for this new and far from predictable opening. And if the problem was new to him, then pondering it at the board should have taken more time. So was it advance preparation on his part, something with a London hallmark? But in the opening phase Karpov had had other urgent problems to contend with, for example in the Nimzowitsch Defence, where he never did suceed in equalising. It was difficult to see how his team could have managed in less than a week to prepare a complex variation with an important strengthening, and more-over not in the main direction, but in a side one. An amazing gift of foresight!

And in game four Karpov had in effect closed a whole variation of the Nimzowitsch Defence by using a continuation which was one of our analytic secrets (see Appendix A). The coincidence of analyses, quite possible in this case, continued until a move by a bishop which Karpov made fairly quickly, but which turned out in fact to be second-rate. The surprising thing was that we, too, had considered it to be the best move. The commentators, on the other hand, quickly found a very strong continuation which neither we nor Karpov had seen. The shortsightedness was easy to explain: we were looking for an advantage for white. But surely Karpov, searching for a defence for black, must have discovered that move if he had done any serious analysis beforehand? So it wasn't just the analyses that coincided, but also the 'holes' in the analyses!

I was faced with puzzles of this kind after almost every game. Either our analyses in one particular area would com-pletely coincide – right down to faulty evaluations of individ-ual moves and positions – or he would inexplicably be able to guess in advance what the theme of the game would be.

After game seven I said I thought that information was being leaked. After game twelve I said that the information was most likely being passed by one of my own people. The situation developed in such a way that suspicion fell on Timoschenko. Because of his extreme individualism there was a certain amount of friction between him and the rest of the team. Before the return match, Timoschenko had switched entirely to working with me alone, without the rest of the team. In London he even lived separately from us, in a hotel. Moreover, Timoschenko was offended that I had not made him my official second. He had announced that he no longer considered himself bound by any obligations, and that after the London half of the match he was going off to take part in an army competition. On one of the occasions that I confided my suspicions about the leak to my trainers, Vladimirov said it was unlikely, but then added immediately: 'Though if the suspicions are correct, then it's Timoschenko.' But all of us were afraid to believe it. 'Karpov must be just guessing,' we decided. But somehow he was guessing just a little bit too often.

In Leningrad I calmed down a little, knowing that I was playing better than Karpov, and I was getting ready to increase my advantage. I succeeded in doing so, as I said, in game fourteen, although Karpov had once again easily found his bearings in an opening position that was new to him. So the joy of victory was tinged with a sense of alarm. Timoschenko had gone, but the miracles continued.

Before game sixteen I warned my mother, 'Today I'm going to sacrifice a knight, so don't faint.' But Karpov, forestalling me with a new move, again avoided the danger I had prepared for him (see Appendix A). It seemed to me, though, that he made his move without enthusiasm. I got the feeling that he had prepared the whole variation in a bit of a hurry. After some hideous complications, Karpov's battle formations were crushed and my lead went up to three points. In the general euphoria no one paid serious attention to my words of bewilderment and alarm: 'What's going on? Karpov scored another bull's-eye!' It was then that Vladimirov let on for the first time that he was leaving the team straight after the match.

The events that followed took a completely unexpected turn: I lost three games in succession. Losing game seventeen, to be honest, didn't upset me too much because I simply wasn't ready for serious play. Game eighteen was another matter. A feature article entitled 'Autumn on Kamennyy Island' written by Karpov's friend, the journalist Igor Akimov, and published in the magazine *Studenchesky Meridian*, said something astounding. A position that occurred in game eighteen, the article said, had given Karpov a sleepless night on the eve of the encounter. Moreover, Karpov was quite sure that that particular position 'will be on the board tomorrow'. Akimov immediately hastened to assure the reader that 'such foresight is in the nature of things'. But questions arise. Why, for example, after two crushing wins using the Spanish opening, was I sure to change tack and open not with a king's pawn, but a queen's pawn? But even if he knew the opening, how could he possibly foresee exactly what would be 'on the board tomorrow', if I was intending to use a continuation that I'd never been known to use before? And how could he be sure the tenth move would come as a surprise to Kasparov? It was impossible to explain, or, on the contrary, easy to explain.

Next day, the incredible happened: from Karpov's chess table at home, the position migrated onto the stage of the concert hall of the Leningrad Hotel. Instead of the natural tenth move with the knight, against which we had prepared a very strong response, my opponent moved his queen, the promised surprise for Kasparov. Of course no one but Karpov and I knew what he was trying to avoid. Unfortunately for him, the position didn't turn out to be his style, and I got out of it completely. But then weird things began to happen, and the game was adjourned with me in a difficult position.

We sat up all night, analysing it. Karpov had three possible continuations. In the first, and most dangerous for me, we discovered a good plan of defence giving a position which would lead easily to a draw. In the second variation we also found an excellent positional draw. But the third continuation we hardly looked at; a draw would be self-evident (and could actually be achieved in a single move). But when we resumed the game, Karpov chose precisely that continuation. So he'd overlooked a draw in one move? Incredible! Yet thanks to that blunder, he won. I had been following our adjournment analysis, which was superficial because of the lack of time and anyway had not demanded any great effort. I myself should have seen at the board the opportunity for a check that we had overlooked in our analysis. But Karpov's choice of an obviously weak continuation spoke volumes.

The atmosphere in our team became very tense. The doubts that had been mounting as the match progressed and had been dispelled each time they bounced against the wall of our contentment at winning, had now risen to their full height and gloated down upon us. I was told for the first time that Vladimirov had been making copies of our opening schemes for the past six months. The other trainers thought he was doing it with my knowledge. We immediately remembered Vladimirov's frequent disappearances and his complete freedom in London: before each game he would go for 'a run'. We remembered that an hour before game eighteen was to be resumed he'd made one of his trips into town, and that Karpov had been ten minutes late back for the continuation of the game. (According to his second, Makarychev, he'd been unable to decide until the very last minute which of the three continuations to choose.)

We decided to take the necessary precautions. No one was to leave the camp compound, and the trainers were to work separately. Vladimirov flatly refused to comply. I told him it wasn't so bad, the match would soon be over, and after all, Karpov's trainers hadn't even attended any of the games throughout the entire match, let alone taken long walks in town. It was something he should just try to put up with. But Vladimirov went off anyway, quietly, no one knew where. This by itself was reason enough to get rid of him.

Then we decided to remove all the trainers' telephones to be on the safe side. Vladimirov handed his telephone set in too. However, when my mother dialled his number at six o'clock the next morning, someone at the other end lifted the receiver without answering. And sure enough, a second telephone which he'd been concealing was later found in Vladimirov's room. We then decided to disconnect all the phones in the house except the main one. When he discovered that his secret telephone had been disconnected, Vladimirov flew off the handle: he accused us of spy mania and announced that he was leaving the team. Then the head of our delegation demanded that he return his chess notes. Vladimirov said he didn't have any. But the trainers quickly refreshed his memory and he was forced to produce them. We then saw what an extensive 'correspondence game' had been going on behind my back. For some reason, Vladimirov's range of interests did not include the openings he usually used, but only the ones that had been my main weapons against Karpov. We asked Vladimirov for a written explanation. Here is what he wrote:

From February 1986 onward I made written notes of the analyses made at G. Kasparov's training sessions in which I took part. Along with the fair copies made by me for A. Shakarov, I made abridged copies for myself for later use in tournaments. I told no one in the team that these notes existed. I kept notes on the following variations:

– Grunfeld Defence (basic variation and variation with 5.Bf4)
– Nimzowitsch Defence (system with 4.Kf3 c5 5.g3)
– Russian game (Rosenthalis system and basic variation).

These notes were exclusively for my own use, and in no circumstances were they passed on to Karpov's team.
Feeling physically and mentally exhausted, I have decided to voluntarily leave G. Kasparov's team.
I promise that I shall not collaborate for at least the next two years with any of G. Kasparov's potential opponents.

Y. Vladimirov, 26 September 1986

We were disheartened by all this. We didn't try to persuade Vladimirov to stay. All night he waited by the telephone for a call, and when it came, he left. Vladimirov kept his word, as far as my *potential* opponents were concerned. On the other hand, as we found out, he helped my *immediate* adversary before the Seville match.

I cannot say unequivocally that Vladimirov's notes were given to Karpov, but in my own mind three consecutive defeats can be explained more easily if they were.

How could it have happened? For years we had lived like a close family, talking about everything under the sun and trusting each other implicitly. We had no chess secrets from each other either: all our theoretical finds were thrown open for general discussion. This helped us look at problems from different angles and ensured that I had a high standard of preparation. We were united by a common aim. Vladimirov's departure had a devastating effect on me. I was used to seeing the enemy in front of me, and now I had been stabbed in the back.

I have often wondered what drove Vladimirov to behave as he did. Was some pressure put on him perhaps? He was an officer of the Soviet Army and a member of the same sporting association as Karpov, the Central Army Sports Club. But he must certainly have had personal motives of some kind. Vladimirov had shown great promise when he was young, but he was weak, a little lazy, and this affected his chess career. I have the impression that he was constantly at odds with himself, and that possibly deep down he resented my success, feeling that with his talent, he deserved it no less than I.

But it would be too simple to put his treachery down to envy alone. There may have been other reasons. Who knows, maybe Vladimirov wanted to play the role of fate for me. Perhaps he felt he was right in stopping someone he thought was aiming too high.

Vladimirov left us on 26 September, and on the following day, before game twenty, Karpov surprised everyone by calling his last time-out. This was a sensation! Many people had been expecting that 'now he had gathered momentum, Karpov would be able to deliver his fourth blow in succession, and Kasparov wouldn't get up'. But Karpov declined to play. The general opinion was that this was a fatal mistake. Here he was for the first time in the match with a chance of winning, and suddenly he was wavering. To take that sort of crucial decision he must have had some pretty strong reasons. But what were they? Karpov was to explain later that he had problems with the opening. Evidently, something had happened to his 'farsightedness', and for the first time in the match Karpov didn't know what would be on the board tomorrow. Just as inexplicable was the way his indomitable fighting spirit evaporated at this crucial stage of the match.

The match had now entered the finishing stretch. The players had used all their time-outs and now knew exactly which day each new encounter would take place. By taking a break, Karpov had lost the psychological initiative and had given me time to lick my wounds. I was exhausted. The previous two years were beginning to take their toll, on top of which I had the burden of this dramatic struggle in the return match.

I needed a breathing-space, so in game twenty we decided on the Catalan opening, something I had previously used against Karpov when I wanted to avoid complications. Whenever I used that opening, he always opted for a sound but unenterprising continuation. Usually throughout these games I would have a slight advantage, but they would end in a truce. Game twenty, in which Karpov brought about innumerable exchanges without too much trouble, ended the same way. One remarkable thing was that in a position he was very familiar with, he spent an unusually large amount of time on the opening phase.

Now that I had broken the depressing series of defeats, I felt my strength returning and began to regain my former self-confidence. 'Game twenty-one will be a draw, and game twenty-two I shall win,' I announced confidently to my team. To achieve that aim, for the next game we chose the New Indian Defence, with its reputation as a sound opening. In addition to the element of surprise, the important thing was the novelty it introduced in our opening relations. Although the score was equal, a draw would mean more to me than half a point. In his post-match interviews, Karpov said this had been the decisive game of the final phase: after it he realised that the most he could hope for was to retain the drawn score. So was this his 'last and decisive' one? It's hard to believe that Karpov's passive play in this game could be called playing to win.

On the day of game twenty-two it had rained incessantly, but when he drove to the hotel it suddenly stopped. Getting out of the car I looked up, and there in the sky above the Leningrad Hotel was the brightest and most beautiful rainbow I had ever seen. To my romantic and slightly superstitious mind, it was a sign from above. The game indeed gave me some unforgettable moments.

In a Queen's Gambit Declined I managed to seize the initiative. Putting on the pressure, white gained the advantage and won a pawn a few moves before the time control; but in exchange, Karpov succeeded in bringing his pieces into highly active play. The position at the adjournment looked like a draw. At the press centre, the pieces on the board were spiritedly shifted this way and that, but no decisive continuation was found. No wonder many of the next day's papers predicted a draw.

I saw the move at once: Ne5–d7!! It was a moment of inspiration. I worked out the various implications for a few minutes, which gave me enormous aesthetic enjoyment, then I wrote down my forty-first move. After a while I wrote something again. People thought I had changed my mind, but I hadn't. I simply wrote the same move again, making it more clear and checking to make sure there was no mistake. There is a photocopy of the scoresheet to prove it, which was published in *Literaturnaya Gazeta*.

Although Karpov tried to appear perfectly calm just before the game was resumed, I'm sure that in his adjournment analysis he had discovered that same move. While the arbiter was opening the envelope, Karpov looked away to the audience as if he didn't care what I had written. But he couldn't keep up this pretence at nonchalance and glanced at the hands of Lothar Schmid as he revealed the sealed move. Even before the move was reproduced on the board, Karpov had seen it and understood everything. After four moves he resigned.

I needed half a point in the remaining two games to retain my title. Karpov had to win both to take it back from me.

At 9.34 p.m. on Monday 6 October, it was all over. After exhausting all his resources in the fight to win game twenty-three, Karpov offered a draw. What made the game unusual was that in the complex standard position of an English opening with the board full of pieces, black sent out his rooks on an extravagant sortie into the centre. This apparently anti-positional decoy action distracted Karpov from pursuing a solid strategy. In an attempt to exploit the provocative location of the black rook, he allowed his position to slightly weaken. When the rook had calmly returned to its own camp, it became evident that white now needed to exercise a certain caution.

The final game was virtually a formality. Karpov could no longer get back his title; all he could do was draw on points and thereby at least go halves with the prize money. But I confidently kept up the pressure; simplifications ensued and we moved into an even end-game. But he behaved with bad grace at the end of the session by refusing to accept an obvious drawn position, dragging out the proceedings until the next day, when I was kindly informed by telephone that the game would not be resumed.

When the famous sports commentator Kote Makharadze was asked for his opinion of the match, he said: 'I don't understand much about chess, but even less do I understand why the victory of one Soviet grandmaster over another is reported on television in such a voice that you'd think the commentator had just lost a close friend.'

The closing ceremony, too, was more like a funeral, with many of the 'select' audience in the hall wearing mournful expressions. There were few people on the stage, and the senior officials of the Sports Committee, and even Sevastyanov, the chairman of the Soviet Chess Federation, were absent. The lavish celebrations that had been planned with another outcome in mind were put off for another occasion. That evening I didn't stumble across any posters congratulating Karpov on his victory like I had in Moscow the previous year. I'm sure the organisers had been no less provident than before; it's just that I didn't have the good fortune to see what they had prepared. But I heard it all right. I shall never forget the shouts from the crowd welcoming the players outside the entrance to the tournament hall: 'Murder him, Tolya!'

TWELVE

The Second Front

Having retained my crown and secured a brief respite before my next match, I decided to concentrate entirely on fighting the chess mafia. First of all, re-elections were coming up in the Soviet Chess Federation, and it seemed to me that if I could get Sevastyanov out, then Campomanes would have a difficult time in the presidential elections in Dubai.

As chairman of the Chess Federation, Sevastyanov was an ideal cover for the sports functionaries, but the shock of Karpov's defeat was such that when Gramov came up against my uncompromising stand, he decided not to tempt fate. My arguments were convincing: there was no doubt that Sevastyanov had had a finger in all kinds of anti-Kasparov operations.

A plenary session of the Chess Federation in late October elected Alexander Davidovich Chikvaidze, a career diplomat, the new chairman. I delivered a keynote speech in which I outlined the paths that Soviet chess should take in order to develop in the same spirit as the changes that were taking place in our country. It met with universal approval.

Seen against this background, the persistent urging by Gramov and Gavrilin that I should not stand in the way of Sevastyanov's election as honorary chairman seemed to me to be merely an attempt to sweeten the pill for him. It's interesting that when Baturinsky made this proposal at the session, it was greeted with deathly silence. Many of the delegates were in a dilemma and swapped puzzled glances. One of them even spoke out strongly against the idea. But I wanted to avoid a fresh conflict and confined myself to a brief conciliatory speech. It wasn't a case of cold feet: it was just that at that time I believed we could achieve general agreement on the problems of chess.

Unfortunately Sevastyanov's honourable retirement virtually reduced all my achievements to nothing: many people now saw the changes in the Federation as just a temporary regrouping of forces. Carried away by my first success, I hoped to beat Campomanes soon as well, and with what appeared to be the guaranteed backing of my Federation I could quite reasonably count on success. What I overlooked completely was the strength of the alliance between the Soviet Sports Committee and Campomanes, an alliance forged by the involvement of both parties in the events of February 1985. Being politically inexperienced, I hadn't the slightest idea that the system was resilient enough to withstand the very strongest blows, and I frantically prepared myself for a frontal attack that was doomed to fail.

Meanwhile, Campomanes was going to enormous lengths to win me over, and he thought up a most original move. At the closing ceremony of the return match in Leningrad, I had been presented with neither a diploma nor a medal as world champion. Instead, Campomanes proposed holding a magnificent coronation in Dubai, and promised there would be a medal of pure gold. I declined. The President evidently decided that this refusal also extended to all future matches, because at the next world championship in Seville I was again deprived of the honorary trophy . . .

Just before our team left for the Olympiad in Dubai, where a FIDE congress was also to be held, the Soviet Sports Committee announced its support for Campomanes. I countered by appealing to Alexander Yakovlev, hoping with his help to get the Sports Committee to change its mind. But even this authoritative opinion wasn't enough; it wasn't just the sporting authorities who sympathised with Campomanes.

Hoping for a miracle, I continued my campaign in Dubai, lobbying delegates late into the night to get their support for

Lincoln Lucena of Brazil. Unfortunately, the official announcement of the view of the Soviet Chess Federation swung the
election. All the pro-Soviet countries voted for Campomanes
and this in turn made up the minds of the delegates who had
been wavering.

Campomanes was held in specially high regard in Dubai,
and the organisers pulled out all the stops for his election
campaign. Local television painted a detailed and glowing
picture of the President's life and extolled his contribution to
world chess. They held several press conferences at which
Campomanes was not, of course, asked any awkward
questions.

I, however, unlike the President, got no chance to put my
point of view to the local press. On someone's secret instructions, the interview in which I called for changes in FIDE was
not published in Dubai. It's probably the only time a world
champion has ever been denied the opportunity to speak to
the press in a worldwide chess forum such as the Olympiad.

In the end we had to admit humiliating defeat. Campomanes was playing his own game on his own ground and on
his own terms. He made us look like amateurs in comparison.
The anti-Campo forces could muster so little support that there
wasn't even a vote. He was actually invited to carry on for a
further period in office. It wasn't that Lucena lost; there was
no contest. I was the one who lost, for I had put my reputation
on the line.

Furthermore, all this late-night campaigning did little to help
my chess. The Soviet team's performance was uneven gener-
ally, and after I lost to Seirawan – which led eventually to our
losing the match to one of our strongest competitors, the
American team – it looked as though we were in dire straits.
In addition to the Americans, the steady and confident British
team were also serious contenders for the gold medal. There
was no doubt that losing the Olympiad would bring recriminations on me for being too busy dabbling in politics to uphold
the honour of Soviet sport.

But a strong final spurt enabled the Soviet team to snatch

victory after all, and by winning the last three games I won three gold medals at once: for the team's victory, for the best result at the first board, and for the absolute best result in the Olympiad.

Having lost the fight in FIDE, I came to the conclusion that what we needed was an independent body of grandmasters which would be able to defend their rights and steer chess onto the path of reform. Many grandmasters responded readily to my suggestion that we should get together there and then in Dubai and discuss our urgent problems. Although we had no advance plan of action and were hardly able to define a clear programme for the future, we all agreed that the deep conflicts that had come to a head in world chess needed to be resolved as soon as possible. This applied above all to the burgeoning administrative apparatus of FIDE, which had virtually completely squeezed the grandmasters out of the system which ran chess. The bureaucrats prevented new competitions from being set up which, if widely supported by Western sponsors and the press, could greatly promote chess.

After two days of lively discussion, we drew up the main points of our programme. We decided to begin by organising a World Cup, competitions consisting of six super-tournaments in which the twenty-four strongest grandmasters would take part. There was no room for a Cup in the two-year cycle of world championship play-offs planned by FIDE, so one of our first demands was a return to the former three-year cycle. In general, Campomanes's high-handed decisions had been a great bone of contention among the grandmasters, but now many of my colleagues at last began to realise that lurking behind all the President's bustling activity was overweening ambition and a striving to consolidate his own personal power. In a letter to the General Assembly of FIDE we said that we were setting up a new association 'to avoid further misunderstandings between FIDE and the leading grandmasters, and also to facilitate the process of decision-making'.

While still in Dubai we set up a provisional seven-man

Grandmasters' Board to carry out the preparatory work. I was elected President, and Anatoly Karpov and Jan Timman Vice-Presidents, the other members being Ljubomir Ljubojevic, Lajos Portisch, Yasser Seirawan and John Nunn. It was these seven men who, on 15 February 1987, were to put their signatures to the documents that were the official birth certificate of a new international organisation, the Association of Grandmasters (AG). It was no surprise that the Board comprised only grandmasters of the highest standing who represented the leading chess-playing nations. This was a natural reaction to the domination of FIDE by incompetent delegates from the lesser chess federations.

The uniting together of the cream of grandmasters was a necessary precondition for forming the Association, but even while we were still in Dubai we could see from the response of the rank-and-file grandmasters that the 'second echelon' might not be too happy about the Board's proposed activities. After all, the Association's main tournament, the World Cup, was designed solely for the top players.

The guarantee that our undertaking would succeed came in the form of active assistance from Bessel Kok, the technical director of SWIFT, the banking computer network based in Brussels. He began his activities in the field of chess by brilliantly organising in April 1986 the SWIFT tournament, which he suggested should be held annually as one of the stages of the World Cup. But the main thing was that he gave the new body, set up under Belgian law, a sound financial and legal basis. One cannot but admire this experienced businessman's feel for a good proposition: he was the first to see the possibilities of the Grandmasters' Association, which at first no one took seriously.

Campomanes didn't believe the grandmasters could create a strong and independent organisation. He thought we wouldn't be able to agree on a united policy. So for the moment he didn't object, or at least, didn't take any action against us. The President was convinced that the Association would function within the framework of the international

Chess Federation, so the question of its founding was discussed at a meeting of FIDE's executive council. After he won the presidential election, Campomanes thought the emergence of a new professional body would actually be grist to his mill, because through it he could re-establish contacts with sponsors and the press. The FIDE leadership had lost all credence in the eyes of the sponsors, who had no desire to put up any further money.

If FIDE could retain its power over chess and be augmented by an active body such as the Association of Grandmasters, then without doubt both Campomanes and FIDE stood to gain.

But in Dubai, when Campomanes tried rapidly (there wasn't much time) to work out the implications, he underestimated a few things: the ability of the grandmasters to unite, the changes in the USSR, my persistence and, above all, the energy of Bessel Kok. Campomanes was slow to realise how far-reaching were Kok's intentions with regard to chess.

Interestingly enough, the first players' conference of this kind took place in the Amstel hotel in Amsterdam fifty years ago. The discussions, which followed the famous AVRO tournament, were about creating a 'Club of the Eight Strongest', the eight at that time being Alekhine, Capablanca, Euwe, Keres, Botvinnik, Fine, Reshevsky and Flohr. Unfortunately, because Alekhine and Capablanca wouldn't speak to each other, they had to take turns to attend the meetings. The players reached a draft agreement but then the war intervened, and after the war FIDE got its act together and took everything over.

By an amazing coincidence, the date that the Association of Grandmasters was launched in Brussels, 15 February 1987, was two years exactly to the day that Campomanes had stopped my first world challenge. Thus the anniversary of an unprecedented act of tyranny in the chess world was marked by the start of organised resistance to the forces which had been behind it.

*   *   *

In April 1988 we succeeded in holding our first assembly. It was not well attended, though many grandmasters did cast their votes by proxy. It was in the passionate arguments at the assembly that the principles of the Association began to take shape. One of our underlying principles was broad-based democracy. We knew that as a newly formed organisation which as yet had no solid financial backing, was not fully recognised in the chess world, and had its own complex internal problems, we would not find the going easy. We could have succumbed to the temptation to run it by simply handing down orders and decrees, but we didn't. We overcame that critical stage and succeeded in keeping our unity intact, despite repeated attempts by FIDE to destroy us.

Our membership now includes some 270 grandmasters. Ultimate success will depend on raising the right amount of commercial sponsorship to meet our ambitious targets, and that will in turn depend on widening the game's popularity around the world. But the money is not just for ourselves: it is to achieve democratic rule in the sport. And at least we are bringing to this task a good deal more energy and initiative than FIDE ever did.

Our Association is going from strength to strength. In the World Cup tournaments we have succeeded in achieving considerable improvements in organisation and financial conditions. The total cost of the six stages was three million dollars, of which 1.2 million was prize money. Judging by the total success of the World Cup, both for the sponsors and in the press, we hope that the prize money will increase by fifty per cent in the next cycle.

But man does not live by bread alone. In December 1988, on the Association's initiative, the first charity match was held in Madrid, between a team of Soviet grandmasters and the Rest of the World. Much was said about it, but few people pointed out one very important fact: the match was held, not under the auspices of the Soviet Children's Fund or the Grandmasters' Association, but primarily under the auspices of UNICEF, the United Nations Children's Fund. To take part in such an event is an enormous honour for any professional, whether he is a chess player, footballer, singer or writer. Donating money to that fund is regarded as one of the most humanitarian acts possible in the world today. These are the grandmasters who handed over the entire prize-money – $160,000 – to UNICEF and the Soviet Children's Fund: Azmayparashvili, Andersson, Belyavsky, Gurevich, Dolmatov, Ilyeskas, Kasparov, Korchnoi, Ljubojevic, Nogeiras, Portisch, Psakhis, Sokolov, Speelman, Hartarson and Chernin.

I consider that the Association's main achievement in 1988, however, was the staging in Belgrade of the first knock-out tournament for the 1991–2 World Cup, which was a considerably better event than the traditional Swiss-system tournaments like those staged in New York and Lugano. At the starting-post there were 258 chess players, including no less than 100 grandmasters. Once it had got some financial muscle, the Association immediately began working not just for the elite, who were not short of tournaments to play in, but for all grandmasters. The Belgrade tournament was the first, but by no means the last. It marked the beginning of a whole series of competitions which allowed every player, every member of the Association, to take part in the play-off for the next World Cup.

In May 1989 Moscow took the baton from Belgrade, and this time the level of organisation silenced even the most stubborn sceptics. At the end of the tournament the Association held its second assembly, which had a far greater attendance than the first: eighty-seven grandmasters had 125 votes, enough for a quorum (which, under our Charter, is not less than half of the members).

The growth of the Association presented the Board with some new problems: with rank-and-file grandmasters in the majority, the privileged position of the elite was beginning to be resented. There were critical speeches at the assembly demanding that a long-term strategic programme be drawn up as soon as possible to take the interests of all the grandmasters into account. Incidentally, the Council itself underwent a few changes: back in 1987, after Nunn retired, his place had been taken by Bent Larsen, and the vacancy that had arisen in September 1988 after the retirement of Seirawan was filled in Moscow. The election was won by another American, Maxim Dlugi, who had the support of most of the 'second echelon' grandmasters. (His rival was a semi-finalist in the candidates matches, Jonathan Speelman.)

The greater democracy within the Association itself showed clearly how far we had come since we first discussed our programme in November 1986. In the future we hope to create a professional union to accommodate all chess players regardless of their standard. This will enable us to bring all levels of professional chess under one wing, which means we'll be able to create an orderly system of tournaments and training.

Behind all these organisational and commercial schemes is my nature as a practical dreamer. I want to promote chess by every means available – games, books, new forms of competition. My first innovation along these lines was the speed challenge match I played with Nigel Short in the winter of 1987 on the revolving stage of the London Hippodrome. I'm ready to experiment even with forms of chess such as this, though they are, of course, mainly for entertainment.

Speed challenge matches and tournaments are good publicity and as a leisure activity for serious chess players they're good fun. As far as grandmasters are concerned, I think the form of competition we hit upon in Madrid is the most suitable. On one hand, it's entertaining for the spectators, and on the other, the whole world benefits when the players donate all their prize money to charity. Not even in my worst imagination, however, could I see speed challenge matches being in any way connected with the play-off for the word title or used to introduce new grandmaster titles.

Sadly, the FIDE officials soon found a way to use speed challenge matches as a weapon against the professional grandmasters. It became clear that the new titles and ranks that could be awarded to players who were sometimes of candidate master standard undermined the traditional hierarchy of classical chess and destroyed the whole system of values in the chess world. It is my hope, however, that we will cope with this new 'speed challenge' from FIDE.

But let us return to the events of 1987. Despite being engrossed in the affairs of the Association and my personal battle with the Soviet Sports Committee, I still had in the forefront of my mind the forthcoming world championship match in the autumn. After Sokolov lost the super-final in Linares, it became clear that I was once again facing a contest against Karpov, the fourth in three years.

When it came to the question of the venue, the United Arab Emirates again cropped up. The Olympiad in Dubai had left no doubt in my mind that counting on the hospitality of the organisers there, who still openly supported Campomanes, was out of the question. No wonder Karpov's preference was Abu Dhabi. The alliance was still alive and well.

That decision turned the whole selection procedure into a farce, because under Campomanes's new rules each player could only choose one city; if there was a disagreement, the match went automatically to whichever had offered the biggest prize money. Since it was well known how I felt about Abu Dhabi, there was no point in stating my choice at all. In principle any city would have suited me except Abu Dhabi. My first choice would have been Seattle. Given the current level of relations between our two countries, it would have been highly symbolic for two Soviet chess players to contest the world title in America. Such a match would have done a great deal to promote chess in the United States, a potentially major market for the game. The final choice was Seville, although I would have preferred Madrid. However, I had been very well received in Seville when I went there on a familiar-isation visit in 1987. Spain is a chess-playing country with many lovers of the ancient game, and fully deserved to host the world championship. Just prior to the match in Seville there was an obvious regrouping of forces. In early 1987, the

Soviet Sports Committee and those of its senior officials who had for the time being tolerated me, changed their attitude. The reason was clear: by speaking out in Dubai against the election of Campomanes, I had become the first Soviet sportsman to openly defy a directive from the Sports Committee. Not content with that, three months later, at the 18th Trades Union Congress, I had declared from the rostrum of the Palace of Congress in the Kremlin that we needed to introduce professional sport in the USSR as the only means of rescuing the Soviet sporting movement from collapse. I had thereby opposed the official stance of the Sports Committee, which categorically rejected the possibility of introducing the status of professional sportsman in our country. It was a question of giving sportsmen, who were humiliatingly dependent on the sports officials, their legitimate rights and, in a broader sense, of abolishing the State monopoly over the individual. Now, many people are unruffled by this demand; but at that stage of *perestroika*, uttering thoughts of that kind immediately increased the number of my enemies in the establishment.

FIDE also got the message that it was no use hoping for peaceful co-existence between me and Campomanes.

Thus the opening of a second front in chess and sport led to the creation of a mighty coalition whose members believed it essential to put a stop to Kasparov's 'destructive activities' as soon as possible.

THIRTEEN

An Evil Spirit

It's probably true to say that for me the match in Seville was psychologically the most difficult of all my four duels with Karpov. That may at first seem paradoxical. After all, I had been through the fantastic tension of the first match, when for two months I had to go out onto the stage under threat of the worst possible defeat, and the unparalleled emotional strain of the second match, in which the goal came so searingly close, and the upheaval in the last lap of the return match in Leningrad after the business with Vladimirov.

Nevertheless, Seville was the worst ordeal of my life. The torments I suffered on the night between games twenty-three and twenty-four were enough for the whole match. To this day, I still have the feeling of having looked into the abyss. I had studied my adversaries pretty closely and knew that they wouldn't be satisfied with merely a chess triumph. It is extremely likely that they had plans ready to launch a public vendetta against me if Karpov won. And it wouldn't just be a series of potshots like the ones fired by a few newspapers in early 1988: it would be an out and out campaign. Fortunately, it didn't happen; the title of world champion saved me from the worst.

But it wasn't only, or rather, it wasn't so much the gloomy thoughts about my own future that depressed me on that terrible night. After all, when I 'overstepped the limits', I was well aware of the threat that confrontation with the mighty apparatus meant for me personally. But I couldn't help thinking also of the people who had put their faith in me and had become actively involved in the fight for changes in the chess world. If Karpov returned to the throne, the shoots of new growth would be ruthlessly trampled underfoot, and exemplary punishment would await those who had been on the side of reform. One by one, the events of the past year floated back through my mind, and I just couldn't understand how, with my enormous experience of top-level contests and my convincing wins in the last two matches, I could once again be, as I was three years ago, on the brink of an abyss.

To this day I am sure that for the Seville match, my superiority as a player was good enough for me to win. But I was not able to put it into effect. The reason is to be found outside chess, above all, in my state of mind at the time. My victory in the return match had in a way disarmed me. The win seemed final, and it didn't appear all that obvious that my next match with Karpov would take place: he still had to play Sokolov. Besides, there had been nearly a year's gap between the matches.

Unfortunately I didn't manage to make fruitful use of the time I had available for chess preparation. From the creative point of view, I can probably count that year as my most undistinguished to date.

In addition to my fight against the sports bureaucracy, I had masses of other important and interesting things on my mind: working at the children's chess school, trying to set up a Soviet–British chess publishing house and chess magazine, and my activities to promote computerisation in our country – for example, the founding of the children's computer club in Moscow, of which I'm the president, and where everyone works on a strictly voluntary basis. In the first two years alone since the club was founded, it has trained more than 500 children between the ages of six and sixteen. Every time I go abroad I bring back software and diskettes for the children, and I take out regular subscriptions to foreign computer magazines on behalf of the club. Incidentally, the games in the first-ever 'starry-chess' session (centred in Cannes), where I played simultaneously with ten cities in various parts of the world, were transmitted from the children's computer club via a telecommunications link.

Who could have imagined that the USSR Sports Committee would contrive to turn even a children's club into an arena to fight me? It all began with an advertising contract I signed with Atari in 1986. By arrangement, my entire fee was paid in computers. So of the fifty series-8 personal computers that were received, the Committee stubbornly tried to appropriate half. As the contract was signed through the Sports Committee, they were the official recipient of the goods; and as such, for two years they refused to fill in the documents transferring the computers to the club. Since the computers themselves were already at the club and they couldn't take them away from the children without a fuss, the Sports Committee simply didn't sign what was a purely formal transfer order. This will seem ridiculous, but requests for the matter to be resolved were sent to the Sports Committee by Velikhov, Vice-President of the USSR Academy of Sciences; Mironenko, First Secretary of the Komsomol Central Committee; and Makarov, Director of the Institute of Economics and Mathematics. None of them received a refusal; the Committee simply didn't sign the order, and that was that. Only after the match in Seville was over did they settle the issue in the children's favour.

Numerous problems prevented me from concentrating on the most important thing, which was preparing for my match with Karpov. The forthcoming battle was somehow very remote from my mind, and I couldn't help wishing that I didn't have to go through with it. That feeling was to remain with me throughout the whole Seville match. Why play again? I'd already proved my superiority. I'd already won and then confirmed my world title, all in the space of two years. I just had no desire for it. My whole being rebelled against the very thought that I must once again, for the Nth time, mobilise myself for battle, even though I knew that far more was at stake this time than in the previous matches. A defeat would go far beyond the bounds of single combat with Karpov, and would affect the whole cause of breathing new life into chess.

After I got back from Seville, someone told me what one of the senior officials of the Sports Committee had said: 'If Garry loses, the Restoration will be bloody!'

As I mentioned before, work on my book *Child of Change*, which I began at the end of 1986, was another distraction from preparing for the match. As the book progressed, it was hard to shake off the feeling that the main struggle for the world title was behind me.

Another difficult problem was that of the team who would go with me to the match, because with Vladimirov and Timoschenko gone, only two of the men with whom I had begun the struggle remained – Nikitin and Dorfman. And there was even an attempt to put one of them out of action. In June 1987, four months before the match, an unexpected visitor came to see me in Baku. His name was Alexander Feldman. He came straight to the point, and told me he was angry at Karpov's ingratitude and wanted to get even with him, so he'd decided to divulge a highly important secret. It was Dorfman, he said – not Vladimirov – who had leaked the information about our work on the openings.

What was interesting was that during the second Moscow match in 1985 it was through Feldman that Dorfman had been offered 100,000 roubles and a Moscow residence permit in exchange for information from my camp. So it wasn't difficult to guess that the main purpose of Feldman's revelations was to compromise Dorfman and deprive me of another of my assistants. But the undercover strategists had overestimated my 'suspiciousness'. (It's interesting to note, by the way, that the leak itself was not denied; only, according to Feldman, it wasn't Vladimirov that did it.)

In March I had talks with the young Georgian master Zurab Azmayparashvili (now a grandmaster), who agreed at once to take part in the preparation work. But still the team lacked another strong grandmaster. A month before the match I approached Sergey Dolmatov, although I knew there would be a serious problem, because he was a close friend and assistant of Artur Yusupov, one of the world title challengers.

But to my joy, Dolmatov agreed. I see this also as evidence of the good will of Yusupov himself, who understood just how important the Seville match was, not only for me, but for chess in general.

I can't agree with the claims that my pre-match preparation was inadequate. In fact, we had found many new ideas; it was just that unfortunately my play was not up to the standard of my preparation. It was already evident at the beginning of the match that my nervous system was not ready for the severe pressure of a world championship match. While experience and intuition occasionally prompted the right solution, some sort of general physical inertia and sluggishness of thought, and above all, complete lack of inspiration made my play heavy and incoherent. It forced me to double-check the variations again and again, and this led to time problems. The first eight games were possibly the most depressing. Two of them – the second (after a splendidly executed opening) and the fifth (in which I found a strong response to an innovation by Karpov and gained a big advantage) – I lost on time because in them I spent two and a half hours on just two moves! Of course you can't allow yourself to spend that sort of time in thought, and it was a good indication of my condition, of the peculiar apathy that I felt about the match.

It didn't escape the notice of the chess experts either. 'After five games you can already draw certain conclusions.' Artur Yusupov told a gathering in the Leningrad Palace of Arts. 'I've known Kasparov since he made his first few moves in chess, and I don't remember ever having seen him in such a bad state. It's not a question of the score. How is he losing?! But as soon as something takes him by surprise, he thinks for a long time. There's severe time pressure. He exposes his rook. He doesn't set the clock. Perhaps he has lost his psychological stability? Before the match Kasparov said, "I've solved the problem of Karpov." But has he solved the problem of himself? The tactics Karpov has chosen in this match are interesting psychologically too. Imagine a tennis player who doesn't go up to the net himself, but forces his opponent to do so time after time: to go up to the net and make a mistake. It looks as if Karpov's playing in this way is a surprise to Kasparov. And I think psychology is what will decide the match.'

Here we should return to the events that took place in Moscow in the last few days before I flew to Spain, and to what preceded them. As you must by now have seen, in my duels with Karpov for the world title, it's not just the black and white pieces that take part: the field of battle extends far beyond the chessboard.

In chapter 7, I wrote about Tofik Dadashev, the Baku psychologist who helped me during the matches in Moscow and Leningrad. In my book *Child of Change*, his name was not mentioned; that was Dadashev's own wish. I called him 'my talisman'.

I don't know whether a talisman can betray you, but Dadashev did. Two days before I left Seville I was told that *Literaturnaya Gazeta* was preparing for publication, and had actually already set up in type, a sensational interview in which Dadashev described how he had used a 'special power emanating from him' to make Kasparov a champion. Almost at the same time, a similar interview was offered to *Moscow News*.

The interview appeared in neither paper, but it was printed during the match, with certain changes, by *Der Spiegel*.

Dadashev said openly in the interview that Karpov had got in touch with him shortly before leaving for Spain, and that Dadashev had given him three pieces of advice on how to fight Kasparov. Dadashev claimed Karpov would win if he followed this advice.

The value of his advice becomes clear if you remember that this undoubtedly gifted psychologist had helped me in the most difficult period of the first match. Dadashev had often talked with me and knew quite a lot about me: my weak and strong points, my suspiciousness, my belief in lucky numbers. Above all, he knew I had faith in him. Dadashev was fairly successful in predicting how the fight would go, and gave me psychological advice. When the score stood at 5-0 he kept telling me I was not going to lose. When he started helping Karpov, he must have known how it would hit me when I found out.

Certainly in Seville, still believing in Dadashev's 'powers', I often racked my brains at night over the question of why he had done it.

The match was being held in the Lope de Vega Theatre, which stands in a beautiful park in the centre of Seville. Built in the Spanish baroque style, the theatre looks like a huge flower, dazzling white in the sun. A few hundred yards away is the Alphonse XIII, one of the best hotels in Seville. It had been planned that both teams would be staying in this ancient hotel, but then a modern hotel with the poetical name of Seville Sol – Sun of Seville – was chosen instead. Karpov and I, however, were given separate villas.

We would arrive for the games separately, just a few minutes before the clocks were started at 4.30 p.m., entering through separate doors depending on which colour we were going to play: one door had a white pawn on it, the other black.

At the back of the stage hung a huge poster advertising the World Fair, which was about to be held in Seville: 'EXPO–92' (the letter 'O' being represented by a pretty orange). Here was the solution to the mystery of the high prize money: the city of Seville had provided half a billion pesetas to finance the match!

The theatre's spacious foyer was dubbed by the spectators 'the casino', and with good reason: it was the place where bets were made on the outcome of the next game. The more bitter the fight on the stage became, the more people rushed from the auditorium into the 'casino'. But of course the laying of bets wasn't the only thing that went on in the foyer. It was a place where you could chat, discuss the game over a cup of coffee, play chess or buy chess books and souvenirs. In the middle of the foyer was an enormous demonstration board at which grandmasters took it in turns to provide a commentary on the games in progress. There were monitor screens everywhere on which you could see the players and the position on the electronic board. Here, too, was the press centre, equipped with so many telex machines and computers that you might think it was covering a disarmament conference.

It was a long drawn-out fight. On the whole, it was Karpov who had the initiative. I just couldn't get into the mood for a full-blooded contest, and did everything I could to avoid taking risks. This was particularly evident in game eleven, where after achieving an excellent position at the opening, I got myself into deep trouble by a series of indecisive manoeuvres. A clumsy oversight by Karpov did give me a point, but I think it was a bad gift: I 'fell asleep' altogether, having decided that what happened next was a matter of technique and that I could simply mark time. Fate, naturally, saw to it that I was duly punished for this. In game sixteen I suddenly charged into the attack, relying not so much on myself as the magical power of the number sixteen, which had twice brought me success in the previous matches. This time the magic didn't work and I lost the game. The bad taste it left behind was due not just to the result but also to my untalented play. We were now equal on points.

After that game I 'woke up', but not for long. Feeling the need to put my inner reserves in motion, in game seventeen I used the Old Indian Defence, an opening that had not been in my repertoire for four years. For a time, things went well for me. In game eighteen, and especially in game twenty, Karpov had a few anxious moments with black, though in the end I made slips which enabled him to avoid the worst. Game twenty-one could have been extremely important for victory in the match: determined to take advantage of playing with white, Karpov in the Grunfeld Defence went in for a complicated double-edged position, but soon made a blunder which allowed me to seize the initiative. Unfortunately, on that day my reaction to the sort of complicated position where I normally feel in my element left a great deal to be desired.

First I failed to press home the advantage I'd gained, and then, sensing that I'd missed the right moment, I forced a draw by repetition of moves, though the position was still one where I could have fought to win.

After game twenty-one it became obvious that I wasn't destined to win the match, but I had to at least hang on to the title. To be perfectly frank, that feeling, that I must at least hang on to the title, never left me throughout the match and was the psychological 'press' that crushed all desire to be active.

'From time to time I ceased to be aware that this was a match for the world championship,' I said in one of my post-match interviews. 'I think that over the past few years the mental fatigue has crept up on me, and it's showing. Usually I'm always looking for the best move and trying to achieve the maximum possible, but in this match with Karpov . . . I somehow felt removed from what was going on. This, incidentally, was the first time that I haven't lost a gram in weight during a match. Of course I got terribly nervous, but usually there is also a physical exhaustion, which this time didn't happen. It was as if the match were taking place somewhere else. I didn't have full concentration, and I began to want to make each move as secure as possible . . .'

The match was actually over after a brief and colourless draw in game twenty-two. Of course, it was a mistake not to play to win, but I had no nervous energy left. That game showed finally that, whatever the outcome of the match, neither of us was in top form. True, Karpov considers that he played well in Seville, that he had some creative achievements, and that in general 'from the creative point of view the contest was of a high standard'. I, on the other hand, feel that the match was inferior in creative content to the previous ones. That's not just my opinion, but the opinion of many grandmasters.

Vitaly Tseshkovsky: 'As sport, it was an uncompromising fight which excited the fans. But the creative standard of the games was not so impressive. I think that both players were under some kind of psychological pressure, and this prevented them from displaying the best aspects of their creativeness. There were far fewer opening innovations and strategic ideas in this match than the previous ones.'

Lev Psakhis: 'In my view, last year's return match was, on any showing, one of the most outstanding competitions for the world title. But I have to say frankly that this battle will not leave such a significant trace in chess.'

Naum Pashkovsky: 'This match shows clearly that many of FIDE's decisions in recent years have proved to be unfruitful. This long rivalry between the world's two strongest chess players is having a bad effect on the quality of their play.'

There is indeed no doubt at all that the games played in the Seville match were considerably inferior in quality to all the previous ones. For that we have to thank the people who thought up the system and made us play annually. Even such a momentous event in a person's life as a world championship match can become humdrum if you have to do it every year. I have always been amazed at the inability of the FIDE leadership to learn from its mistakes.

Although the match contained numerous interesting ideas, both in the openings and the middle-game, the battle never reached the high pitch that people were expecting – except for the finale, which left no-one cold: it was an incredible, fantastic denouement!

The opening of game twenty-three turned out successfully for me; black managed to solve all the problems. But then I made two impulsive moves in succession, enabling Karpov to gain a clear strategic advantage. When both of us got into time trouble, however, he lost most of it, and at the fortieth move I could probably have achieved a draw, something, incidentally, that the commentators have overlooked. But of the two possible continuations I chose the worse, and if Karpov had sealed a really strong move, I would have been faced with insoluble problems. However, as we'd hoped, his sealed move also turned out not to be the best, but black succeeded by subtle manoeuvres in creating counterplay. Moreover, it was complicated counterplay that even away from the game we found it impossible to analyse in all its detail (besides, while we were analysing it at night, we were nagged by the awful thought of what would happen if Karpov had in fact sealed the best move.

It's not surprising that it took us a lot of time to solve the problems at the board, and we both found ourselves once again under time pressure. Karpov began repeating moves, and then something incredible happened. Instead of also repeating moves, leaving it to white to find a way of strengthening his position, I suddenly embarked on a combination whose refutation we had actually found in our adjournment analysis. In fact, the refutation was lying on the surface, and wasn't difficult to find even at the board. Karpov found it, and when the time threat had passed, I had to resign.

Grandmaster Sergey Makarychev prefaced his commentary on this game with an interesting psychological sketch: 'Even before the dramatic twenty-third game had come to an end I heard some of Kasparov's fans speaking of their bewilderment and even dissatisfaction at the unusual way their idol was playing. I'd like to give my view on it. I believe that what influences a player most in his choice of tactics is not his conscious decision as to whether he is going to play this way or that, but his subconscious feelings, and here the player will sometimes begin to deceive even himself, using hindsight to make what has happened on the board fit the right answer. This is true of any master or grandmaster: not even the world's top players are free from the pressure of objective psychological circumstances. And it seems to me that Kasparov, throughout this whole game, was constantly struggling with his own inner self trying to hold him back. That's why at crucial moments in the game he made moves such as 12 . . . Ba6; 34 . . . ba?! and 50 . . . R7f3 . . . Yes, no one can now accuse the 13th world champion of dry pragmatism, but the split between his mind as Kasparov the sportsman and Kasparov the creative player was brilliantly exploited by Karpov in that second last game. Anticipating possible questions, let me quote the opinion of Mikhail Tal, who commented in a TV chess programme that in Seville, the sporting factor clearly prevailed over all others – it was a battle for results, for the chess crown.'

Yes, that's right. A world championship match is, first and foremost, sport. But the opponents' tasks are different: the challenger's task is to win the match, while the champion's is to retain his title. As you can see, it all boils down to the world title. After game twenty-three it became obvious that I'd already lost it. Even now I shudder when I recall those first few minutes after we resumed the game, the road back, the state of doom and prostration into which I sank.

But even clearly realising that all was lost, I was nevertheless conscious of having one last chance – just one. Maybe one in a thousand, maybe one in a million, but one chance remained, although everyone knows that if you desperately need to win the final game, you never do. (On the morning of the day we were to play game twenty-four, the grandmaster Milunka Lazarevic telephoned my mother from Switzerland and said, 'Clara, tell Garik only two people could win a decisive game to order: Alekhine, who didn't have occasion to, and Fischer, who didn't need to. Tell Garry he has to do it.' But my mother didn't pass that message on to me until after the game. Evidently even she didn't believe in a miracle.)

In 1985, in a similar situation, Karpov had thrown himself into a desperate attack and lost the twenty-fourth game. Not a pleasant comparison. But even while preparing myself mentally for the moment where I'd have to concede the match, I didn't forget this was the one game I had to put everything into.

For a start, I had to get into a calm frame of mind. I therefore went to the Seville Sol Hotel, where the team were staying. I went in smiling, forcing myself to remain outwardly calm. I sat with my team in their room all evening playing cards, laughing and joking. We all tried not to think of tomorrow, but tomorrow was relentlessly drawing nearer. I didn't get to sleep until just before dawn.

And so the day came. Before the game began, I saw a huge crowd outside the Lope de Vega Theatre. Even on ordinary days the match drew big crowds, but never so many people as on that day. I said sadly to Litvinov: 'I suppose they've come to see me buried.' But no sooner had I got out of the car, when I heard shouts of 'Suerte! – Good Luck! Suerto, Kasparov!' This support from the people of Seville gave me extra confidence. This buzzing crowd of Spaniards wishing me well as I went into the crucial battle reminded me of the millions of fans back home who had faith in me and were hoping for a miracle. A woman broke through the police cordon and pushed something into my pocket. In the hall I discovered that it was an image of the Virgin of Macarena, protector of the city.

We had decided I should play as calmly as possible, not pushing things, so as to draw my opponent into a slow contest of manoeuvring. The hope was that, in trying to bring about simplifications, Karpov would falter.

'I think,' Makarychev wrote, 'that the world champion, having seriously risked sitting down at the board as the holder of that title for the last time (at least for the next three years), chose the only correct tactic. Just as his opponent had done two days before, he played a closed opening system in an attempt to safeguard himself first and foremost against premature exchanges and the forcing of simplifying variations. However, the sporting purpose of that strategy was a little different. Whereas Kasparov, although "striving for a draw", at times strayed from the straight and narrow into unpragmatically risky play because of his inner aversion to that "striving", Karpov could not overcome his natural desire to play safe, even though experience has repeatedly shown that this is a disastrous course. Each senses the other so well that there are times when they find it far easier to "programme" their opponent than to cope with particular character traits of their own.' Never a truer word!

I well remembered how I felt before the last game of the Moscow match which brought me the world title. What I had been most afraid of then was just this sort of stodgy, drawn-out play that would have delayed my triumph. Fortunately, in that game Karpov had fallen upon me with all his might, forcing me to defend myself and find the only right response; in other words, he'd given me concrete problems to solve, and in so doing, he had lifted from me the entire burden of psychological problems. By avoiding that mistake, I put Karpov psychologically in a most unpleasant situation. Throughout the whole game he was forced to agonise over whether it was better to make the strongest moves, or the safest. Karpov chose safety. His position worsened a little, but was still entirely defensible.

Because he was hoping for an easy draw, Karpov was slow to sense the impending danger. When he did sense it, he lost his nerve. He was frantic and got into time trouble. With both of us in time trouble, we swapped mistakes. First Karpov gave me an opportunity to create a winning combination, and I didn't see it. Then he missed a draw, after which I again overlooked a forced win and the battle was adjourned in an end-game in which the chances of winning or drawing seemed to me about equal; in practice, however, if you have a staunch opponent, saving such an end-game is far from easy. It later emerged that Karpov had lost his faith in a successful outcome and assessed his chances more pessimistically, thirty per cent for a draw against seventy for a win. Thus I had the psychological advantage on my side too.

Although analysis showed no clear way of winning, I resumed the game with one sole desire – victory. What happened when I went on to the stage only increased my confidence: I was greeted by an ovation which convinced me that my fans in the hall were very much in the majority.

That final part of the game was to be one of the most memorable moments in my life. Karpov couldn't stand the strain and soon made a strategic error which was, in my view, decisive. I then went on playing with precision, not giving my opponent a single chance to win the game.

Karpov's defeat in game twenty-four, which smashed his near accomplished dream of a return to the chess Olympus, was like a psychological knock-out. To Karpov's credit, he did find the strength to appear at the closing ceremony two hours later and watch dispassionately as his 'eternal' rival received the award. But Campomanes and the other top FIDE officials, who had converged on Seville practically in full strength, were a sorry sight. With their hopes of Karpov's return lying in ruins, they were plunged into despair. One of the onlookers laughed: 'The future of Campomanes and his minions is written all over their faces.'

'Karpov has now had a chance to prove that he plays chess better than me,' I said at a press conference in Seville. 'Yet another chance. But he didn't. For a player who didn't get his title back, it must be cold comfort that the match as a whole ended in a draw. Two years ago we were in a very similar situation: I was winning 12-11, and Karpov needed to win the last game. It never occurred to me or anyone on my side that if the match were drawn, at least I could be content with the moral victory. And I don't think Karpov was in the least interested in the moral problem of whether he retained his title by drawing or winning the match. So I have kept my title by playing, actually for the first time in history, two return matches against the same person. And please note that I didn't have a return match behind me! I regard the result of this match, which gives me a three-year respite, as victory for me. And the way the match ended – I mean games twenty-three and twenty-four – makes it a very convincing victory. I won the last game to order, against a player like Karpov. And you can take my word for it that you can't win the last game on psychology alone. You have to play better chess, and also believe that you are playing better chess . . .'

The Seville match shows clearly that chess, like any other form of creative art, demands everything that you can put into it.

But it is difficult to agree with those people who try to restrict a chess player's sphere of activity to chess alone. Of course it's only in chess that I can fully satisfy my desire to be creative, but it's in my nature to want a broad field of action. In my case, the fight for change and new social structures is probably something I need in order to maintain a healthy way of life. You just have to be able to isolate what is important and concentrate your energy in that area.

It may be that in 1987 I didn't calculate the energy I had available and was unable to concentrate properly on preparation for the match, by which I mean psychological preparation, because, as I have said, I had no complaints about my chess preparation. What's more, we succeeded in eliminating the shortcomings in our analysis of adjourned games, and managed to achieve substantial superiority in that area. In all the adjourned games, our team's analysis was first class (even including game twenty-three, which I lost), and the plans of defence we drew up in games nine and nineteen were undoubtedly some of our best creative achievements.

As far as the openings are concerned, and the way they affected the match, mention should be made of the good result I achieved with the Grunfeld Defence (+1−1=6). When he encountered it for the first time in the return match, Karpov kept finding areas of vulnerability in my preparation, achieving in the Grunfeld Defence an impressive victory (+30−0=6). It seems surprising that just a year later in Seville, Karpov was unable to repeat the performance.

The match was very well organised, especially for a city that had no great tradition of chess-playing. Altogether it passed off without a hitch, except for the incident over the resumption of game fifteen, which showed vividly how the massive latent tension could lead to any trifle sparking off a row.

What happened was this. The game had been adjourned in a dead-drawn position – quite simply, no other outcome could have been possible. It could be argued, of course, as to whether adjourning the game in that situation was the right thing to do. However, to offer a draw the next day, just three and a half hours before the game was due to resume, was in my view a totally wrong thing to do. The very fact that he waited so long to do it indicates that Karpov couldn't care less about the rules of common decency in chess. Things then developed as follows. After receiving Karpov's offer of a draw, Gijsen, the chief arbiter, telephoned me but the call came while our team were having their traditional afternoon rest. He wasn't able to speak to me until three o'clock, when I woke up. I naturally agreed to the draw, although I was unhappy that it had been offered so late. Karpov, however, then told Gijsen he was annoyed at my behaviour (by the fact that I was asleep?), and that he wanted to continue the game and was retracting his offer. But the chief arbiter stood firm, and the game wasn't resumed.

Another significant fact about the Seville match is that it took place entirely outside the Soviet Union. For many people this symbolised a major change in policy by the Soviet Sports Committee: a whole competition had been farmed out to foreigners. Personally, I think that what was uppermost in their minds were commercial considerations: there was a huge prize in foreign currency, which we had to hand over to the Sports Committee. A special government decree was issued for the purpose, signed by Nikolai Ryzhkov, Chairman of the USSR Council of Ministers. With support from such high quarters, the Sports Committee won an easy victory in its financial duel against the world's two top chess players. Of the 2,280,000 Swiss francs we were awarded, each of us was actually given 137,000 francs plus the equivalent of the same sum in Soviet currency (about 60,000 roubles).

But let us go back to the 'evil spirit'.

Karpov was known to have had his own 'talisman', another famous parapsychologist. Dadashev often said he was struggling with the latter's aura, and that was one reason why he was helping me. It was said that after he lost the return match, Karpov dispensed with this man's assistance. But he didn't refuse the advice of my psychologist. Dadashev stood to benefit enormously if Karpov won in Seville. His fame as a parapsychologist and champion-maker would have surpassed even the fame of the legendary Juna. After game twenty-three, it seemed that Dadashev's prediction had come true. But he was out of luck. The 'miracle' of game twenty-four delivered chess from the snare of parapsychology.

'Open-ended Fight'

On 9 November 1985, when I won the most important game in my life, I had no idea that I would logically become drawn into the social confrontation that was initiated by *perestroika*. It is not just a battle about justice in chess, but a fight for more important values, ones that are common to all humanity. These values have special relevance to the Soviet Union, because they are directly linked with the truly historic changes that are now taking place in our country. I am a child of those changes, since I belong to the left wing of society, both by conviction and by destiny. By conviction, because I have never been able to accept the authoritarian ideology which has held sway in the USSR. By destiny, because it was only the changes in our country that enabled me to surmount the many barriers erected on my path to the world championship.

I grew up under an administrative system whose supreme aim seemed to be to suppress the personality of the individual. I stood my ground. Naturally, I could not avoid certain compromises and certain losses, and it would be senseless to deny that I did. My enemies brazenly made use of the full might of the establishment, and if I was not to be crushed, I needed to look for influential support.

There was a serious test in store for me when I won the world championship title, something which opened many doors. The bureaucrats assumed that there would merely be a change of decoration on the chess Olympus. But I knew that under the patronage of the system, the only freedom of self-expression that was going to be granted to me would be at the chessboard. To have accepted that would have been an act of self-betrayal. It is a well-known truth that freedom is not something you've been given, but something that cannot be taken away from you.

I regard 1987 as a turning-point in my life. The publication of my book *Child of Change* in the West and the ensuing rift with the Soviet Sports Committee can really be said to have determined my relations with the system.

Unfortunately, the war waged for many years by the chess bureaucracy against challenger, later world champion, Kasparov, the competition rules that were so frequently altered, and ultimately infringed anyway, and no less than four world championship matches in three years – all these unattractive features of recent chess history have still not been given the assessment they deserve. The bureaucratic apparatus is still strong. It controls the State purse, which it can spend as it sees fit, and it has behind it the spirit and ideology of an administrative system founded upon the suppression of all free thinking.

Chess, like every other sport, is a part of that system, so it's no surprise that for a great many years it languished under bureaucratic oppression with no question of any kind of democracy or freedom of opinion. Many chess players themselves experienced the utter ruthlessness of that machine. The dozens of Soviet chess players who now live outside their own country are another indication that there has long been something wrong in Soviet chess.

In my public statement I try to avoid the subject of my relations with Karpov, although in many respects it was through them that the major conflicts between me and the administrative apparatus began. I know that basically everyone is tired of the subject, and that each person has his own opinion about it. But it has to be said that the Soviet Sports Committee and the Presidium of the USSR Chess Federation, which from the outset took a very definite line on the issue, very largely predetermined both the beginning of the conflict and the way it developed.

We often ignore the fact that the system also reacts rapidly to changes in the country's political and social climate. Realising that the axe-like wielding of administrative power has become extremely unpopular, the more far-sighted proponents of the system bring their best people forward to the front of the stage. One concept is then surreptitiously replaced by another: an exceptional individual begins, through his reputation and success, to act as a cover-up for what the system is doing. This is a process that we regularly encounter in the ideological sphere of confrontation between the old and the new.

I have to admit that from the propaganda point of view, in Karpov's case this scheme was brilliantly realised. After being elevated by the semi-official press to unattainable ideological heights and having become an integral part of the system in the period of stagnation, Karpov accepted the new rules of the game, and thanks to his outstanding qualities and achievements in the realm of sport he was able to divert public attention from the chronic problems of chess and, indeed, sport in general. Having turned Karpov into a political counterbalance to my activities, the system has all these years taken great care to maintain the immaculate reputation of its idol in the eyes of the people.

What we have witnessed is the conflict between the 'two K's' – Karpov and Kasparov – blown up out of all proportion and used in an attempt to cover up the lawlessness and tyranny that are being perpetrated in the world of chess.

Take the fiasco at the end of the 55th USSR championship in August 1988. After Karpov and I had shared first and second place, the regulations prescribed that a match for the title of USSR Champion should take place. But it never did. As for the myth that was put about by the organisers and taken up by a number of journalists that there were 'irreconcilable differences' between us, that was no more than a ruse designed to conceal the answer to the main question of who cancelled the match after it had already begun, and on what grounds. I say it had already begun, because the draw had taken place, with both Karpov and myself included, which means in effect that the competition had started. Yet when I turned up for the first game, I found myself instead at a press conference – yet another one!

When I asked who had cancelled the match, I was told that it had been done on the verbal instructions of Gavrilin, vice-chairman of the Sports Committee . . .

I can't help pointing out that once again the decision by the sports officials was in full accord with the demands of Karpov, who had expressed displeasure not only at having to play a match to the first win, but also at the fact the starting date was too early. A draft decision by the Presidium of the USSR Chess Federation said: 'In view of . . . the fatigue of both players . . .' Which medical document was used to draw this sudden conclusion? And since when have competitions been stopped because the players didn't feel like playing, or because they were tired?

The simple answer to that last question is 15 February 1985, the day Campomanes interrupted our first world championship match, saying that it was because of the critical state of the players' health and the fatigue of the referees, organisers, spectators, etc. Campomanes alleged that he was acting 'in the best interests of chess', and supported this by reference to the letter from the Soviet Chess Federation signed by Sevastyanov. After the row erupted at the 55th USSR Championship, what unconcealed glee must there have been in Campomanes's comment: 'Now you see that you are exporting your problems to FIDE!'

When I began work on *Child of Change*, I thought the end of my struggle for the world title meant that the struggle on the entire chess front was over too. At one time, that would have been so. The champion would automatically receive royal prerogatives and his opinion on important issues would be definitive. But by challenging the foundations of the established system of chess administration, I had deprived myself of my 'immunity' as champion. It was only myself, however: the ex-champion continued to enjoy his former 'immunity'! So there you have the answer to the question asked in May 1989 by Viktor Vasilyev, the chess columnist of the weekly *Nedelya*: 'What is the explanation for the undoubted anomaly that no one permits himself to criticise Karpov except Kasparov, while criticisms about Kasparov are uttered regularly and freely by just about anyone who has the time and inclination?' He then went on to give an impressive list of those who had made 'sharp and direct or veiled attacks' on me: *Studenchesky Meridian*, *Nash Sovremennik*, *Sovietskaya Rossiya*, *64-Chess Review*, *Sportivnaya Moskva*, *Sovietsky Sport*, *Tass* observer, the *Pravda* commentator grandmaster A. Suetin, and others.

I don't regret the loss of that dubious champion's privilege, because I know that fighting for democratic values is incompatible with dictatorship, regardless of who the dictator is!

Many people wonder why I go on with this gruelling struggle. Why do I take the risk? I'm young, financially well off and have reached the peak of my profession. What more do I want? There was a time, after the fourth match, when I also thought: that's it, the war's over. But it was an illusion. All that had ended was a certain stage of my life. And time after time, as I've outgrown another problem or defeated another opponent, I have seen that the main battles are yet to come. There was a time when I didn't see that behind the chess department of the Soviet Sports Committee were the bureaucrats of FIDE, and that behind Campomanes were the officials of the Sports Committee. Today I am free of illusions; in the word of Robert Jordan in Hemingway's *For Whom the Bell Tolls*: 'There were fifty years of undeclared war against fascism ahead, and I had signed on for the duration.'

My fight is open-ended . . .

APPENDIX A: **Illustrative Games**

Black v. Tukmanov. USSR Championship 1981

See page 49

1	d4	Nf6
2	c4	g6
3	Nc3	Bg7
4	e4	d6
5	Be2	0–0
6	Bg5	c5
7	d5	b5
8	cb	a6
9	a4	h6
10	Bd2	e6
11	de	Bxe6
12	Nf3	ab
13	Bxb5	Na6
14	0–0	Nc7
15	Rel	Nxb5
16	Nxb5	d5
17	ed	Nxd5
18	Ne5	Re8
19	Rcl	Bf5
20	Nc6	Qd7
21	Rxc5	Rxel+
22	Qxel	Re8
23	Qcl	Nb6
24	b3	Re2
25	Ba5	Be4
26	Ne5	Qe7
27	Nd4	Ra2
28	Bxb6	Bxe5
29	Qe3	Qxc5

0-1

Black v. Korchnoi, the Lucerne Olympiad, 1982

See page 78

1	d4	Nf6
2	c4	g6
3	g3	Bg7
4	Bg2	c5
5	d5	d6
6	Nc3	0–0
7	Nf3	e6
8	0–0	ed
9	cd	a6
10	a4	Re8
11	Nd2	Nbd7
12	h3	Rb8
13	Nc4	Ne5
14	Na3	Nh5
15	e4	Rf8
16	Kh2	f5
17	f4	b5
18	ab	ab
19	Naxb5	fe
20	Bxe4	Bd7
21	Qe2	Qb6
22	Na3	Rbe8
23	Bd2	Qxb2
24	fe	Bxe5
25	Nc4	Nxg3
26	Rxf8+	Rxf8
27	Qe1	Nxe4+
28	Kg2	Qc2
29	Nxe5	Rf2+
30	Qxf2	Nxf2
31	Ra2	Qf5
32	Nxd7	Nd3
33	Bh6	Qxd7
34	Ra8+	Kf7
35	Rh8	Kf6
36	Kf3	Qxh3+

0-1 (on time)

Black v. Korchnoi, London 1983

See page 93

1	d4	d5
2	c4	e6
3	Nf3	c5
4	cd	ed
5	g3	Nc6
6	Bg2	Nf6
7	0-0	Be7
8	Be3	c4
9	Ne5	0-0
10	b3	cb
11	Qxb3	Qb6
12	Rc1	Qxb3
13	ab	Nb4
14	Na3	a6
15	Bd2	Rb8
16	Bxb4	Bxb4
17	Nd3	Bd6
18	Nc2	Bg4
19	Kf1	Bf5
20	Nc5	Rfc8
21	Ne3	Be6
22	b4	Kf8
23	Rc2	Ke7
24	Ke1	h5
25	Rb2	Rc7
26	Nd3	Ra8
27	b5	a5
28	b6	Rc6
29	Rb5	a4
30	Nxd5+	Nxd5
31	Bxd5	Bxd5
32	Rxd5	Rxb6
33	Rxh5	Rb3
34	Kd2	b5
35	h4	Rc8
36	g4	a3
37	f4	Rcc3
38	Rd5	Ke6
39	Rh5	b4
40	Ra5	Rxd3+
41	ed	Bxf4+
42	Ke2	Rc3
43	g5	Bc1
44	h5	b3
45	R5xa3	Bxa3

46	Rxa3	b2
47	Ra6+	Kf5
48	Rb6	Rc2+
49	Ke3	Kxg5
50	d5	Kxh5
51	Kd4	g5
52	Rb8	g4
53	d6	Rc6
54	Ke5	Rc5+
55	Kf6	g3
56	Rxb2	Rd5
57	Kxf7	Rxd6
58	Rd2	Kg4
59	d4	Kf5
60	Ke7	Rd5
61	Rd3	Kf4
62	Ke6	Rg5
63	d5	Rg6+
64	Ke7	g2
65	Rd1	Ke5
66	d6	Re6+
67	Kd7	Rxd6+
68	Rxd6	g1Q
69	Re6+	Kf5
70	Rd6	Qa7+
71	Kd8	Ke5
72	Rg6	Qa5+
73	Kd7	Qa4+
74	Ke7	Qh4+
75	Kf8	Qd8+
76	Kf7	Kf5
77	Rh6	Qd7+

0-1

White v. Karpov, Moscow, 1985 (first match, game 48)

See page 113

1	e4	e5
2	Nf3	Nf6
3	Nxe5	d6
4	Nf3	Nxe4
5	d4	d5
6	Bd3	Nc6
7	0–0	Be7
8	c4	Nf6
9	Nc3	0–0
10	h3	dc
11	Bxc4	Na5
12	Bd3	Be6
13	Re1	Nc6
14	a3	a6
15	Bf4	Qd7
16	Ne5	Nxe5
17	de	Nd5
18	Nxd5	Bxd5
19	Qc2	g6
20	Rad1	c6
21	Bh6	Rfd8
22	e6!	fe
23	Bxg6	Bf8
24	Bxf8	Rxf8
25	Be4	Rf7
26	Re3	Rg7
27	R1d3	Rf8
28	Rg3	Kh8
29	Qc3	Rf7
30	Rde3	Kg8
31	Qe5	Qc7
32	Rxg7+	Rxg7
33	Bxd5	Qxe5
34	Bxe6+	Qxe6
35	Rxe6	Rd7
36	b4	Kf7
37	Re3	Rd1+
38	Kh2	Rc1
39	g4	b5
40	f4	c5
41	bc	Rxc5
42	Rd3	Ke7
43	Kg3	a5
44	Kf3	b4
45	ab	ab

46	Ke4	Rb5
47	Rb3	Rb8
48	Kd5	Kf6
49	Kc5	Re8
50	Rxb4	Re3
51	h4	Rh3
52	h5	Rh4
53	f5	Rh1
54	Kd5	Rd1+
55	Rd4	Re1
56	Kd6	Re8
57	Kd7	Rg8
58	h6	Kf7
59	Rc4	Kf6
60	Re4	Kf7
61	Kd6	Kf6
62	Re6+	Kf7
63	Re7+	Kf6
64	Rg7	Rd8+
65	Kc5	Rd5+
66	Kc4	Rd4+
67	Kc3	

1-0

Black v. Karpov, Moscow 1985 (second match, game 16)

See page 169

1	e4	c5
2	Nf3	e6
3	d4	cd
4	Nxd4	Nc6
5	Nb5	d6
6	c4	Nf6
7	N1c3	a6
8	Na3	d5
9	cd	ed
10	ed	Nb4
11	Be2	Bc5
12	0–0	0–0
13	Bf3	Bf5
14	Bg5	Re8
15	Qd2	b5
16	Rad1	Nd3
17	Nab1	h6
18	Bh4	b4
19	Na4	Bd6
20	Bg3	Rc8
21	b3	g5
22	Bxd6	Qxd6
23	g3	Nd7
24	Bg2	Qf6
25	a3	a5
26	ab	ab
27	Qa2	Bg6
28	d6	g4
29	Qd2	Kg7
30	f3	Qxd6
31	fg	Qd4+
32	Kh1	Nf6
33	Rf4	Ne4
34	Qxd3	Nf2+
35	Rxf2	Bxd3
36	Rfd2	Qe3
37	Rxd3	Rc1
38	Nb2	Qf2
39	Nd2	Rxd1+
40	Nxd1	Re1+

0-1

Black v. Karpov. Moscow 1985 (second match, game 24)

See page 172

1	e4	c5
2	Nf3	d6
3	d4	cd
4	Nxd4	Nf6
5	Nc3	a6
6	Be2	e6
7	0–0	Be7
8	f4	0–0
9	Kh1	Qc7
10	a4	Nc6
11	Be3	Re8
12	Bf3	Rb8
13	Qd2	Bd7
14	Nb3	b6
15	g4	Bc8
16	g5	Nd7
17	Qf2	Bf8
18	Bg2	Bb7
19	Rad1	g6
20	Bc1	Rbc8
21	Rd3	Nb4
22	Rh3	Bg7
23	Be3	Re7
24	Kg1	Rce8
25	Rd1	f5
26	gf	Nxf6
27	Rg3	Rf7
28	Bxb6	Qb8
29	Be3	Nh5
30	Rg4	Nf6
31	Rh4	g5
32	fg	Ng4
33	Qd2	Nxe3
34	Qxe3	Nxc2
35	Qb6	Ba8
36	Rxd6	Rb7
37	Qxa6	Rxb3
38	Rxe6	Rxb2
39	Qc4	Kh8
40	e5	Qa7+
41	Kh1	Bxg2+
42	Kxg2	Nd4+

0-1

White v. Karpov, London 1986 (third match, game 4)

See page 207

1	d4	Nf6
2	c4	e6
3	Nc3	Bb4
4	Nf3	c5
5	g3	cd
6	Nxd4	0–0
7	Bg2	d5
8	Qb3	Bxc3+
9	bc	Nc6
10	cd	Na5
11	Qc2	Nxd5
12	Qd3	Bd7
13	c4	Ne7
14	0–0	Rc8
15	Nb3	Nxc4
16	Bxb7	Rc7
17	Ba6	Ne5
18	Qe3	Nc4
19	Qe4	Nd6
20	Qd3	Rc6
21	Ba3	Bc8
22	Bxc8	Ndxc8
23	Rfd1	Qxd3
24	Rxd3	Re8
25	Rad1	f6
26	Nd4	Rb6
27	Bc5	Ra6
28	Nb5	Rc6
29	Bxe7	Nxe7
30	Rd7	Ng6
31	Rxa7	Nf8
32	a4	Rb8
33	e3	h5
34	Kg2	e5
35	Rd3	Kh7
36	Rc3	Rbc8
37	Rxc6	Rxc6
38	Nc7	Ne6
39	Nd5	Kh6
40	a5	e4
41	a6 (sealed);	but Karpov resigned without resuming play

1-0

White v. Karpov, Leningrad 1986 (third match, game 16)

See page 208

1	e4	e5
2	Nf3	Nc6
3	Bb5	a6
4	Ba4	Nf6
5	0–0	Be7
6	Re1	b5
7	Bb3	d6
8	c3	0–0
9	h3	Bb7
10	d4	Re8
11	Nbd2	Bf8
12	a4	h6
13	Bc2	ed
14	cd	Nb4
15	Bb1	c5
16	d5	Nd7
17	Ra3	c4
18	Nd4	Qf6
19	N2f3	Nc5
20	ab	ab
21	Nxb5	Rxa3
22	Nxa3	Ba6
23	Re3	Rb8
24	e5	de
25	Nxe5	Nbd3
26	Ng4	Qb6
27	Rg3	g6
28	Bxh6	Qxb2
29	Qf3	Nd7
30	Bxf8	Kxf8
31	Kh2	Rb3
32	Bxd3	cd
33	Qf4	Qxa3
34	Nh6	Qe7
35	Rxg6	Qe5
36	Rg8+	Ke7
37	d6+	Ke6
38	Re8+	Kd5
39	Rxe5+	Nxe5
40	d7	Rb8
41	Nxf7	

1-0

APPENDIX B: Chief Tournament and Match Results of Garry Kasparov

Year	Competition	+	−	=	Place
1976	USSR youth championship, Tbilisi	5	−	4	1
1976	World junior championship, Wattigny	5	2	2	3–6
1977	USSR youth championship, Riga	8	−	1	1
1977	World junior championship, Cagnes-sur-Mer	6	2	3	3
1978	A. Sokolsky memorial trophy, Minsk	11	2	4	1
1978	National selection tournament, Daugavpils	6	1	6	1
1978	46th USSR championship	4	4	9	9
1979	International tournament, Banja Luka	8	−	7	1
1979	47th USSR championship, Minsk	6	3	8	3–4
1980	International tournament, Baku	8	−	7	1
1980	World youth championship, Dortmund	8	−	5	1
1980	24th Olympiad, Malta (2nd reserve)	8	1	3	2
1981	International tournament, Moscow	3	1	9	2–4
1981	International tournament, Tilburg	3	3	5	6–8
1981	49th USSR championship, Frunze	10	2	5	1–2
1982	International tournament, Bugojno	6	−	7	1
1982	Interzonal tournament, Moscow	7	−	6	1
1982	25th Olympiad, Lucerne (2nd board)	6	−	5	3
1983	Quarter-final candidates match v. A. Belyavsky, Moscow	4	1	4	
1983	International tournament, Niksic	9	1	4	1
1983	Semi-final candidates match v. V. Korchnoi, London	4	1	6	
1984	Final candidates match v. V. Smyslov, Vilnius	4	−	9	
1984–5	World championship match v. A. Karpov, Moscow	3	5	40	
1985	Match v. R. Hübner, Hamburg	3	−	3	
1985	Match v. U. Andersson, Belgrade	2	−	4	
1985	World championship match v. A. Karpov, Moscow	5	3	16	

Year	Competition	+	−	=	Place
1985	Match v. J. Timman, Hilversum	3	1	2	
1986	Match v. A. Miles, Basel	5	−	1	
1986	World championship return match				
	v. A. Karpov, London–Leningrad	5	4	15	
1986	27th Olympiad, Dubai (1st board)	7	1	3	1
1986	International tournament, Brussels	6	1	3	1
1987	International tournament, Brussels	6	−	5	1–2
1987	World championship match				
	v. A. Karpov, Seville	4	4	16	
1988	International tournament, Amsterdam	6	−	6	1
1988	International tournament, Belfort	9	1	5	1
1988	55th USSR championship, Moscow	6	−	11	1–2
1988	International tournament, Reykjavik	6	1	10	1
1988	28th Olympiad, Salonika (1st board)	7	−	3	1
1989	International tournament, Barcelona	7	1	8	1–2
1989	International tournament, Skelleftea	4	−	11	1–2
1989	International tournament, Tilburg	10	−	4	1

INDEX